A Science and Religion
PRIMER

A Science and Religion
PRIMER

Edited by
Heidi A. Campbell
and Heather Looy

B
Baker Academic
a division of Baker Publishing Group
Grand Rapids, Michigan

Published by Baker Academic
a division of Baker Publishing Group
P.O. Box 6287, Grand Rapids, MI 49516-6287
www.bakeracademic.com

Printed in the United States of America

Library of Congress Cataloging-in-Publication Data
A science and religion primer / edited by Heidi A. Campbell and Heather Looy.
    p. cm.
    Includes index.
    ISBN: 978-0-8010-3150-2 (pbk.)
    1. Religion and science. I. Campbell, Heidi, 1970– II. Looy, Heather, 1961–
BL240.3.S349 2009
201′.65—dc22   2008037973

For
John Roche
A beloved mentor and friend

Contents

Editorial and Advisory Board

Entries

Introduction

HEATHER LOOY, THE KING'S UNIVERSITY COLLEGE

AND

HEIDI A. CAMPBELL, TEXAS A&M UNIVERSITY

The Need for a Science and Religion Dialogue

"A dialogue on science and religion? Must be a short conversation!" quipped a British customs officer at Heathrow Airport to one of us on her way to attend a monthlong seminar on science and religion at Oxford University. The customs officer's surprise and skepticism reflects a widespread myth that science and religion are antagonistic, or at best unrelated, ways of viewing the world. Yet science and religion have always been inextricably intertwined, and recent years have seen a surge toward open, explicit dialogue and research on their relationships. "Science and Religion" is emerging as an interdisciplinary academic field of study, a claim that is justified by the growing number of undergraduate courses, graduate degree programs, and research institutes in this area.

The idea that science and religion are in conflict has been promoted by proponents of the secularization thesis and cultural critics of religion. Recently several well-publicized voices—such as Richard Dawkins in *The God Delusion* and Daniel Dennett in *Breaking the Spell: Religion as a Natural Phenomenon*—have decried religion in all its forms as "childish superstition," "irrational," and the main reason for current environmental and geopolitical crises. Religion is characterized as something to be discarded, rather than integrated. In their view, rational science must take the place of irrational religion if we are to find a way through our current and future crises.

Yet those who become even superficially familiar with the history and complexity of the relationships between science and religion quickly realize that these recent claims of the triumph of atheism are neither new nor do they acknowledge the very real, vital, and subtle ways in which religion and science have always been inextricably intertwined. The popular view that the relationship between science and religion is primarily antagonistic (based on a mythologized and grossly distorted telling of the Galileo story) is simply wrong. There is a tendency to simplify, polarize, and turn public discussion into science *against* religion, with little reflection on what is meant by either term, and to perceive a conflict or dialogue between two utterly independent entities.

There is a real need for thoughtful, historical, philosophical, and scientific engagement with questions of science and religion. How have we come to perceive science and religion as separate and often incompatible entities? How do we understand their historic and current interactions? In what ways does science challenge or confirm religion? And how does religion challenge or even enrich science? Whether one is a student of science, theology, philosophy, or history, engaging these questions and conversations in the public sphere requires a certain understanding of the real and the perceived relations between science and religion.

Conversations between science and religion have taken many forms and currently bring together diverse disciplines, from biology and physics to philosophy and theology. Those trying to enter into the conversation may feel like strangers in a foreign country where a hybrid of multiple languages and customs prevail, some familiar and many utterly new and bewildering. The *Science and Religion Primer* is intended to serve as a "phrase book" and cultural crib sheet that provides a basic and essential guide for those seeking to navigate this fascinating but potentially confusing territory.

The *Science and Religion Primer* Story

The *Science and Religion Primer* was born from the experience of the editors as participants in the John Templeton Oxford Seminars in Science and Christianity, organized by the Council for Christian Colleges and Universities (http://www.cccu.org/projects/templeton/default.asp). For three summers (2003–5), thirty-five scholars from around the world met in Wycliffe Hall in Oxford, England, to listen, learn, and engage in dialogue with many luminaries in the broad terrain of science and religion (SR), including among many others Simon Conway Morris, Malcolm Jeeves, Wolfhart Pannenberg, and Arthur Peacocke. This was the second such series (the first occurring from 1998 to 2001) seeking to bring together scholars from a variety of disciplines who had common research interests in the interrelationships between the sciences and religion.

During the first seminar session in 2003 it quickly became apparent that, due to the interdisciplinary nature of the conversation, some key concepts and contributors in the science/religion dialogue (SRD) were not widely known or understood by all the participants. Scientists needed to become more familiar with basic philosophical concepts and historical figures, while philosophers were often unfamiliar with basic scientific terms and issues. Most of the suggested readings for the seminars assumed a working knowledge of these concepts and key individuals. Even more difficult to grasp were the contexts and controversies associated with key ideas. Collectively, the participants had all the needed knowledge, so through networking, library interactions, and intense conversations around the dinner table during the seminars they were able to seek out the necessary information with relative ease. However, outside of the seminar context access to this important pool of knowledge proved to be difficult. What was needed was a quick guide into this world, something one could carry in a briefcase and consult during a lecture or while reading books about SR.

Other excellent guides to SRD exist, such as the *Science and Religion Encyclopedia* (Van Huyssteen 2003) and *The Oxford Handbook on Science and Religion* (Clayton and Simpson 2006). However, these are far more in-depth and require a preliminary working knowledge of SR, or are expensive and so available only in libraries. Online SR resources are available, including Metanexus (http://www.metanexus.net/Institute/) and Counterbalance (http://www.counterbalance.net/), that provide brief biographies, definitions, and useful links related to SR. However, one cannot always access the Internet while reading or listening. This primer is meant to provide a relatively inexpensive and portable guide for new scholars and students interested in SR, and to serve as a companion for those doing interdisciplinary work. Herein one will find the collective wisdom and insight of noted senior and junior scholars in SR who seek to provide a succinct introduction to key concepts and figures in the field.

How to Use This Book

We hope the *Science and Religion Primer* will be a valuable tool for many individuals and communities, such as those in science and religion courses and programs, discussion groups, adult education classes, individual scholars venturing into this territory, and anyone with an interest in the historical and current dialogues between science and religion. We encourage you to take this book along to lectures or seminars on SR topics, to keep it beside you when you read popular books or academic literature on SR, and to use it as a crib sheet to get a very basic understanding of the concepts or key figures encountered. The book focuses on four core areas: history, philosophy of science, science and technology, and theology, with key concepts and individuals from each of these areas represented. The primer places emphasis on science and Christianity, rather than religion in general, in an effort to focus the discussion on the dominant discourse of much of the historical and current SRD.

No book of this scale can cover all the relevant concepts and figures, and as you read you may well wish for entries we have not included. We have tried to cover a basic spectrum of core concepts and figures, those we repeatedly encountered and about which we wanted further information. Consider this primer as a "way in," just as a foreign language phrase book merely gets you started. Once you enter the "culture" of SR, you will find other resources (books, online sources, colleagues, and mentors) that will bring depth to your understanding.

The book is divided into two sections. Section one provides insight into SRD through introductory essays in each of the four main topic areas of the primer, written by leaders in SR. Peter Harrison, the Andreas Idreos Professor of Science and Religion and Fellow of Harris Manchester College, Oxford University, provides a succinct introduction to historical aspects of SRD by discussing the myths, realities, and complexities of the relationships between science and religion throughout Western history.

Nancey Murphy, professor of Christian philosophy at Fuller Theological Seminary, offers a clear synthesis of the role philosophy has played in shaping SRD. For Murphy, philosophy is crucial in developing conceptual schemes that are consonant with, and enable us to make sense of, the data of science and of theology. Philosophers are challenged to bring coherence to what is often a "balkanized intellectual world."

Holmes Rolston III, University Distinguished Professor of Philosophy at Colorado State University and recipient of the Templeton Prize, highlights how discoveries in and development of the sciences and technology have led scientists to raise questions of truth, beauty, and being that engage religious beliefs and discourse. He reveals the power, the potential, and the dangers of science and technology, and points to religion as offering a necessary dimension to our meaningful engagement with the natural and human-manipulated worlds.

Celia Deane-Drummond, professor of theology and biological sciences at the University of Chester, shows how Christian theologies approach and respond to science on issues ranging from human personhood, origins, and the environment. She underscores the postmodern view that no approach, including scientific approaches, is truly neutral, and that engagement with science requires acknowledgment of one's foundational beliefs.

The second section is an alphabetical listing of entries dealing with a variety of philosophical, historical, scientific, and theological concepts, individuals, and events related to SRD. Each entry is divided into three parts: a brief summary/definition of the concept; a section on key points and challenges, identifying significant issues or debating the way the entry relates to SRD; and a section on "further reading" that lists key sources addressing the topic in more detail. This key sources section will enable readers to explore issues of interest related to these topics in greater depth.

Acknowledgments

This project would not have been possible without the assistance and inspiration of a number of groups and individuals. First we are grateful that the John Templeton Foundation provided generous and key financial resources to make this project a reality.

We also give special thanks to the Council for Christian Colleges and Universities (CCCU) and the work of Ronald Mahurin and Stanley Rosenberg in their organization of the John Templeton Oxford Seminars in Science and Christianity, and the tireless and gracious efforts of Nita Stemmler, who made the seminars a rich and pleasant experience.

Many senior scholars in SR offered mentoring, support, encouragement, and feedback. We want to thank Seminar Director Alister McGrath, who has a more extensive bibliography in his head than most people have in their libraries, for his leadership and mentoring during the summer sessions. Also John Roche, senior consultant and administrator, who valiantly served as seminar organizer, administrator, punting tutor extraordinaire, and humble mentor to many, even in the face of significant health issues.

We would have been lost without the astoundingly generous and patient assistance of the members of our first class advisory board of recognized scholars in SR, who gave of their time and expertise through every stage of developing and editing the primer. They include Craig Boyd, Celia Deane-Drummond, George Ellis, Peter Harrison, Nancey Murphy, and Holmes Rolston III. We thank them for their advice, which greatly improved the quality of the primer. Any remaining errors or omissions are our responsibility.

The development of the primer was informed and encouraged by our fellow seminar participants, many of whom contributed entries to this project. We appreciate every one of you. Particular thanks go the "Isis Frogs" (you know who you are!) for their friendship and support.

Many thanks to project research assistants Zachary Rathke and Tara Oslick, whose careful work and attention helped make the primer come to reality. We also thank Erin Welke, whose teaching assistance freed up time to work on the primer, and who also diligently completed the index. Last, but by no means least, we thank our patient contributors and the remarkably helpful and encouraging staff at Baker Academic, most notably our editor Bob Hosack.

Bibliography

Clayton, Philip, and Zachary Simpson, eds. 2006. *The Oxford Handbook on Science and Religion*. Oxford: Oxford University Press.

Counterbalance Foundation, http://www.counterbalance.net/.

Metanexus Institute on Religion, Science and the Humanities, http://www.metanexus.net/Institute/.

Van Huyssteen, Wentzel, ed. 2003. *Encyclopedia of Science and Religion*. 2 Vols. New York: MacMillan.

Introductory Essays on Science and Religion

History of the Science/Religion Dialogue

PETER HARRISON, UNIVERSITY OF OXFORD

History has always played a significant role in discussions of the relationship between science and religion. Some have made appeals to history to support general theses of a perennial conflict between these two disciplines. Others have argued that science—modern science in particular—has religious foundations, and could have arisen only in the Christian West. While there is, perhaps, more merit in the second view, historians of science have become increasingly wary of global claims of either kind. Simple categories such as *conflict* or *congruence* fail to do justice to the historical realities. Moreover, questions have been asked about whether the categories *science* and *religion* are themselves too abstract to capture the human elements of the activities they purport to describe.

The Conflict Myth

One of the most pervasive conceptions of the historical relationship between science and religion has been that of perennial conflict. This view, first set out in the late nineteenth century by Andrew Dickson White and John Draper, has exercised a tenacious hold over popular imagination ever since. The key episodes from which this stance derives most of its force are the condemnation of **Galileo** in 1623 and the religious reception of the ideas of **Darwin** about evolution and natural selection in the second half of the nineteenth century. On closer examination these historical episodes fall well short of establishing the conflict thesis. The case of Galileo was at least in part a conflict between two competing scientific worldviews. The Catholic Church supported the **Ptolemaic system**, which at the time enjoyed the support of most of the scientific community and was consistent with much of the observational evidence.

The religious upheavals of this period also played an important role in this episode, with the Catholic hierarchy wanting to retain its authority as the sole legitimate interpreter of Scripture. Finally, no vital religious issue was at stake in the controversy. To characterize the Galileo affair as essentially a conflict between science and religion is to misunderstand the complexities of the situation.

The case of the reception of Darwinism is similar in certain respects. There were scientific opponents of evolution by natural selection, although in this case there were scientific supporters too. From a scientific perspective, what Darwin lacked was an adequate genetic explanation of how advantageous adaptations increased in frequency in successive generations. In time this problem was solved with the neo-Darwinian synthesis, which brought together natural selection and genetics. Darwin also had both supporters and detractors among the religious community. Arguably, genuine religious issues were at stake in this controversy, but to regard this historical episode as primarily a conflict between science and religion vastly oversimplifies a complicated situation. Finally, even if the religious responses to Galileo and Darwin were uniformly negative—which they were not—they would form a rather flimsy foundation for a general case that, throughout history, religion and science have been in opposition.

The Religious Origins of Science?

In contrast to proponents of the conflict thesis, some have suggested a rather more positive relationship between science and religion. In its most familiar guise this takes the form of an argument that modern science has religious origins. Supporters of this view include Reijer Hoykaas, Stanley Jaki, and most recently the sociologist Rodney Stark. This view has more to commend it; after all, Christianity was a pervasive feature of the culture in which science arose and religious factors would almost inevitably have played a role. There is little doubt, moreover, about the religious commitments of most of the leading figures of the scientific revolution. Some have also pointed to how modern science emerged in the West but not elsewhere, suggesting that some distinctive feature of Western culture—such as its religion—must be responsible. Granting that Christian ideas or institutions may have played a positive role in the birth of modern science, it is important not to overlook the lingering influence of the ideas of the ancient Greeks, or of the less distant custodians of classical thought, medieval Islamic thinkers. A more defensible position might be that religion was a necessary but insufficient condition for the emergence of modern science.

More cautious than those who suggest that religious influences were the sine qua non of modern science are those who posit midrange theories about the possible interactions of science and religion. The best known is that of sociologist Robert K. Merton (see **Merton thesis**), who in the 1930s pointed to a correlation between Puritanism and scientific activity. This idea has been subjected to searching criticism over the years but still finds qualified support among a minority of historians. In a similar vein, Oxford historian Charles Webster has suggested that the remarkable efflorescence of scientific activity in mid-seventeenth-century England was motivated by puritan millenarianism.

Another theory links particular religious commitments with certain scientific attitudes. Margaret Osler and others have suggested a connection between theological voluntarism—a view that emphasizes divine will, rather than divine rationality—and the empirical approach to the natural world that characterizes the experimental **natural philosophy** of the seventeenth century. My own work has pointed to possible connections between changes in biblical hermeneutics and the new approaches to nature that emerged during the scientific revolution. Also important, in my view, was the renewed Augustinian (see **Augustine**) anthropology of the early modern period that promoted the probabilistic methods of experimental science.

Much recent writing on the historical relationship between science and religion, such as that of John Hedley Brooke, David Lindberg, and Ronald Numbers, has affirmed neither the conflict model nor the idea that science and religion have always been congenial partners. Rather, the situation is complex and defies simple categorization. The relationship between science and religion has been highly dependent on time and place and on the varying commitments of the relevant historical actors. Accordingly, it defies such simple categories as conflict or congruence.

Categorizing Historical Relations between Science and Religion

If the nature of relations between science and religion has indeed been complex, it may be necessary to reconsider some of the ways in which we have typically thought about these historical interactions. Perhaps the most common way to classify the relationship between science and religion has been Ian Barbour's fourfold typology: conflict, independence, dialogue, integration. While this typology has proven to be a very useful pedagogical tool, it is not always sufficiently sensitive when applied in specific historical contexts. John Brooke has suggested other ways in which we might think about the role played by religious ideas and practices in the history of science. Theological notions might provide the presuppositions on which science rests. The modern idea of **laws of nature**, for example, arose from the idea of a divine lawgiver. Those involved in scientific activity may have had religious motivations. **Johannes Kepler** and **Robert Boyle** are good examples of individuals who understood their scientific investigations to be essentially religious activities. Theological considerations might also underpin methods of investigation, as has been suggested with regard to the experimental approach to nature. Sometimes religious beliefs have provided a social sanction for the sciences, as was the case in seventeenth-century England, where there was a religious environment that was particularly conducive to the flourishing of the natural sciences. Finally, theological convictions may actually provide the content of science, as witnessed in the eighteenth-century amalgamation of natural history and **natural theology** (see **handmaiden metaphor**).

This last example—in which the boundaries between science and religion are blurred—also illustrates how the distinction between science and religion with which we are now familiar may not have applied in previous eras. It is significant, for instance, that prior to the nineteenth century those engaged in the study of nature were not designated "scientists," and the activities they conducted were usually referred to as "natural philosophy" or "natural history." This is not merely a semantic point, for natural history and natural philosophy differ in significant ways from modern science. Whereas the latter usually requires the adoption of a methodological **naturalism** that excludes theistic explanations, natural history and **natural philosophy** could both have a theological orientation. It has even been suggested that part of what distinguishes natural philosophy from modern science is that the earlier discipline is ultimately "about God." The lesson here applies to all attempts to understand the past: while history provides rich resources for understanding the present, we must be careful not to impose on previous periods of history distorting categories that are really only appropriate for our time.

Bibliography

Brooke, John Hedley. 1991. *Science and Religion: Some Historical Perspectives*. Cambridge: Cambridge University Press.

Ferngren, Gary B., ed. 2000. *The History of Science and Religion in the Western Tradition: An Encyclopedia*. New York: Garland.

Harrison, Peter. 1998. *The Bible, Protestantism and the Rise of Natural Science*. Cambridge: Cambridge University Press.

———. 2007. *The Fall of Man and the Foundations of Science*. Cambridge: Cambridge University Press.

Hoykaas, Reijer. 1972. *Religion and the Rise of Science*. Grand Rapids: Eerdmans.

Lindberg, David C., and Ronald L. Numbers, eds. 2003. *When Science and Christianity Meet*. Chicago: University of Chicago Press.

Merton, Robert K. 1970. *Science, Technology and Society in Seventeenth-Century England*. New York: Howard Fertig.

Osler, Margaret J. 1994. *Divine Will and the Mechanical Philosophy: Gassendi and Descartes on Contingency and Necessity in the Created World*. Cambridge: Cambridge University Press.

Webster, Charles. 1975. *The Great Instauration: Science, Medicine, and Reform, 1626–1660*. London: Duckworth.

The Role of Philosophy
in the Science/Religion Dialogue

NANCEY MURPHY, FULLER THEOLOGICAL SEMINARY

Reflection on the role of philosophy in the science/religion dialogue (SRD) requires, first, an answer to the question of what philosophy is. Most disagreements about the proper place of philosophy in SRD stem from disagreements about the nature of philosophy itself. Here, I first trace some history of ideas about the nature of philosophy, concentrating on spelling out what a "postanalytic" philosophy might entail. I then turn to the sorts of contributions philosophy so understood can make to SRD, both critically and constructively.

In ancient Greece *philosophy* simply meant "organized knowledge." Aristotle's system covered everything from theology to the reproduction of plants. The chronology of Western intellectual life can be put in terms of the differentiation of disciplines from their origins in ancient philosophy. In the middle ages positive theology, based on revelation, was distinguished from what the philosopher could know through natural reason alone. In the modern era the empirical sciences (optics, astronomy/cosmology, physics, chemistry, and biology) developed in ways that distinguished them from philosophy. More recently, the social sciences and psychology have competed with philosophy to define human nature. Richard Rorty says that "the notion that there is an autonomous discipline called 'philosophy,' distinct from both religion and science, is of quite recent origin" (1979, 131).

So if science and theology have taken over (most of) the original content of philosophy, what is left for philosophers to do? The predominant answer during the modern period was to make philosophy the arbiter of the rational status of other disciplines. So **epistemology** became first philosophy, and the rest of philosophy became (largely) a second-order discipline—we have philosophy of history, philosophy of science, philosophy of religion, and so on. Yet in the mid-twentieth century the very notion that the various academic disciplines needed special "philosopher-approved" rational foundations was called into question by philosophers themselves.

To bring this thumbnail sketch up to date we have to distinguish between the Continental and Anglo-American traditions in late modern and contemporary philosophy. Each provided its own answer to the question regarding the philosopher's proper sphere. I believe it is fair to say that Continental philosophy, taking its phenomenological and existentialist turns, took the description and analysis of human experience to be its *raison d'être*. This tradition has little influence in SRD.

The analytic movement took root primarily in the English-speaking world, although many of its important resources were German and Austrian. There have been a variety of forms of analytic philosophy, but central to all of them is the notion of conceptual analysis. Immanuel Kant prepared the way with his distinction between analytic and synthetic propositions, that is, propositions true by virtue of conceptual content alone and propositions true by virtue of both conceptual content and empirical information. "All bachelors are unmarried" is true solely by virtue of the meanings of the words; "grass is green" is true by virtue of both the meanings of "grass" and "green" and of a fact about the world.

If science had taken over the realm of empirical knowledge, then philosophy could take conceptual knowledge as its proper domain. Two (supposed) characteristics of such knowledge made it appealing. First, the philosopher's job appeared to be immune from further encroachment by science since empirical investigation was thought to be irrelevant to conceptual analysis. One of the first lessons undergraduates had to learn during the heyday of analytic philosophy was not to confuse conceptual questions about the meaning and use of concepts such as *mind, knowledge,* and *justification* with empirical questions regarding cognitive functions and decision making. Second, whereas science yields only probability, conceptual analysis was taken to yield necessary truths.

While the analytic style now dominates current philosophy of religion in America, Robert Hanna states that elsewhere the movement was widely regarded as defunct by the end of the 1970s (1998, 519). Hanna cites technical problems within the movement, but I claim that the problem with analytic philosophy is its inadequate sensitivity to historical location—to the fact that concepts evolve over time and vary from one worldview to another. The beginning of the end of philosophy's analytic period is found in W. V. O. Quine's "Two Dogmas of Empiricism" (1951). Quine is famously taken to have shown that there is no way to draw a clear distinction between analytic and synthetic sentences. If the distinction cannot be drawn sharply, then neither can the distinction between conceptual analysis and empirical investigation (see **Quine-Duhem thesis**).

Since Quine first delivered this address in 1950 a variety of developments in philosophy have confirmed his position. Thomas Kuhn's *Structure of Scientific Revolutions* (1970) dramatically made the point that basic concepts in science undergo significant shifts, despite surface similarities in language. In moral philosophy Charles Taylor and

Alasdair MacIntyre have made it clear that basic concepts of the self (Taylor 1989) as well as the entirety of our moral discourse (MacIntyre 1984) have a history. MacIntyre and Stephen Toulmin have each, in different ways, provided insightful diagnoses and criticisms of modernity's attempt at ahistorical reason (Toulmin 1990; MacIntyre 1977).

According to this approach, philosophical arguments based on current linguistic practices are suspect. While analytic philosopher J. L. Austin claimed that our common stock of words embodies all of the distinctions and connections worth making (1961), philosopher of science Paul Feyerabend pointed out that common ways of speaking are adapted to beliefs, not facts, and the acquisition of new knowledge ought to be allowed to call such beliefs into question (1981). So this postanalytic view of philosophy—philosophy "naturalized"—demotes philosophers from the role of cultural magistrates and encourages them to investigate the frontiers of knowledge, looking for ways in which traditional patterns of use may need to be modified.

Another distinction needs to be drawn here. While the majority of English-language philosophers take a modest view of the possibility of constructing philosophical systems, there has also been the tradition of **process philosophy**, based on the view that existing patterns of thought need to be changed radically to encompass current knowledge. Philosophers such as Alfred North Whitehead have proposed new systems of concepts intended to replace the inherited scheme wholesale. Process philosophy and other related metaphysical ventures have influenced some theologians and are used as resources for relating religion and science.

For those who reject philosophy's claim to devise new metaphysical systems (see **metaphysics**), what can philosophy justly aspire to be? We can still say that, as for Aristotle, philosophy is about everything, but in a different sense; it is largely second-order discourse about other fields of inquiry. And we can say with the analytic philosophers that its method is primarily attention to the language and concepts of those other discourses. Yet it cannot be mere conceptual analysis; we have to ask, analysis of whose concepts, in which phase of their development? So one of philosophy's roles is a (modest, not wholesale) constructive task.

There is a therapeutic task as well. Ludwig Wittgenstein has been most influential in developing the notion that philosophy is akin to therapy. One of the lasting achievements of the analytic movement is the recognition that many (some would say all) philosophical problems are the result of misconstruing concepts or, in other words, of beguilement by the inept use of language. Some proponents of the view of philosophy as therapy, such as D. Z. Phillips, eschew theology/science dialogue on principle because they believe it is motivated by conceptions of religion that need instead to be diagnosed and cured. Yet there is room in SRD for recognition of problems that need to be dissolved rather than solved. One area where Wittgensteinian cautions are in order is in discussions of time. If science says that time originated with the big bang, and Augustine said that time was a part of creation, then God cannot be in time. Instead, God is eternal. But how can the eternal interact with the temporal? If we cannot answer this question, how can we claim that God acts in nature or human history? Has language led us astray here?

Much of the philosophical work related to SRD in the past forty years is of the modest constructive sort. There is a tendency to speak of a "conceptual scheme" as though, lying behind our various spheres of discourse, there is a single unified network of interrelated concepts. As a matter of fact, there is a great deal of inconsistency and indefiniteness. Consider the concept of **causation**. It has multifarious manifestations in science and ordinary life. Yet there is no agreement even on the "simple" matter of whether *things* or *events* serve as causes. Other problematic concepts include truth, justification, meaning, goodness, and human nature. So the constructive role for philosophers generally, and especially for philosophers involved in SRD, is to examine nests of interrelated concepts, whether from philosophy or science, in order to sniff out inconsistencies and other problems, and then to make proposals for less problematic ways of thinking—which means, in effect, proposals for more felicitous language. Topics include methodological issues, the nature of language, realism and truth, causation and agency, goodness and evil, and time.

Current work on the nature of the human person provides a particularly fine illustration of positive interaction between philosophy and theology. Our culture has no shared concept of human nature, even at the most basic ontological level. Many lay Christians hold a trichotomous view—humans comprise body, soul, and spirit. Body-soul or body-mind dualism has been a significant position in academia for centuries (see **mind/body problem**). Currently most philosophers and many scientists promote materialist or physicalist accounts. A crucial question is whether physicalist accounts are consistent with Christian teaching. Part of the answer here depends on whether we can make sense of a *nonreductive* version—can we show that a physicalist ontology (in relation to the person) does not entail that our thoughts and behavior are simply determined by the laws of neurobiology?

Many current academicians are happy with the proliferation of a variety of unrelated discourses. SRD, however, grows out of discomfort with such a balkanized intellectual world. So while there is no clear, consistent, and unified conceptual scheme lying behind our assorted linguistic practices, the search for unity and consistency seems a worthy goal for the philosopher. The works of Quine and others show that philosophers need to listen to scientists, and many of the most interesting and important philosophers today are the ones who are attempting to warp philosophical theories to fit new scientific discoveries. If theology, too, provides genuine knowledge about reality—and most participants in SRD agree that it does—then the opportunity to think philosophically in the midst of both theologians and scientists is a great opportunity indeed.

Bibliography

Austin, J. L. 1961. "A Plea for Excuses." In *Philosophical Papers*, edited by J. O. Urmson and G. J. Warnock, 123–52. Oxford: Clarendon.

Feyerabend, Paul. 1981. "Materialism and the Mind-Body Problem." In *Realism, Rationalism, and Scientific Method: Philosophical Papers*, 1:161–75. Cambridge: Cambridge University Press.

Hanna, Robert. 1998. "Conceptual Analysis." In *The New Routledge Encyclopedia of Philosophy*, edited by Edward Craig, 2:518–22. London and New York: Routledge.

Kuhn, Thomas. 1970. *The Structure of Scientific Revolutions*. 2nd ed. Chicago: University of Chicago Press.

MacIntyre, Alasdair. 1977. "Epistemological Crises, Dramatic Narrative, and the Philosophy of Science." *The Monist* 60:453–72.

———. 1984. *After Virtue*. 2nd ed. Notre Dame, IN: University of Notre Dame Press.

Quine, W. V. O. 1951. "Two Dogmas of Empiricism." *Philosophical Review* 60:20–43.

Rorty, Richard. 1979. *Philosophy and the Mirror of Nature*. Princeton, NJ: Princeton University Press.

Taylor, Charles. 1989. *Sources of the Self: The Making of Modern Identity*. Cambridge, MA: Harvard University Press.

Toulmin, Stephen. 1990. *Cosmopolis: The Hidden Agenda of Modernity*. Chicago and New York: Free Press.

Theology's Intersection with the Science/Religion Dialogue

CELIA DEANE-DRUMMOND, UNIVERSITY OF CHESTER

Theology, as the name implies, is rational deliberation about religious beliefs (Ford 1999). It differs from religious studies in that it asks questions about what people believe and the basis for such beliefs, rather than describing particular practices or rituals as an external observer. While other works helpfully summarize different faith positions in relation to science (Eisen and Laderman 2007), the purpose of this essay is to concentrate attention on Christian theology.

There is vigorous debate over the extent to which it is necessary or proper for theologians to be believers. While one can study theology without any form of religious faith, at least one school of thought argues that generating theology requires at least an appreciation of what it means to have faith. The earliest traditions of theology therefore speak of it as "faith seeking understanding" (see **Augustine**). Of course, there may be resistance to this tradition among members of certain academic communities who believe that faith amounts to a bias that prevents fully rational analysis of different concepts. The belief that it is possible to be entirely neutral in one's stance toward belief, and therefore stand outside religious traditions, stems from confidence in modern forms of Enlightenment rationality. Such confidence also led to the burgeoning rise in experimental science that seemed to the casual observer to be detached from any religious position. However, such confidence has itself come under scrutiny through incorporation of postmodern criticism of modernist ideals. In this case, postmodernity challenges the possibility of *any* neutral stance toward reality, including religious reality. It also resists any claims for overarching universalistic foundations as being out of touch with the varied human contexts in which ideas ferment and take shape.

Given this ferment in discussion about what theology is and what it might contribute to academic discourse, theology can adopt a number of different methodologies. Almost all will include a combination of philosophy, Scripture, tradition, and experience (which will include the experience of faith or its rejection). David Ford suggests that given the multiplicity of different dimensions to theology, it can be summarized as a form of wisdom (1999, 157–58). Within the academic setting the study of theology is less likely to take a confessional stance, reflected in the dogmatic proclamation of a particular church tradition, and more likely to be open to inquiry and revision drawing on particular styles of theological reasoning. As it engages with science and other aspects of contemporary culture, theology is increasingly likely to become ecumenical, drawing on various church traditions as they seem useful for the debates at hand. The commonality of particular issues or problems, such as those arising from debates in science and religion, has the effect of breaking down denominational barriers and allowing a mutual exchange of ideas and concepts.

Historically, the relationship between science and theology came into focus in the seventeenth century through the development of various forms of **natural theology**. Such theologies sought to find evidence of God in the workings of the natural world; the "book of nature" became a place for divine revelation. This contrasted with traditional theology that put more emphasis on the Word of God, that is, God revealed in Holy Scripture. This approach, also known as revealed theology, was often suspicious of ways of finding God outside scriptural revelation. The roots of this suspicion are reflected in contemporary movements such as **creationism**, except in this case the interpretation of Scripture (or **hermeneutics**) has followed a particular ideology that assumes that the first books of Genesis are about the literal origin of the world. Here the revealed Word of God is considered as a source for creation "science" that itself has little scientific credibility. In other words, instead of rejecting the scientific view of the world and naming revelation as the path to God, creationists claim scientific credence for their own view. Science has become subsumed under the category of scriptural revelation. Of course, it is not necessary to interpret the Bible in this way, but it is used as a bulwark against perceived fears of evolutionary science becoming a source of meaning.

One of the key ideas for those working at the boundary of science and religion (Clayton 2006) is to seek to understand how God can be understood as Creator of all that is, given the knowledge that we have gained in cosmology, physics, biology, and all the sciences. Ever since David Hume challenged natural theology by pointing to natural evil in the world, theologians have struggled to make sense of belief in a Creator. Envisaging **miracles** as divine interventions from outside the material world seemed to pose God as detached from the world and active only in special and unique events that were outside the explanatory powers of science. Instead, theologians have sought to come to terms with belief in God as Creator by envisaging God as creating those physical laws and biological systems that allow life and all its processes to emerge. Of course, precisely how God might do this is also a matter of philosophical debate about the nature of God's involvement with the world.

One of the key differences between Christian theology and other religious traditions is the belief in Christ as God incarnate; Jesus is divine humanity on earth. Moreover, the scandal of this belief is not just that he is claimed to have been born through the power of the Holy Spirit, but also that he died and was raised again, his resurrection becoming the source of life for the world. Such belief in the universal significance of the particular man, Jesus, has remained a stumbling block for nonbelievers from the earliest time to the present day. In theological parlance the discussion about Christ's significance is termed **Christology**. The aspects of Christology that have come to the fore in science and religion debates concern in particular the significance of his incarnation and resurrection and their meaning in a scientific age.

Christ's relationship to creation raises many questions. How is Christ related to evolutionary concepts of human becoming? What does his resurrection mean in the light of projections of heat death or the eventual collapse of the universe predicted by theoretical physics? What about more immediate portents of ecological collapse identified by environmental science and predictions of climate change? What might be the future of creation as a whole in light of these concerns? The latter, of course, brings us into the territory of **eschatology**.

The science of the earliest origins of the cosmos and life (see **cosmology**) and the science of future projections of life's history include speculative elements and prompt continuous debate among scientists. In these areas, therefore, theology is able to make a contribution to the debate, which may explain why some physicists, such as Stephen Hawking, speak of God when describing discoveries about the origin of the cosmos and time (Hawking 1988). The question that theologians need to ask here is how far such renditions of God are adequate in the theological sense.

Theologians who draw on traditional concepts will also be concerned to portray God as **Trinity**. Some philosophical and scientific portrayals of God, as in Paul Davies (1989), speak of God in general rather than the Trinity. This is because Davies' ideas appeal to the religious imagination in detachment from Christian classical reflection. The concept of the Trinity is important as it allows theologians to understand more deeply how God can be both intimately connected to the world yet remain transcendent over it.

Of course, some theologians will resist viewing God as having any transcendence on the basis that God is identified with the natural world and its processes. **Pantheism** identifies God with the world, while **process thought** sees God as emerging through such world processes, even though process thought also allows for a conception of God as being more than these processes. **Panentheism** is the view that the world is somehow contained in God, and this is a satisfying alternative for those who wish to acknowledge both the immanence and transcendence of God simultaneously. Not all panentheists view the relationship of immanence to transcendence in trinitarian ways, that is, in terms of God understood not just as the One, but as the Three in One, the Father, the Son, and the Spirit.

For a trinitarian theologian the mutual indwelling of each of the persons of the Trinity in love overflows to the love of the world and initiates its creation and continual creativity. Such a process cannot be categorized in scientific terms, and it would be inappropriate to try to force the work of the Trinity into such categories. There remain, therefore, some areas where theology cannot be corroborated by science. However, theologians seek to develop theology in such a way that scientific ideas can also be acknowledged for the truths they contain. Evolution (see **evolutionary biology**), for example, is accepted by most of those in the science and religion debate as being compatible with biblical faith in a Creator God. Both are aspects of one reality, that is, one world in its diversity and complexity.

Clearly there are still problems, even if we accept some accommodation between theology and the natural sciences. Many of these problems are not necessarily unique to the present day, but can be intensified by current issues and challenges. One such problem is that of **theodicy**. How can theologians claim belief in a good God when there is so much evil and suffering, particularly in light of millions of years of evolutionary struggle and extinctions? Portraying such horrendous changes as mere stages on the way to an evolving humanity seems unconvincing. Debates about how to come to terms with such problems continue apace.

Also, given what we know of the evolutionary history of humanity, how might a theological anthropology be developed? What does it mean to speak of humans as in the image of God, given our knowledge of natural science through biological, social, scientific, psychological, and anthropological knowledge of the human person? What does freedom of the will mean in the light of such understanding (see **determinism and free will**)? Does human nature even exist, given our knowledge of genetics? All such questions impinge on traditional theological understandings of the human person.

Theology is also concerned today about the human contexts in which it develops. Within the science and religion debate the application of science in **technology** also needs to come to the fore. The relationship between theology and technology raises particular questions about human identity, how we might perceive ourselves in light of burgeoning technologies, many of which are **biotechnologies** that seek to manipulate the pattern of creation itself. Is such manipulation a gift of God or a crime against God's good creation (Deane-Drummond 2001)? Such discussions also slip into the area of theological **ethics**, and overlap with secular discourse about the role of the human person in manipulating nature.

Concern with humanity's impact on the natural world (see **environmentalism**) has culminated in **ecotheologies** and various forms of feminist theology (see **ecofeminism**). Feminist thought challenges the androcentric language that has dominated traditional theological discourse and seeks to find new ways to think about God that give proper attention to feminist ideas. All aspects of theological discussion can come under scrutiny from feminist theologians, from God-talk to theological themes such as creation and redemption. Feminist theologians generally will resist all forms of hierarchical thinking, though there is variety in feminism that needs to be acknowledged, just as there is variety within traditional discourse. Feminists who have a particular concern with environmental issues are known as ecofeminists, but not all ecotheologians are feminists. Many feminists are similarly concerned with the social impact of technologies, especially the new reproductive technologies, insofar as they preferentially affect women and women's communities.

Bibliography

Clayton, Philip, ed. 2006. *The Oxford Handbook of Religion and Science.* Oxford: Oxford University Press.

Davies, Paul. 1989. *The Cosmic Blueprint.* London: Unwin.

Deane-Drummond, Celia. 2001. *Biology and Theology Today: Exploring the Boundaries.* London: SCM.

Eisen, Arri, and Gary Laderman, eds. 2007. *Science, Religion and Society: An Encyclopedia of History, Culture and Controversy.* 2 vols. London: M. E. Sharpe.

Ford, David. 1999. *Theology: A Very Short Introduction.* Oxford: Oxford University Press.

Hawking, Stephen. 1988. *A Brief History of Time.* New York: Bantam.

Science and Technology in Light of Religion

Holmes Rolston III, Colorado State University

Physics and biology are the two principal natural sciences affecting contemporary religious thought. Both have developed at microscopic and megascale levels, unknown when the Christian or other world faiths were founded. Astronomy opens up vast space and time; atomic physics reveals strange elemental particles. Evolutionary biology finds deep time on Earth, molecular biology reveals the building blocks and coding for life. Geology first raised the question of vast time scales. Technical sciences, such as medical science and computer science, raise both theoretical and ethical issues, often because they make possible novel, sometimes quite unprecedented, human actions; examples include questions about therapeutic genetics made possible by sequencing human DNA, or about cloning. Theologians also interact with the social sciences—psychology, anthropology, economics, history—although they are not addressed directly here.

Science as we know it today arose in the Christian West, with both Greek and Hebrew roots. Historians often find that such science required the monotheist worldview for its origins, providing the belief that the world is ordered and rational, knowable by observation, and that humans have the power and destiny, as Kepler said, to "think God's thoughts after him."

Scientists often insist that the **scientific method**, especially since the European Enlightenment (the last four centuries), is based on reason and observation; they seek theory corroborated by evidence. Currently they often contrast this with "faith," or belief in things not seen and not proved. They advocate repeatability or testability, although many of the phenomena scientists investigate (such as the big bang or origin of life) are historical and not directly repeatable or testable. Further, scientists often "believe" in what their theories suggest should be there—for example, spending decades looking for the neutrino, a massless, chargeless minute particle, or entelechy, a vital life force supposed to be in living things (biology) and absent in physics and chemistry.

Scientists also increasingly realize that theory, models, data, and description are more entwined than once supposed. When moving beyond immediate, native-range observation, scientists see mostly what their constructed theories and instruments enable them to see. This, together with discoveries in physics and shifting scientific theories over time, has softened the hard objectivity earlier advocated in science in favor of more historical and culture-bound accounts. Western science is but one way to look at the world; it features laws, natural causes, empirical facts.

But the world we inhabit is complex and multileveled; any scientific account is partial and abstracts from the real world, somewhat as a map only partially depicts the whole landscape. One also needs accounts of meaning, significance, and guidance for life to make one's way around in the real world. Critics of science, especially postmodernists, press these claims about the social construction of science further than many scientists wish, and theologians debate whether to welcome these developments (Rolston 2006).

Science and religion may relate in four ways, according to an analysis made popular by Ian Barbour (1990). There may be conflict, independence, dialogue, or integration. Scientific materialism and biblical literalism will be in direct conflict. But perhaps science works with causes, religion with meanings. The two are as independent as law and poetry. Or perhaps, though each has its own integrity, they overlap and complement each other in ongoing dialogue. Perhaps a comprehensive science even points toward God, launching a theology with which it can integrate, as in the tradition of natural theology (Van Huyssteen 2003).

The relations between physics and theology are surprisingly cordial at present; the relations between biology and theology are more difficult. Astrophysics and nuclear physics, combining quantum mechanics and relativity theory, are describing a universe fine-tuned for life, while evolutionary and molecular biology seem to be discovering that the history of life is a random walk with much struggle and chance, driven by selfish genes.

Physics has made dramatic discoveries at astronomical and submicroscopic ranges, remote from ordinary, native-range experience. Physics has discovered that the universe (this universe at least) originated thirteen billion years ago in a big bang and has since been expanding. From the primal burst of energy elementary particles formed, and afterward hydrogen, the simplest element, which serves a fuel for the stars. In the stellar furnaces all the heavier atoms were forged. Some stars subsequently exploded (supernovae). The heavier elements were collected to form, in our case, the solar system and planet Earth. Startling interrelationships are required for these creative processes to work.

These results have been summarized as the **anthropic principle**, which argues that the universe has been fine-tuned from the beginning and in its fundamental construction for the subsequent construction of stars, planets, life, and mind (Barr

2003). There are nontheological, naturalistic ways of interpreting these discoveries, but a plausible interpretation is divine design. Theologians and philosophers have often been wary of design arguments, remembering **William Paley**, his fine-tuned watch, and the many telling criticisms of such arguments. Nevertheless the physical world has again begun to resemble a fine-tuned watch, and now many quantitative calculations support the argument.

Biology stands in stark contrast to the above—at least at first glance. Molecular biology, discovering DNA, has decoded the "secret of life" (once ascribed to the Spirit of God). Evolutionary history has located the secret of life in natural selection operating over incremental variations across enormous time spans, with the fittest selected to survive (see **evolutionary biology**). Speciation begins with the simple and results in the complex, from microbes to persons. As with physics, the two levels have been theoretically interrelated. The genetic level supplies variations, through the coding of life in DNA. Organisms cope at their native-range levels, inhabiting ecosystems, and across deep evolutionary time species are selected as they track changing environments, transforming one into another.

The process is prolific but no longer fine-tuned. To the contrary, evolutionary history can seem tinkering and make-shift at the same time that, within structural constraints and mutations available, it optimizes adapted fit. Natural selection is thought to be blind, both in the genetic variations bubbling up without regard to the needs of the organism, some few of which by chance are beneficial, and also in the evolutionary selective forces, which select for survival without active agency or direction. Evolutionary theorists insist that nothing in natural selection theory guarantees progress; many doubt that the theory predicts the long-term historical innovations that have occurred, such as a centered nucleus, multiple-celled life, capacities to acquire information, enlarging brains, and the emergence of humans.

Theological reaction to the biological sciences is mixed. Fundamentalist theology denies much of (or all of) evolution and sometimes seeks to prevent its teaching in public schools. Others construct an evolutionary theism, emphasizing the continuing vital creative processes over time, the ascent of life from the simple to the complex, the increase of information, the effective and efficient results of genetic creativity and natural selection, producing a quasi-design, the production of more out of less over long millennia (see **creationism**). Increasing knowledge of the sophistication of molecular structures has led some to look for **intelligent design** there (see also **William Paley**). Many geneticists are now speaking of genetic programs as sophisticated problem-solving processes (see **genomics/genetics**). Some suppose divine intervention at quantum levels (see **quantum theory**). The watchmaker-design approach to the concept of a Creator, if appropriate in physics, may not be the model for biology, where more autonomy and self-creativity is combined with the divine will for life, a divine parenting entwined with spontaneous creative process (Rolston 1999).

Science is both pure and applied, and the application of science has brought an explosion of **technology**. This is true in two main areas: medicine and industry, the latter including industrialized, high-tech agriculture. Communication and transportation are also spectacularly advanced. Consider the transformations on Earth in the last century resulting from automobiles and airplanes, electricity and electronics. Although long in coming, a threshold was crossed with the coming of the steam engine. Prior to that the work of the world was done by muscle and blood, with some windpower and waterpower. But with the switch to motors and gears and the escalating technology thereafter, humans gained vast powers for the transformation of their world. The result has been a population explosion by one species, *Homo sapiens*, unprecedented in Earth history. Combined with the technological explosion of powers, this has brought escalating consumption, as well as increasing differential in the distribution of these resources. With world capitalism, as it has developed in recent times, the rich get richer and the poor poorer.

Science here is both pivotal and puzzling. Hard science has a soft underbelly: conscience. Phrased less metaphorically, science can answer *is* questions, but not *ought* questions. Science has made us increasingly competent in knowledge and power, but it has also left us decreasingly confident about right and wrong. Indeed, there is no scientific guidance for life. With due admiration for its successes, science leaves the ultimate value questions still urgent and unresolved. If one requires proof of that, one need only read the newspaper: the Iraqi war, the 9/11 terrorist attacks, Enron, protests at G-8 summits, health care for the poor, corruption in government, deforestation, global warming—the list goes on and on.

Scientists may object that these are not issues in science, though they may deal with its application in economics, technology, and public policy. They are, however, issues arising from the powers launched by science and technology. What do scientists who launch these powers care about? What do those to whom their science becomes available care about? Science is a magnificent enterprise, but many, including theologians and scientists themselves, probe the logic of science and worry about its zest for mastery, fearful lest this become a lust for mastery. Science is the quest for knowledge, and knowledge is power.

Even pure science is driven by a desire to understand, and that, ipso facto, is a desire to conquer. The fundamental posture of science is analysis, the discovery of laws and generalizations, theory with implications, prediction, testability, repeatability. One wants better probes, better techniques, higher-resolution detectors, more computing power. Such attitudes always invite control, but more than that, this very approach to nature is driven by the desire to control. The underlying premise of all scientific logic is mastery, and with that insight the claims to detachment, objectivity, and independence take on a different color.

Fueling technology, science brings escalating know-how without know-whether. More than any people before, as a result of our technological prowess through science and industry we have the capacity to do good and evil, to make war or to feed others, to act in justice and in love, or in self-interested aggrandizement. Allegedly objective science is inevitably bent, sooner or later, into the service of technology, and such scientific knowledge coupled with technological power is neither detached nor objective. Thus relativity theory is used to make nuclear weapons; the human genome, mapped, invites first medical therapy and later genetic engineering. Such utility is not simply an outcome of science, it is part of its worldview.

Science is the product of the powerful urge to dominate nature, and those who have it are ready enough to colonize elsewhere and harvest whatever resources they can wherever they can, to build machines of industry and of war, to dominate other peoples and races. There are three problems: overpopulation, overconsumption, and underdistribution.

When moving from pure to applied science, scientists seem to care; the benefits of science in the service of humans are preached incessantly. While often such caring and benefits are present, it is also certain that science without critical caring for others, by scientists or those who exploit their science, is what has produced the present triple crisis. And caring for others—loving one's neighbor—is the central claim in religious ethics. Science is not theology. Theology cannot suggest the content of any science, but theologians can notice the forms into which such content is being poured. One can do science without adverting explicitly to theology, but one cannot live by science alone.

Indeed, science cannot teach us what we most need to know—that about which we most should care. Science could be as much part of the problem as part of the solution. Science can, and often does, serve noble interests. Science can, and often does, become self-serving, a means of perpetuating injustice, violating human rights, making war, degrading the environment. Science is used for Western domination over nature and over other nations. As a result of the powers of science-based technology, humans are altering the natural history of the planet, threatening alike the future of life, the fauna and the flora, and human life (Gottlieb 2006). The values associated with the pursuit of science, as well as those that govern the uses to which science is put, are not generated out of the sciences. Nothing in science ensures against philosophical confusions, against rationalizing, against mistaking evil for good, against loving the wrong gods.

Despite the evident progress in the sciences in today's world the value questions remain as acute and painful as ever. There lie crises ahead, not for the lack of science but for the lack of wisdom, a wisdom that only religion in the broad sense can supply—worldviews that orient us philosophically and that can redeem our human nature from its perennial failings. The need for justice, for love, for caring will remain undiminished, and science will need conscience in the next century more than ever before.

What on Earth are we doing? What on Earth can we do? What on Earth ought we to be doing? There is no figuring this out without both science and religion; there is no doing it right without integration of the two.

Bibliography

Barbour, Ian G. 1990. *Religion in an Age of Science*. San Francisco: Harper & Row.

Barr, Stephen M. 2003. *Modern Physics and Ancient Faith*. Notre Dame, IN: University of Notre Dame Press.

Gottlieb, Roger S., ed. 2006. *The Oxford Handbook of Religion and Ecology*. New York: Oxford University Press.

Rolston, Holmes, III. 1999. *Genes, Genesis and God*. Cambridge: Cambridge University Press.

———. 2006. *Science and Religion: A Critical Survey*. New ed. Philadelphia: Templeton Foundation Press.

Van Huyssteen, Wentzel, ed. 2003. *Encyclopedia of Science and Religion*. 2 vols. New York: Macmillan.

Entries

☐ Altruism

The word *altruism* was coined by the nineteenth-century philosopher Auguste Comte. In its barest sense the word means acting for the benefit of the other. Discerning which actions should be considered altruistic and which should not depends on whether one judges an actor's motive or the action's consequences. If a person acts with someone else's benefit chiefly in mind but that action results in harm, should this be called an altruistic act? Virtue ethicists emphasize motives, whereas many sociobiologists emphasize the consequences related to promoting a "genetic heritage." Related to this is the debate over whether an action should be regarded as altruistic if the actor enjoys personal benefit in addition to acting for the good of the other. *Absolute altruism* says that the altruist can receive no benefit whatsoever. *Relative altruism*, according to C. Daniel Batson (1991), says that the altruist can benefit if the action was done with the primary motive of helping another.

Altruism is understood differently in various philosophical traditions, scientific disciplines, and religious orientations. In common parlance, altruism is closely related to, if not identical with, loving others. When altruism is understood as acting to help others, the link between it and love seems obvious. But when altruism is defined as self-sacrifice or self-denial, some suggest that an altruistic action is not always loving. For instance, those in codependent relationships may not be acting in love when they allow others to abuse them or take them for granted.

Most biologists define altruism as acting to enhance the reproductive success of others at the expense of one's own reproductive success. Accordingly, *reciprocal altruism* suggests that some act to help others only when expecting some benefit in response. *Kin altruism* predicts that actors will help those whose genetic lineage is similar to their own. *Group altruism* argues that groups of self-sacrificial altruists can out-compete groups comprised of selfish individuals. In group altruism, in-group cooperation occurs, but out-group competition can be vicious.

Key Points/Challenges

- Altruism is important in discussions of science and religion because all of the world's major religions promote ways of living in relation to others and the sciences recognize the importance environment plays in scientific study.

41

- Some see in nature the impetus and explanation for extravagant altruism. Organisms might be altruistic toward relatives or for the sake of the members of their group when in competition with other groups. Others suggest that genuine altruism is unnatural, unreasonable, and radically impractical. Colin Grant (2001) argues that altruism is a modern notion that has little or no true meaning apart from the Christian gospel from which it originally emerged.

- Some feminist scholars have argued that sometimes acting for the good of oneself is more important than giving priority to the desires of others. When love is defined as acting intentionally, in sympathetic response to others (including God), to promote overall well-being, an altruistic act is not loving if overall well-being is not promoted.

- Some religious traditions consider God the model altruist; these traditions teach that God has acted for the benefit of the universe as a whole, or individuals and groups in particular. Many Christians view the crucifixion as the ultimate altruistic act—Jesus laying down his life for the benefit (salvation) of others. Believers ought to imitate God by acting for the good of others.

- Altruism is seen by Stephen Post as a primary goal of all the major world religions. However, this is true only if altruism is not understood in the sense of absolute altruism. After all, most theistic religions suggest that God rewards those who help others. And nontheistic religious traditions do not neatly distinguish between self and others. In such an interrelated universe, actions done to benefit others almost inevitably also help the actor.

Further Reading

Batson, C. Daniel. 1991. *The Altruism Question: Toward a Social-Psychological Answer.* Hillsdale, NJ: Lawrence Erlbaum Associates.

Provides recent social science research on altruism.

Grant, Colin. 2001. *Altruism and Christian Ethics.* Cambridge: Cambridge University Press.

Surveys theories of altruism and suggests a theological response.

Oord, Thomas J. 2004. *Science of Love: The Wisdom of Well-Being.* Philadelphia: Templeton Foundation Press.

Defines love and explores scientific and theological implications of love research.

Post, Stephen G. 2003. *Unlimited Love: Altruism, Compassion, and Service.* Philadelphia: Templeton Foundation Press.

President of the Institute for Research on Unlimited Love offers arguments for the importance of studying love.

Sober, Elliott, and David S. Wilson. 1998. *Unto Others: The Evolution and Psychology of Unselfish Behavior.* Cambridge, MA: Harvard University Press.

Addresses questions of altruism and egoism from biological, anthropological, and philosophical perspectives.

Thomas Jay Oord, Northwest Nazarene University

□ Anthropic Principle

Anthropic principles (AP) are statements frequently cited in response to the phenomenon of fine-tuning, the sensitive dependence of life on values of the fundamental constants of nature (e.g., electron mass and charge, relative strengths of gravitational and electromagnetic forces) and on the conditions of the universe near the time of the big bang. *Sensitive dependence* means that if the values of these constants or initial conditions were changed very slightly, then life as we know it could not exist.

One formulation of the AP is the "weak" AP (WAP): "What we can expect to observe must be restricted by the conditions necessary for our presence as observers" (Carter 1974, 132). This is a methodological principle, specifically, a reminder that our existence imposes a selection effect. A selection effect occurs whenever our observation methods restrict us to only a subset of the possible phenomena. In the case of cosmology, our very existence restricts our observations to only those universes that are fine-tuned such that we *can* exist.

A second version of the AP is the "strong" AP (SAP): "The universe (and hence, the fundamental parameters on which it depends) must be such as to admit the creation of observers within it at some stage" (Carter 1974, 135). There are two ways to interpret the SAP: as a design or as an ensemble hypothesis. According to the design view, "must" implies that observers are a necessary feature of a universe, and that their existence causally explains fine-tuning. In some versions of the design hypothesis, the cause of fine-tuning is the intention of a designer for a universe with intelligent life. In the ensemble version, the SAP consists of the WAP plus the hypothesis of a large ensemble of universes, each universe having different values of the fundamental constants. The WAP then implies that no matter how unlikely it is that intelligent life could appear in the universe, the only universe we could ever observe would be one in which such life is possible. For example, astronomers observe that the expansion rate of the universe is increasing. This implies a surprisingly low value for a fundamental constant called the "cosmological constant," whereas a higher value would characterize a universe in which stars and planets could not form and thus presumably no life would exist. Both versions of the SAP go beyond methodological considerations and attempt to explain fine-tuning by means of arguments in which the existence of human life plays a key role—that is, anthropic arguments.

Key Points/Challenges

- There is disagreement over whether APs are scientifically useful ideas. McMullin (1993) sees the WAP as merely a reminder of a methodological principle of which scientists are already aware.

- McMullin, Barrow, and Tipler (1986), and a number of other scientists, see the design version of the SAP as metaphysical speculation (since they interpret "must" as implying necessity).

- McMullin warns that fine-tuning may not provide support for either a design or an ensemble hypothesis.

- Bostrum (2002) argues that if the WAP is invoked, then the observation of fine-tuning lends support to an ensemble theory.

- The WAP is sometimes used—by Susskind (2006) and possibly by Barrow and Tipler—as a crucial step in arguing that an ensemble hypothesis is preferable to a design hypothesis when trying to understand the origin of fine-tuning.

Further Reading

Barrow, John D., and Frank J. Tipler. 1986. *The Anthropic Cosmological Principle*. Oxford: Oxford University Press.

> A comprehensive and detailed description (requiring some familiarity with physics and cosmology to be appreciated) of fine-tuning phenomena and examples of how APs can be used in a scientifically fruitful way.

Bostrum, Nick. 2002. *Anthropic Bias: Observation Selection Effects in Science and Philosophy*. New York: Routledge.

> A helpful survey of the applications of selection effects to questions in science and philosophy (strongly recommended).

Carter, Brandon. 1974. "Large Number Coincidences and the Anthropic Principle in Cosmology." In *Modern Cosmology and Philosophy*, edited by John Leslie, 131–39. Amherst, New York: Prometheus.

> The paper in which the WAP and SAP were first introduced along with examples of their application to cosmology.

Craig, William Lane. 1987. "Barrow and Tipler on the Anthropic Principle vs. Divine Design." http://www.leaderu.com/offices/billcraig/docs/barrow.html.

> A theist's response to the claim that the best explanation for fine-tuning is not design but instead a multiple-universe hypothesis combined with the WAP.

Davies, Paul W. C. 1982. *The Accidental Universe*. Cambridge: Cambridge University Press.

> A clear description of fine-tuning phenomena, more concise than Barrow and Tipler.

McMullin, Ernan. 1993. "Indifference Principle and Anthropic Principle in Cosmology." *Studies in History and Philosophy of Science* 24:359–89.

Insightfully places APs in historical and theological contexts.

Susskind, Leonard. 2006. *The Cosmic Landscape: String Theory and the Illusion of Intelligent Design*. New York: Little, Brown.

A detailed, well-argued exploration of why the fundamental constants of physics have the values they do, and how these values support life, without resorting to a hypothesis of supernatural agency.

James K. Simmons, Shawnee State University

☐ Aquinas (Thomas Aquinas 1225–74)

The work of Thomas Aquinas represents the most complete synthesis of Aristotelian metaphysics and Christian theology. Aquinas was a Dominican monk who studied under Albert the Great and taught at the University of Paris in the mid-thirteenth century when the works of Aristotle had only recently been translated into Latin. However, Aquinas is no mere commentator on Aristotle; he transforms and shapes the ancient philosopher's work for his own purposes. For Aquinas, humans come to know through two complementary sources: the natural light of reason and the light of faith. The "natural light of reason" refers to the universal human capacity to know particular things by means of an empirical investigation. The various sciences (as bodies of knowledge) provide all people with basic truths concerning the world—for example, that there is a God, that all people recognize basic precepts of morality, and that each kind of thing has a particular nature, or essence. The "light of faith" refers to knowledge that only Christians possess by virtue of the Holy Scriptures and the traditions of the church. Such truths include the doctrines of the Trinity, the incarnation, and the resurrection of the body.

Aquinas's most famous contribution to the history of philosophy is his "five ways" (or "proofs") for God's existence (*Summa Theologiae*, Ia, 2; see also Kenny 1977). Using the Aristotelian language of causation, Aquinas argues that the radical contingency of the cosmos requires a *necessary* cause, an Unmoved Mover whom all people recognize as God. This Uncaused Cause is responsible for the apparent design in the universe: since creatures other than humans seem to be guided to their various activities without the benefit of possessing free will, they must do so because of some designing agent external to themselves. Of particular importance here was Aquinas's use of Aristotle's ideas of *formal* and *final* causes, which later scientists found superfluous (see **Aristotle** and **causation**).

Aquinas also developed two critical themes in **ethics**: natural law morality and virtue ethics. **Natural law** refers to those universally known moral truths that apply across cultures. A virtue is an acquired quality of the soul that can be used only for the pursuit of the good. Aquinas concentrates on developing a complete taxonomy of the virtues.

In addition to the classical pagan virtues of prudence, justice, courage, and temperance, Aquinas adds faith, hope, and charity, which radically alter the pagan virtues.

Key Points/Challenges

- Aristotle believed that the cosmos was eternal, that the soul was not immortal, and that the object of God's contemplation was God's own self. In contrast, Aquinas argued for the temporality of the cosmos, the immortality of the soul, and the idea that God not only knew God's own nature but had knowledge of the entire terrestrial world.

- Aquinas's essentialism has been challenged on at least three counts. First, Sartre argued that "existence precedes essence" (i.e., human nature is nothing until we create it by our own choice; see his *Existentialism and Humanism* [1948]). This criticism has been absorbed by postmodernists who charge Aquinas with subscribing to a grand metanarrative that reflects only his own cultural context and the power structures inherent in it. They see human autonomy as threatened and confined by its "nature." Second, Wittgenstein challenged essentialism by arguing that language does not refer to real essences but reflects the dynamic and fluid "forms of life" in which we find ourselves (see his *Philosophical Investigations* [1953]). Third, process thinkers (see **process philosophy/theology**) argue that the universe is not composed of discrete essences but of "events" or beings "in process" (see Whitehead, *Process and Reality* [1929]).

- With the recent interest in big bang cosmology and intelligent design Aquinas's arguments for God's existence have merited more interest, especially with regard to the idea that the universe is finely tuned (see **anthropic principle**).

Further Reading

Gilson, Etienne. 1994. *The Christian Philosophy of St. Thomas Aquinas*. Notre Dame, IN: University of Notre Dame Press.

> The standard interpretation of Aquinas representing the approach known as "existential Thomism."

Kenny, Anthony. 1977. *The Five Ways*. Notre Dame, IN: University of Notre Dame Press.

> A careful exposition of Aquinas's arguments for God's existence with particular attention to how the arguments employ Aristotelian causes.

McInerny, Ralph. 1990. *A First Glance at Thomas Aquinas: A Handbook for Peeping Thomists*. Notre Dame, IN: University of Notre Dame Press.

> The most accessible introduction to the spectrum of Aquinas's thought, including brief translations of primary sources from Aquinas.

Craig A. Boyd, Azusa Pacific University

☐ Aristotle (384–322 BC)

Aristotle is one of the most significant philosophers and scientific thinkers of all time. He was originally from Macedonia and studied under Plato at the Academy in Athens, taught Alexander the Great, and later started a rival school (called the Lyceum). Aristotle traveled widely, observed carefully, and wrote extensively. We have his writings on logic, physics, metaphysics, ethics, politics, psychology, poetry, theater, and other subjects. Although Aristotle's works were lost to the West for several centuries, they were preserved by Muslim scholars and reintroduced to Western Europe during the High Middle Ages. They greatly influenced the work of St. **Thomas Aquinas** and provided a catalyst for medieval science and the early **scientific revolution**.

Aristotle's influence on scientific thinking is immeasurable. In many ways he can be regarded as the first scientist and a catalyst for both Greek and late-medieval science. Aristotle's influence on science was sometimes detrimental; since he was regarded as such an authority, it became difficult to challenge his thinking on any point. This had especially injurious effects on the **Galileo** controversy. He was also the first to divide knowledge into various subjects or "disciplines" (although he saw them as closely connected). His idea of what constitutes "scientific" research or knowledge still shapes the structure of university education and of scholarly research. This is particularly true of the division of the disciplines in liberal arts education.

Although Aristotle's physics, mechanics, and biology were slowly replaced with developing scientific insight, his logic and ethics continue to exercise a strong role in contemporary debates, and contemporary Thomist thought (see **Aquinas**) is still deeply Aristotelian.

Key Points/Challenges

- Aristotle identified four types of causes for natural phenomena: formal, material, efficient, and final (see **causation**).

- He also viewed reality as teleological, increasingly moving toward greater and greater actuality (see **teleology**). This implied notions of prime matter and a prime mover.

- Aristotle's notion of the prime mover and the agent intellect had a strong impact on medieval formulations of the divine, especially those of Aquinas. The latter's proofs for God's existence (his "five ways") are essentially Aristotelian. Particularly influential—some would say detrimental—was Aristotle's definition of the divine as pure actuality, incapable of change since change implies defect.

- Aristotle, like many Greek thinkers, made a clear division between "earthly" science—the study of change and matter—and "heavenly" science—the study of the eternal and "spiritual." This division was overcome by the **scientific revolution**.

- Aristotle's distinction between accidental and substantial change (and his definition of substance) profoundly shaped Western thinking on what constitutes the identity of a being. His contention that species are unalterable was not challenged until **Darwin**.
- Aristotle laid the groundwork for the medieval "great chain of being," which organized all beings into a hierarchy of increasing complexity. It both enabled and conflicted with later theories of natural **evolution**.
- Aristotle's divisions of the soul—nutritive, vegetative, and rational—and especially his definition of the human person as "rational animal" not only exercised great influence in the past (e.g., by defining reason as the most important human capacity), but are beginning to be recovered in environmental debates (e.g., realizing that "soul" is not a merely "human" prerogative, but also denotes our connectivity to the rest of nature).
- Aristotle's ethics, as concerned with the development of virtue and character, are still very influential in contemporary ethical debates, especially in the areas of medical ethics and bioethics.

Further Reading

Barnes, Jonathan, ed. 1995. *The Cambridge Companion to Aristotle*. New York: Cambridge University Press.

>   A clear, reasonably accessible collection of essays on Aristotle's philosophy. Particularly relevant to SRD are the essays by R. J. Hankinson on "Philosophy of Science" and "Science," and by Stephen Everson on "Psychology."

Grant, Edward. 2000. "Aristotle and Aristotelianism." In *The History of Science and Religion in the Western Tradition: An Encyclopedia*, edited by Gary B. Ferngren, 115–21. New York: Garland.

>   A discussion of Aristotle placed within the context of SRD.

Lindberg, David C. 1992. *The Beginnings of Western Science: The European Scientific Tradition in Philosophical, Religious, and Institutional Context, 600 B.C. to A.D. 1450*. Chicago: University of Chicago Press.

>   This accessible survey of the history of ancient and medieval science contains an entire chapter on Aristotle (chapter 3).

Christina M. Gschwandtner, University of Scranton

☐ Augustine (AD 354–430)

Augustine was the most important thinker of late antiquity and the most influential theologian of the Middle Ages and early modern period. He converted to Christianity in 387 after years of searching. He began his adult Christian life in a quasi-monastic community in his hometown of Tagaste (North Africa), where he was ordained, and finished his career as bishop of Hippo. During much of his ecclesiastical career he was engaged in literary disputes with several groups, and his writings are far ranging, covering matters of doctrine, history, philosophical theology, autobiography, and moral and civic life in such influential treatises as his *Confessions*, *The City of God*, and *On the Trinity*.

Augustine's epistemology significantly influenced western European theology and philosophy throughout the Middle Ages. He believed the only knowledge worth having is the knowledge of God and of self. Other knowledge is valuable only insofar as it contributes to this. He taught that the Word of God illuminates the mind's perception or radiates into the soul immutable and eternal truths.

Though we first turn outward for knowledge of things perceptible by the senses (*scientia*), we progress inwardly to the knowledge of higher truths of God and the soul by wisdom (*sapientia*), until we arrive at knowledge of God and immutable truth by intuition apart from sensation. Beyond this is ineffable union with God. For Augustine, the mind does not discover truth in the world of sense, due to the world's changeability and the fallibility of the senses.

The soul is dominant and superior to the body; it is not acted upon directly by the external world, but it attends to changes in the body due to external stimuli. As humans, we make rational judgments about sensible objects; the mind judges their approximation to eternal ideas or concepts. In a Platonic sense Augustine understood that appearance and reality do not always agree, but this knowledge, which is somewhere between mere animal sensation and the soul's higher contemplation, is still necessary for practical everyday life.

Augustine's metaphysics adapted Plotinus, by locating in the divine Mind the platonic Ideas or Forms, the eternal and unchangeable archetypes, essences, or models by which God creates the sensible world. Thus God created unformed matter with Forms and the capacity of matter to receive those Forms. With the creation of matter, time and space followed.

For exegetical purposes (such as resolving the contradiction between Genesis 1, which teaches that God created the world in seven days, and the fact that some things come into being much later), Augustine's doctrine of "seminal principles," influenced by Plotinus and Stoic ideas, taught that God implanted formative principles (germs, invisible powers, potentialities) in matter at creation—like seeds that ultimately germinate into the corporeal organisms we now know. In this way God is said to have created all things— even those things that have yet to develop fully—out of nothing by a free divine act. All created things that emerge in time contribute to the goodness and perfection of the whole created universe. God first knew the things of creation before they came into existence, because from eternity he saw in himself, as Exemplar, the things he could and would create. That is, they were created as external and finite reflections of his divine essence, so that there are vestiges or traces of God throughout creation.

Key Points/Challenges

- Augustine followed the platonic notion that knowledge of truth does not come through observations of the sensible world, though it does begin there (see **Plato**). He also taught that we cannot prove historical events with the certainty we achieve in mathematics; historical knowledge relies on the witness of trustworthy authorities. In fact, Augustine's dictum "faith seeks understanding" reminds the modernist who equates objectivity with truth that we must not only live our lives content with much that cannot be held with absolute certainty, but that the Christian must *begin* with the facts of revelation as God has disclosed them in Scripture. In some respects this is a postmodern position.

- Augustine's caution about the reliability of our knowledge of the sensible world foreshadows the *Meditations* of **René Descartes**, one of the fathers of modernism. Similarly, Augustine's discussion of the relation of the mind to the body and external stimuli is in line with future discussions in Descartes, Malebranche (who cites Augustine), Berkeley, and others (see **mind/body problem**).

- Some have accused Augustine of failing to clarify the relationship of faith to science. To this one might reply, first, that his interest was primarily spiritual knowledge; the mutable and sensible creation points beyond itself to the immutable Beauty it reflects. Second, in *On Christian Doctrine* Augustine insists that careful study of nature, history, math, language, and such is necessary for understanding Scripture well.

Further Reading

Bourke, Vernon J., ed. 1974. *The Essential Augustine*. 2nd ed. Indianapolis: Hackett.

    A wonderful compendium of key excerpts from Augustine's writings arranged by topic, with excellent indices and a glossary of terms.

Stump, Eleonore, and Norman Kretzmann, eds. 2001. *The Cambridge Companion to Augustine*. Cambridge: Cambridge University Press.

    A series of essays in which Augustine's understanding of many topics (such as time, memory, and creation) are discussed by scholars current in the field.

Wilken, Robert Louis. 2003. "The Reasonableness of Faith." In *The Spirit of Early Christian Thought*, 162–85. New Haven: Yale University Press.

    Exquisitely written explanation of Augustine's epistemology.

Dennis Okholm, Azusa Pacific University

☐ Bacon, Francis (1561–1626)

It may seem peculiar that the author of the modern scientific method was not a natural philosopher (i.e., a scientist) but rather a politician and statesman. Francis Bacon gained renown in many areas, serving the English courts of Elizabeth I and James I, initially as a member of Parliament, then as Solicitor General, attorney general, a member of the Privy Council, Lord Keeper of the Great Seal, and Lord Chancellor. Bacon's most enduring recognition is derived from his influential writings, some of which articulate specific viewpoints regarding natural philosophy and religion. Most noted among these are *The Proficiency and Advancement of Learning, Divine and Humane* (1605), *Novum Organum* (1620), and *The New Atlantis* (1626).

Bacon opposed the centuries-long dogmatic acceptance of Aristotelian (see **Aristotle**) doctrine as the ultimate authority on nature. Rather, in order to gain a deeper and more truthful understanding of the natural world, Bacon advocated for a new method, best articulated in his *Novum Organum*. Instead of accepting generalized Aristotelian hypotheses about the operations of the natural world and accommodating specific interpretations within that framework, Bacon proposed that a multitude of specific observations of nature must first be gathered directly through experience or experimentation; only then could generalizations be made. This process, a form of inductive reasoning, became the foundation for the "new science" (also called Baconian science) that was based on an experimental method.

Bacon's experimental method became the principal form of investigation adopted by the Royal Society of London at its founding in 1660. Though helpful in advancing the Society's goal of "improving natural knowledge" and adherent to its motto, *nullius in verba* ("upon the word or authority of no one"), Baconian science was viewed by some to forge a lasting wedge between science and religion. Although Bacon fully appreciated the importance of religion to a natural philosopher, he argued that science and religion should not be "unwisely mingled." This view was represented in the form of Bacon's "two books" analogy. One book, that of God's work or Nature, provided knowledge that was accessible through human reason, observation, and the senses. Ultimately, this book served as a preparation to better understand the other book, God's Word in the Bible. However, unlike knowledge of the natural world, knowledge of God was attainable only through divine revelation.

Key Points/Challenges

- Bacon opposed the Christianized view of Aristotle promulgated in university education, which claimed that **natural philosophy** (science) was a form of **natural theology** through which divine information was revealed. Bacon's own view was later challenged by the physico-theological writings of authors including John Ray, William Derham, and **William Paley**.

- Bacon also opposed the traditional **teleological** belief that the aim of natural philosophy was to identify and invoke God as the First Cause or Prime Mover of all things. Since, in Bacon's view, God has "nothing in common with any creature," nothing "revealing of the nature of God" is obtainable through natural philosophy's inquiry into "sensible and material things." Later authors interpreted the limits that Bacon imposed on natural philosophy inquiry as indicative of atheism.

- As a matter of clarification Bacon distinguished religion and science by using the analogy of a chess game. In chess the rules must be "received as they are, and not disputed." That part of the game, he argued, was comparable to religion. But learning "how to play a skillful and winning game" is a "scientific and rational" process.

- Bacon promoted the Reformation belief that human dominion over nature, a quest that had been lost in the biblical fall of humankind, would be righteously restored through his new method of accumulating knowledge of nature. Contemporary science and religion dialogue has focused on this point as arousing fear about the degradation of our natural environment (see **environmentalism**). Bacon viewed such a restoration as charitable and as fulfilling Daniel's prophecy: "Many shall run to and fro and knowledge shall be increased" (Dan. 12:4 KJV).

Further Reading

McKnight, Stephen A. 2006. *The Religious Foundations of Francis Bacon's Thought*. Columbia: University of Missouri Press.

> Surveys important religious motifs in Bacon's work. A helpful corrective to studies that ignore Bacon's emphasis on Christian charity and the use of science to relieve human misery.

Peltonen, Markku, ed. 1996. *The Cambridge Companion to Bacon*. Cambridge: Cambridge University Press.

> A series of essays from scholars in many fields, including science and religion, that nicely contextualize Bacon, his ideas, and the centuries of scholarship that have been devoted to Bacon's influence.

Quinton, Anthony. 1980. *Francis Bacon*. Oxford: Oxford University Press.

> An accessible and brief overview of the life, writings, and historical period within which Bacon developed his influential thoughts.

Webster, Charles. 1975. *The Great Instauration: Science, Medicine, and Reform 1626–1660*. London: Duckworth.

> A key study of the evolution of Baconian ideas into the reformation of natural philosophy. Webster refined the now scarcely-accepted **Merton thesis** that sociologist Robert K. Merton advanced in 1938, claiming that a clear connection existed between the growth of Baconian science and Puritanism in seventeenth-century England.

Philip K. Wilson, Penn State University College of Medicine

☐ Biotechnology

Biotechnology—any technique that uses living organisms to make or modify products, to improve plants or animals, or to develop micro-organisms for specific uses—has been part of the repertoire of human techniques since civilization began. The Sumerians (7000 to 5000 BC) used microbes to make beer and the Egyptians (4000 BC) invented leavened bread. Today biotechnology is a recognizable, market-driven, corpus of profit-driven businesses.

By 1936 a research and educational program in "biological engineering" had been initiated at the Massachusetts Institute of Technology, and similar programs emerged rapidly in other universities. Simultaneously, industrial microbiology saw significant expansion. Japan was producing ethanol as a substitute for oil by 1935, and after World War II the US pharmaceutical industry took off with the development of antibiotics. Thus the union of medicine, engineering, and agriculture produced the modern biotechnology industry.

The 1970s witnessed the development of the new genetics and provided a novel field for application of the techniques that could, by then, be called, "biotechnology." By the 1980s the commercialization of biotechnology was seen as critical to the fortunes of the developed world.

Key Points/Challenges

- Technics has a decidedly ethical dimension. For instance, "geography is descriptive science (*geo* earth, *graphy* describe); it tells what *is*. Geotechnics is applied science (*geo* earth, *technics* use); it shows what *ought to be*" (Bud 1993, 68; see also **technology**).

- Theologically, this raises the question, "Can we have a theology of technology that comprehends, gives meaning to, dares to influence the direction and set limits to this explosion of new powers?" (Cole-Turner 2000, 101). Recently, theologians have portrayed humans as "created co-creators" as a way of exploring this question (Hefner 1993).

- Biotechnology emerged as the culmination of a series of preindustrial and industrial revolutions (Mumford 1934). The "machine" metaphor became a powerful conceptual apparatus, with the engineering model applied to biology containing an implicit paradigm shift in the way organisms, tissues, cells, and genes were valued. This model may conflict with other ways of viewing nature (Deane-Drummond, Grove-White, and Szerszynski 2001).

- Like other technologies, biotechnology enables humans to achieve goods they desire: improved quality of life, relief of human and animal suffering, and conservation and recovery of the environment. Yet biotechnologies may also contribute to human, animal, and environmental destruction because of unintended consequences. Since at least the mid-1970s scientists have studied the unique ethical, social, and legal implications of emerging biotechnologies. In 1974, for instance, scientists called for a voluntary moratorium on certain recombinant DNA experiments (Berg 2004).

- Emerging biotechnologies, including regenerative medicine, artificial intelligence, and synthetic biology, present formidable challenges for the future. Harnessing the power of these technologies for human good without eroding respect for human dignity will be especially difficult (Waters 2007; Mitchell et al. 2007).

Further Reading

Berg, Paul. 2004. *Asilomar and Recombinant DNA.* http://nobelprize.org/nobel_prizes/chemistry/articles/berg/index.html.
> An eyewitness account of a history-making conference by a Nobel Prize-winning scientist.

Biotechnology Industry Organization. 2007. *Milestones 2006–2007.* Washington, DC: Biotechnology Industry Organization.
> BIO's annual report on membership, outreach and advocacy efforts, and expenditures.

Bud, Robert. 1993. *The Uses of Life: A History of Biotechnology.* Cambridge: Cambridge University Press.
> A sweeping history of biotechnology by the head of information and research at the Science Museum of London.

Cole-Turner, Ronald. 2000. "Science, Technology and Mission." In *The Local Church in a Global Era: Reflections for a New Century*, edited by Max L. Stackhouse, Tim Dearborn, and Scott Paeth, 100–112. Grand Rapids: Eerdmans.
> An argument for the development of a comprehensive theology of technology, with particular reference to biotechnology.

Deane-Drummond, Celia, Robin Grove-White, and Bronislaw Szerszynski. 2001. "Genetically Modified Theology: The Religious Dimensions of Public Concerns about Agricultural Biotechnology." *Studies in Christian Ethics* 14 (2):23–41.
> A survey of some of the religious dimensions related to public concerns about biotechnology.

Hefner, Philip. 1993. *The Human Factor: Evolution, Culture and Religion, Theology and the Sciences.* Minneapolis: Fortress.
> An introduction of the concept of the created co-creator to the science/religion/technology conversation.

Mitchell, C. Ben, Edmund D. Pellegrino, Jean Bethke Elshtain, John F. Kilner, and Scott Rae. 2007. *Biotechnology and the Human Good.* Washington, DC: Georgetown University Press.

A multi-authored critical analysis of how cybernetics, nanotechnology, and genetics might affect our future and how they might be shepherded to contribute to human flourishing.

Mumford, Lewis. 1934. *Technics and Civilization.* New York: Harcourt, Brace & Company.

A groundbreaking examination of the human impact of technology by a celebrated historian of science and technology.

Ratledge, Colin. 1992. "Biotechnology: The Socio-Economic Revolution? A Synoptic View of the World Status of Biotechnology." In *Biotechnology: Economic and Social Aspects*, edited by E. J. Da Silva, C. Ratledge, and A. Sasson, 1–22. Cambridge: Cambridge University Press.

An essay arguing that biotechnology is a set of enabling technologies, a means to apply science for the purpose of creating wealth.

Waters, Brent. 2007. *From Human to Posthuman: Christian Theology and Technology in a Postmodern World.* Burlington, VT: Ashgate.

An analysis of technology in the late modern context, especially as it is shaped by Fredrick Nietzsche. Application is made both to the transhumanism movement and to a robust theology of technology.

C. Ben Mitchell, Trinity International University,
and Stephen Garner, University of Auckland

☐ Boyle, Robert (1627–91)

The seventeenth century saw a growing acceptance of empirical experiments as a source of truth about nature. Simultaneously, many **natural philosophers** (i.e., scientists) were attracted to mechanical philosophy, a way to understand nature in terms of matter and motion. Robert Boyle, the youngest son of the powerful and wealthy Richard Boyle, Earl of Cork, made important contributions to both of these key aspects of early modern science.

In laboratories at the London home of his older sister, Katherine (Lady Ranelagh), and in other locations, Boyle supervised several assistants who conducted fundamental investigations in chemistry and physiology. These focused especially on the properties of air and its components but extended further to matter theory and pharmacology. He also reflected on the practical difficulties of conducting experiments and drawing the correct conclusions from them, establishing himself as an experimental philosopher and practitioner of the first rank, whose books were read throughout Europe and colonial North America for decades. In several works he argued directly for or otherwise tried to demonstrate the superior explanatory efficacy of mechanical philosophy over scholastic conceptions of nature. The "Mechanical Hypothesis or Philosophy," as Boyle explained it, "explicates things by Corpuscles, or minute Bodies" of matter; it tries "to give an account of the Phenomena of Nature by the Motion and other Affections of the minute Particles of Matter" (*Certain Physiological Essays*, in Hunter and Davis 1999–2000, 2:87). This overall approach remains central to science today.

The modern edition of his works lists sixty titles, of which more than a dozen are largely or entirely religious in nature. One defends the cogency of the Bible as a divinely inspired book, a few are strongly moralistic, and others explore the deep consistency of mechanical philosophy with Christian theology. Boyle was arguably the leading **natural theologian** of his age, and his will established a lectureship dedicated to "proving the Christian Religion against notorious Infidels (*viz*) Atheists, Theists [that is, deists], Pagans, Jews and Mahometans, not descending lower to any Controversies that are among Christians themselves" (Maddison 1969, 274).

Key Points/Challenges

- Boyle opposed the views of nature prevalent in his day, views drawn from the ancient Greek philosopher **Aristotle** and the Greco-Roman physician Galen. Proponents of these views tended to attribute wisdom and beneficence to a personified Nature. Boyle believed this was unbiblical, elevating Nature to a kind of goddess. Instead he promoted mechanical philosophy, which he felt focused one's attention more properly on the divine author of the properties and powers given to creation.
- As Boyle presented it, mechanical philosophy had other positive theological implications. The great clockwork (the world) required a clockmaker (God) to design it, set it into motion, maintain it, and sustain its very existence until such time that it would be replaced by a new heaven and a new earth (see **Paley**).
- Boyle's enthusiasm for the clock metaphor has led some readers to interpret him as a deist, but this ignores his reverence for Scripture, his deep sense of God's immediate presence, his belief in biblical miracles, and his belief that God's power and wisdom are required continually to uphold the world in being. Boyle's subtle theology of creation, with its balance between the immanence and transcendence of God, remains a viable alternative to process theism and other modern views that tend to diminish God's traditional role as the maker of heaven and earth.

Further Reading

Boyle, Robert. 1996. *A Free Enquiry into the Vulgarly Received Notion of Nature*. Edited by Edward B. Davis and Michael Hunter. Cambridge: Cambridge University Press.

Boyle's chief work on the theological and scientific advantages of mechanical philosophy, edited (but not abridged) for modern readers. The introduction places Boyle in the context of the scientific revolution and outlines the range and depth of his scientific interests.

Hunter, Michael. 2004a. "Boyle, Robert (1627–1691)." In *Oxford Dictionary of National Biography*, edited by H. C. G. Matthew and Brian Harrison, 7:100–108. Oxford: Oxford University Press.

A reliable, comprehensive, and up-to-date biographical essay.

———. 2004b. *Robert Boyle Project*. http://www.bbk.ac.uk/boyle/.

Supervised by Michael Hunter, the best electronic source of information about Boyle's life and thought.

Hunter, Michael, and Edward B. Davis, eds. 1999–2000. *The Works of Robert Boyle*. London: Pickering & Chatto.

A complete edition of Boyle's published works, with full scholarly apparatus and supplemented by two volumes of previously unpublished writings.

Maddison, Robert E. W. 1969. *The Life of the Honorable Robert Boyle F. R. S.* London: Taylor & Francis.

The standard modern biography, but very limited in scope.

Edward B. Davis, Messiah College

☐ Causation

Causation has aptly been described as the cement of the universe; aside from the possible exception of quantum indeterminacy, it is believed that everything has a cause and that the way objects relate depends on what causes what (see **quantum theory** and **indeterminacy**). Causation may thus be characterized as a fundamental relation that binds causes to their effects and "holds things together." Causal explanations may be understood as attempts to render intelligible the workings and structure of the world. It is no surprise, then, that the notion of causation has been central to scientific and religious theorizing about the universe.

Aristotle first delineated a fourfold classification of causes whose categories correspond to four ways in which the existence and characteristics of an object may be explained: efficient cause, material cause, formal cause, and final cause. For illustration, a statue has as its *efficient cause* the sculptor who produced it; its *material cause*, the stuff out of which it is made; its *formal cause*, the structure according to which the matter composing it is arranged; and its *final cause*, the purpose (*telos*) for which it was made. Each category helps to explain the existence, motion, and change of particular objects. However, Aristotle further argued that this classification system does not explain the origin of causation. According to Aristotle, a series of objects in motion, each moved by another, must begin with a mover that is not itself moved by anything else, thus motion demands an *un*moved mover. This motion begun by the unmoved mover is the First Cause. Aristotle's reasoning proved influential to philosophers who saw in it a viable proof for the existence of a Creator, and his category of final causation likewise pointed toward an Intelligence behind natural order.

During the **scientific revolution** each of these categories was rejected except efficient causation, which is thought to involve the transference of energy or force. The concept of force, however, was challenged by David Hume, who argued that we possess no adequate idea of force (and therefore of causation) unless it refers to (1) the constant conjunction of types of objects, or (2) our anticipation, upon seeing one object typically conjoined with another, that its usual concomitant will follow. Humeans thus view causation as no more than either a mere succession of natural occurrences or a subjective feeling of expectation based on past experience.

Key Points/Challenges

- While few today subscribe to all of Aristotle's causal categories, many find it difficult to avoid giving **teleological** explanations of biological and psychological phenomena since they appear to be essentially goal-oriented. Naturalists typically seek efficient causes for goal-directed behavior in the natural order, but it remains an open question whether teleological processes can be successfully reduced to efficient causes.

- Contemporary philosophers continue to advance causal arguments for the existence of God, based mainly on efficient causality. Those who identify God as the *primary* cause, however, disagree over the way God's causal activity is distinguished from the activity of created things, considered as *secondary* causes. There are two extreme perspectives: occasionalism and deism. Occasionalists argue that all natural events are merely occasions in which God directly produces the effects associated with those events. Deists assign God responsibility for the initial creative act but view the world as subsequently self-sufficient. Between these extremes are intermediate positions according to which God sustains the universe by continuously causing all created entities to exist (sometimes called "productive" causation), but without robbing such created entities of the power to cause changes in other created objects ("alterational" causation).

- Some causal arguments for God's existence assume that the universe must have had a beginning, or that everything has a sufficient reason for its existence, or that an infinite regress of causes is impossible. Since some of these doctrines have fallen into disrepute, and since contemporary defenders of the causal argument must operate with a narrower conception of causation than what was in use during the premodern era, they cannot generally rely on the arguments as they were formulated in the past.

Further Reading

Craig, William Lane. 2001. *The Cosmological Argument from Plato to Leibniz*. Eugene, OR: Wipf and Stock.

Analysis of arguments from the world (cosmos) to God's existence based on causation, including some discussion of primary/secondary causation.

Tooley, Michael, and Ernest Sosa, eds. 1993. *Causation*. Oxford: Oxford University Press.

An anthology containing classical and contemporary readings on causation, with a historical and philosophical introduction.

Neal Judisch, University of Oklahoma

☐ Chaos Theory

Chaos theory describes the behavior of systems that exhibit sensitive dependence on initial conditions, such as the weather, or turbulent smoke from a fire. While most of classical Newtonian mechanics studies linear systems—in which, for example, doubling the cause (e.g., force) doubles the effect (e.g., acceleration)—the behavior of nonlinear systems (in which doubling a cause could triple or negate the effect) has been shown to exhibit chaos. This does not mean that nonlinear systems behave in completely random or arbitrary ways; instead, stable patterns (known as "strange attractors") of an intricate geometrical ("fractal") nature do emerge when the mathematical representation of the system's development over time is examined. The "butterfly effect" is a general property of chaotic systems: the tiny difference between any two starting points grows exponentially as time goes on. The term *butterfly effect* comes from the belief that the precise way a single butterfly flutters significantly affects large-scale features of the atmosphere, such as the fizzling of a hurricane, over time.

Because we cannot know all such long-range interactions, a nonlinear chaotic system cannot be truly isolated or indefinitely predicted, even if we were to know its initial conditions perfectly (which is impossible).

Key Points/Challenges

- Chaos theory is controversially suggested by some, most notably Polkinghorne (1998), as a means of divine and/or human free action in the world, in which "active information" allows for selection of particular paths along the strange attractors.

- There is some debate about whether chaos is deterministic (see **determinism**) or whether this matters. Most authors suggest that it is, citing the well-understood classical physics that leads to chaos. But Polkinghorne's critical realist position (see **critical realism**) emphasizes a holistic treatment, because of a chaotic system's dependence on its total environment, and points out that the deterministic Newtonian mechanics in which chaos arises is exact only in a limiting sense (slow motion, for example). Insofar as chaos is indeterministic, similar questions regarding divine action arise as they do in quantum theory.

- Precisely how **quantum mechanics** adjusts chaos theory remains an area of research in physics; different views of how this might be resolved are played out in the science/religion field as well.
- The holistic character of chaotic systems, in which there is dependence on literally everything in the universe, is a grand theme evoking thoughts of the unity of the creation due to its one Creator.
- In the face of chaotic systems, humankind's lack of universal knowledge demonstrates a fundamental limitation to a goal to attain to a "theory of everything" in physics. Such limits, because they show our humble position, are often considered an impetus to draw us to God.

Further Reading

Gleick, James. 1987. *Chaos: Making a New Science*. New York: Viking.
    The most frequently cited introduction to the historical development and conceptual ideas of chaos theory.

Murphy, Nancey, Robert J. Russell, and Arthur Peacocke, eds. 1995. *Chaos and Complexity: Scientific Perspectives on Divine Action*. Vatican City: Vatican Observatory Publications; Berkeley: Center for Theology and the Natural Sciences.
    A substantial volume presenting a range of scholarly opinion by leading thinkers on the possibility that chaos theory might help in understanding God's interaction with creation, particularly because of its sensitivity to small changes.

Polkinghorne, John. 1998. "Does God Act in the Physical World?" In *Belief in God in an Age of Science*, 48–75. New Haven: Yale University Press.
    An explanation and promotion of the view that chaotic dynamics is the "causal joint" of divine action, the means through which God acts in the physical world.

Smedes, Taede A. 2004. *Chaos, Complexity, and God: Divine Action and Scientism*. Leuven: Peeters.
    A significant clarification of the questions concerning divine action in the world, giving thorough critical reviews of the positions of Polkinghorne and Peacocke.

Stewart, Ian. 1997. *Does God Play Dice? The New Mathematics of Chaos*. New York: Penguin.
    A rare and accessible combination of all of the technical aspects, with philosophical and everyday ramifications presented in a witty conversational style. This book proposes a chaotic answer to Einstein's famous question about quantum theory.

Arnold E. Sikkema, Trinity Western University

☐ Christology (Incarnation)

Belief in the incarnation of the divine Logos (the "Word" made flesh) in the life of Jesus of Nazareth is one of the distinctive doctrines of the Christian religion. Articulating this belief has traditionally been understood as the main task of Christology, the study of Jesus Christ. The term *incarnation* is derived from the Bible: "The Word became flesh" (John 1:14 NRSV). The classical formulation of this doctrine, developed at the Council of Chalcedon (AD 451), asserted that "one and the same Son," our "Lord Jesus Christ," was of the same substance with God the Father (and thus truly divine) and of the same substance with humanity (and thus truly human).

For the science/religion dialogue, it is important to note the mutually shaping relationship between anthropology and Christology that structured the debates among the early church fathers over the nature of Christ. Two schools of thought emerged in early Christianity: Alexandrians and Antiochenes. The Alexandrians tended to place a strong emphasis on the substantial unity of the soul and the body in each person. The Antiochenes preferred a more dualistic anthropology, in which the substances of the body and soul were more radically distinguished. These philosophical intuitions about human nature affected their understanding of the relationship between the divine nature and the human nature in the person of Jesus Christ. Both schools took the soul/body relationship as an analogy for the deity/humanity relationship. The underlying question is the same: how can two different substances truly be united in one person? Alexandrians emphasized that Jesus's divinity and humanity were not divided or separated but substantially united in one person, while the Antiochenes stressed that the two distinct natures that made up the one person of Christ were not fused or changed in the union. Both positions were affirmed at the Council of Chalcedon (AD 451). Among the early Reformers one can trace an Alexandrian tendency in Martin Luther and an Antiochene influence in John Calvin; this difference continues to shape many of the ongoing debates related to Christology.

Key Points/Challenges

- Because this Christian doctrine has to do with the relationship between divinity and humanity, its formulation is inherently shaped by assumptions of the doctrine of God and theological anthropology. Contemporary sciences such as psychology and neurobiology have challenged ancient models of human nature, and this has implications for the way theologians articulate the doctrine of the incarnation (see **mind/body problem**).

- Much of Western philosophy relied on the categories of "substance" and "sameness," but many late modern philosophers have emphasized the concepts of "relationality" and "difference." Many sciences also reflect the significance of relationships and differentiation in their interpretations of the world (e.g., "object relations" or "systems" theory in psychology). This shift has altered the conceptual space within which interdisciplinary discourse now occurs, providing an opportunity for theology to explore new ways of formulating the relationality between God and humanity revealed in Jesus Christ.

- The science/religion dialogue has tended to focus more on generic ideas of God and on the problems inherent in body/soul dualism than it has on the particular claims of Christology. The late modern embrace of the particularity of religious experience has opened up new opportunities for reconstructing Christology in dialogue with contemporary science, illustrated in some of the references below.

Further Reading

Peacocke, Arthur. 1993. *Theology for a Scientific Age*. Minneapolis: Fortress.

> A depiction of the incarnation in light of the biological and natural sciences, as the communication of divine self-limitation in Jesus of Nazareth, who manifests the ideal of human becoming.

Shults, F. LeRon. 2008. *Christology and Science*. Aldershot, UK: Ashgate.

> An exploration of the relationship between philosophy, science, and Christology, providing three case studies on incarnation and evolutionary biology, atonement and cultural anthropology, and parousia and physical cosmology.

Torrance, T. F. 1969. *Space, Time and Incarnation*. Oxford: Oxford University Press.

> An examination of the way that conceptions of space and time shaped the doctrine of the incarnation in the patristic and Reformation periods, and an explanation of the implications for Christology after Einstein's relativity theory.

Wildman, Wesley. 1998. *Fidelity with Plausibility: Modest Christologies in the Twentieth Century*. Albany: State University of New York Press.

> An overview of the social scientific challenges to Christology, including the popular debates over "the myth of God incarnate."

F. LeRon Shults, University of Agder

☐ Consciousness

Consciousness is subjective awareness, the ability to "experience" objects at all. The separation of consciousness from other attributes of mind, such as rationality and emotion, is a modern phenomenon, implied in the writings of **René Descartes** (1596–1650) and then developed explicitly by later philosophers and theologians (e.g., John Locke, Friedrich Schleiermacher). In the twentieth century, consciousness became a contested category as scholars either dismissed its significance or saw the use of consciousness and other psychological terms as the result of linguistic confusion or as a vestige of a prescientific psychology that would soon be swept away by developments in scientific psychology and neuroscience.

While these views are still present, the 1980s and 1990s witnessed a renewal of interest in the topic of consciousness, both scientifically and philosophically. Advances in neuroscience and, in particular, the development of brain-scanning techniques have encouraged neuroscientists to ask what structures of the brain give rise to subjective awareness and to what extent and in what way consciousness can be said to result from brain activity. This research is ongoing, and although certain areas of the brain have been identified as important for consciousness, there is a great deal that remains unknown at the neuroscientific level.

Scientific research on consciousness raises the more general question of the relationship of mind and body (see **mind/body problem**) and the nature of personhood (see **person**). Contemporary theologians and philosophers of religion have developed a number of proposals to reconcile scientific data and theories with theological accounts of personhood.

Key Points/Challenges

- Especially since Descartes, the popular view of the mind/body relationship in Western culture has been that of substance dualism, which posits that the mind or soul is a completely separate thing from the body, nonmaterial and immortal. This view has been widely criticized by both philosophers and scientists as incompatible with modern scientific knowledge. Many twentieth-century thinkers tried to eliminate talk about consciousness and the mind altogether, resulting in psychological and philosophical behaviorism, associated with John B. Watson and Gilbert Ryle respectively, and more recently in the eliminative materialist views (which reduce consciousness to a property of neural organization) of such thinkers as Paul and Patricia Churchland. Although dualism still has its advocates, among them the notable Christian philosophers Richard Swinburne and Alvin Plantinga, and the Nobel Prize-winning neuroscientist John Eccles, it is an embattled position that most scholars consider difficult to defend.

- Many scholars have proposed a number of intermediate positions, appealing to a nonreductive physicalism or the category of **emergence**. These positions suggest that consciousness does arise out of the brain but they are critical of attempts to reduce states of consciousness to brain states. They suggest that consciousness is fundamentally irreducible and is an emergent property in a way that is consonant with both science and a theological perspective. A number of theologians and philosophers of religion, including Nancey Murphy and Philip Clayton, have defended sophisticated versions of either nonreductive physicalism or emergence.

- Process theologians such as David Ray Griffin have argued for a panexperientialism that sees the seeds of consciousness present in the very basic structures of the world (see **process philosophy/theology**), and some philosophers and scientists, most notably the physicist Roger Penrose, have suggested that the mystery of consciousness may lie in the secrets of **quantum mechanics** or some future theory of physics. Although both approaches might be seen as versions of emergence, they are sometimes seen as alternatives to both emergence and nonreductive physicalism.

- A key question is the causal role of consciousness. Reductive approaches tend to see consciousness as a kind of epiphenomenon, meaning that consciousness is produced as a byproduct of the operations of the brain but plays no actual role in behavior. On this account, the feeling of being "in control" and having "freedom of choice" is simply dismissed as an illusion. By contrast, advocates of emergence and nonreductive physicalism have suggested that consciousness does play a causal role. A distinction is made between the bottom-up causality characterized by the parts of the system, and the top-down causation imposed by the whole of a system. Consciousness, being a property of the whole of the brain and not just one individual part, might be understood as having precisely this kind of top-down effect (see **supervenience** [**top-down causation**]).

- Part of the theological discussion has been a reevaluation of biblical texts regarding human nature. Most modern biblical scholars now argue that the doctrine of the immortality of the soul is foreign to the biblical tradition and entered Western thought through the philosopher **Plato**. Rather, the Bible speaks of a resurrection of the dead, which seems to imply a more unified understanding of body and soul, a view of human nature that is largely consonant with the developments in neuroscience. On this understanding the soul, and thus consciousness, is not separable from the body but is in intimate connection with it.

Further Reading

Damasio, Antonio. 1999. *The Feeling of What Happens: Body and Emotion in the Making of Consciousness*. New York: Harvest Books.

    A sophisticated attempt to explain consciousness from a neuroscientific perspective.

Green, Joel, ed. 2005. *In Search of the Soul: Four Views of the Mind-Body Problem*. Downers Grove, IL: InterVarsity.

    An introduction to some of the major alternatives currently taken with regard to the mind/body problem.

Peterson, Gregory R. 2003. *Minding God: Theology and Cognitive Science*. Minneapolis: Fortress.

    An introductory survey of scientific and theological accounts of personhood, including consciousness.

Searle, John. 1997. *The Mystery of Consciousness*. New York: New York Review of Books.

An accessible introduction to the study of consciousness from both scientific and philosophical perspectives.

Gregory R. Peterson, South Dakota State University

☐ Contingency

The idea of contingency occurs in several ways in science and has various meanings, including "not necessary," "random" or "chance," "dependent," "unexplained," and even "unexplainable." In the simplest case, contingency refers to an event, process, or property that occurs but that apparently might not have occurred. The roll of dice, a car accident, a change in weather, the color of hair all seem to be chance events, dependent on factors beyond our knowledge.

Though we loosely say "it occurred by chance," we should not think of chance as a cause; instead, chance means a lack of a known or actual cause. In some cases, one may assume that adequate causes do exist and could, in principle, be known. Future discoveries and theories in science may reduce the varieties of ways we currently view contingency, or they may uncover new forms of contingency not yet recognized and suggestive of various philosophical and theological responses.

Many scientists and philosophers, however, argue that processes and events at the subatomic level involve genuine contingency. Nature, according to **quantum physics**, is ontologically indeterministic (see **determinism**): certain events at the quantum level lack a sufficient efficient cause. Such contingency may extend into the "classical" level in processes ranging from genetic mutations and their expression to superfluidity and quantum **chaos theory**, as well as the amplification of quantum processes in lasers, photocells, chips, and the visual cortex.

Key Points/Challenges

- Why is there anything, and not nothing? Natural processes might be accounted for by the laws of nature (including statistical and indeterministic ones), but the sheer existence of the universe per se may forever lie outside the power of science to explain. Standard big bang **cosmology**, whose finite age suggests a beginning of time, leaves the existence of the universe a mystery and points to God as the Creator. However, inflation and quantum cosmology may explain our universe in terms of a many universes account.

- The **laws of nature**, as well as the fundamental physical constants (the speed of light, c; Planck's constant, h; etc.), can be seen as contingent: they could have been other than they are. The **anthropic principle** suggests to some that they were fine-tuned by God, while to others they are once again explained via a many universes account. Still the existence of the universe, however it is described, represents the fundamental contingency of nature and opens the door to theological explanation.

- Contingency may be formalized in a number of ways. We may speak of the universe as (1) "globally contingent" (contingent as a whole), regarding both its existence per se and the particular laws and constants of nature that characterize the universe as a whole; (2) "locally contingent" regarding both the existence of any or all particular events, properties, and processes and the laws that characterize them; or (3) "nomologically contingent," regarding the laws of nature in the sense that their form and the value of the natural constants included in them need not take this form or value, and in the sense that before their first instantiation in nature the world could have been other than it, in fact, now is.

- Also relevant are factors in the history of science through which theories arise and are replaced, including experimental, theoretical, philosophical, sociological, aesthetic, and religious factors, and the contingency they bring to our scientific worldview as such. Any worldview we hold based on current scientific theory is subject to change as these theories are modified or replaced.

Further Reading

Cushing, James T. 1998. *Philosophical Concepts in Physics: The Historical Relation between Philosophy and Scientific Theories*. Cambridge: Cambridge University Press.

> A description of the essential role philosophy plays in the practice of science and the construction of scientific theories.

Jammer, Max. 1974. *The Philosophy of Quantum Mechanics*. New York: John Wiley & Sons.

> A classic text presenting a comprehensive analysis of the different and conflicting philosophical interpretations of quantum mechanics (including contingency as indeterminism) with a particular focus on its historical development in the early twentieth century.

Leslie, John. 1989. *Universes*. London: Routledge.

> A detailed treatment of the scientific basis for claiming our universe is fine-tuned for life, its relationship to the anthropic principle, and such responses as "many universes" versus "God."

Russell, Robert J., Nancey Murphy, and C. J. Isham, eds. 1993. *Quantum Cosmology and the Laws of Nature: Scientific Perspectives on Divine Action*. Vatican City: Vatican Observatory Publications; Berkeley: Center for Theology and the Natural Sciences.

> A technical publication providing an introduction to big bang and quantum cosmologies, laying out their philosophical implications, and presenting a variety of theological interpretations.

Torrance, Thomas F. 1981. *Divine and Contingent Order*. Oxford: Oxford University Press.

Addresses the relationship between the theology of creation and the contingency and rationality of the universe as presupposed by modern science and cosmology.

Robert J. Russell, Center for Theology and the Natural Sciences and Graduate Theological Union, Berkeley

☐ Copernicus, Nicholas (1473–1543)

In 1543 Copernicus published a sun-centered astronomical system. His work challenged the earth-centered physics and astronomy adopted by the medieval church and became the basis for a frequently misunderstood confrontation between science and religion. During the Middle Ages most educated people in the West accepted the physical and cosmological ideas of **Aristotle**, who taught that the earth was the center of the universe and that planets and stars were embedded in concentric shells of ether that revolved around it. These ideas were assimilated by many Catholic theologians who used them to interpret several passages in the Bible (e.g., Josh. 10:12–13; Eccles. 1:4–5). In addition to Aristotle, medieval scholars used mathematical models devised by Claudius **Ptolemy** to calculate and predict the positions of the heavenly bodies. Such calculations became the basis for church calendars and were important in astrology, which was a key component of medieval medicine.

Sometime before 1514 Copernicus composed a short account of a system in which planets moved around the sun, not the earth, adapting mathematical techniques pioneered by Islamic astronomers. Although his ideas required a radical departure from accepted physics and cosmology, he relied on improved versions of Ptolemaic mathematical models. Copernicus spent his adult life as a canon attached to the cathedral in Frauenburg (Frombork) in modern-day Poland. His major public presentation of his ideas, *On the Revolutions of the Celestial Spheres*, appeared in 1543, the year of his death.

Key Points/Challenges

- Although Copernicus remained a practicing Catholic throughout his life, Protestants have claimed credit for promulgating his ideas. There is some truth to this. Joachim Rheticus, a protégé of Lutheran reformer Philip Melanchthon, published the *First Account* of Copernicus's astronomical system and protected him by securing the patronage of Albrecht, Duke of Prussia, another Lutheran. Rheticus also supervised the preparation of *On the Revolutions* for publication by Protestants in Nuremberg. Ultimately, Melanchthon and his students at the University of Wittenberg embraced Copernicus as a reformer of astronomy. They disseminated his mathematical methods in new astronomical tables and textbooks but retained the idea that the earth was the center of the cosmos on physical and biblical grounds. Their position is now known as the Wittenberg interpretation of Copernicus. Later Lutherans, especially **Johannes Kepler**, accepted heliocentrism and introduced the modern form of Copernicanism by freeing the planets from supporting spheres, introducing the concept of elliptical orbits, and establishing the centrality and physical role of the sun in moving the planets.

- Contrary to popular belief, Copernicus's work was never banned by the Catholic Church. Copernicus dedicated his book to Pope Paul III, and several Catholics affirmed his ideas over the next fifty years. Giordano Bruno, a Copernican, was executed in 1600 for his opinions on religion, not his opinions on cosmology. After hearings in 1616 the proposition that the sun is immobile and the center of the world was declared "formally heretical" and the proposition that the earth moves was declared "at least erroneous in faith." Both propositions were declared "foolish and absurd in philosophy," or "physically false," to use modern terms ("Consultants' Report on Copernicanism"). Catholic readers of Copernicus were not ordered to destroy his book, only to correct the small number of passages containing objectionable ideas. But outside of Italy few copies of *On the Revolutions* show the amendments. In 1632 **Galileo** built on Copernicus's work and faced persecution for mainly political reasons. However, the restrictions on Copernicus's book were officially removed by the Catholic Church in 1758.

Further Reading

Barker, P. 2000. "The Role of Religion in the Lutheran Response to Copernicus." In *Rethinking the Scientific Revolution*, edited by M. J. Osler, 59–88. Cambridge: Cambridge University Press.

> Accessible paper on early Lutheran Copernicans.

Barker, P., and B. R. Goldstein. 2003. "Patronage and the Production of *De revolutionibus.*" *Journal for the History of Astronomy* 34:345–68.

> Reconstructs the story of how Rheticus saved Copernicus, showing the role of Protestants in the publication of *On the Revolutions*.

Copernicus, Nicholas. 1976. *On the Revolutions of the Heavenly Spheres*. Translated by A. M. Duncan. New York: Barnes and Noble.

> Accessible translation of *De revolutionibus orbium coelestium* (1543). Book 1 presents Copernicus's main arguments for the motion of the earth, without mathematical technicalities.

Danielson, Dennis. 2006. *The First Copernican: Georg Joachim Rheticus and the Rise of the Copernican Revolution*. New York: Walker.

> Nontechnical but historically sophisticated account of Rheticus and Copernicus, including their religious background.

Westman, Robert S. 1986. "The Copernicans and the Churches." In *God and Nature: Historical Essays on the Encounter between Christianity and Science*, edited by D. C. Lindberg and R. L. Numbers, 76–113. Berkeley: University of California Press.

Covers Protestant and Catholic responses to Copernicus up to the time of Galileo.

Peter Barker, University of Oklahoma

☐ Cosmology

Historically, cosmology was widely defined as both a branch of philosophy (in which one can explore not only the realm of physics but also such topics as causality and freedom and metaphysics) and as a branch of theology (in which one may focus on the relationship of the universe, as creation, to its creator and the creator's purposes for the created order). In the modern era cosmology is usually defined more narrowly as the subdiscipline of astronomy that studies the large-scale structures of the universe and formulates theories to explain their origin and development through time.

Until the early twentieth century everything in the "visible universe" was understood to be somewhere within the structure of what we now call our galaxy, the Milky Way. But observations since then (starting with Edwin Hubble) made it clear that our galaxy is merely one of trillions. More startling was the discovery—by means of the red shift in the light spectra of galaxies—that the universe is expanding. This and several other observations have led to the major theory about the origin of the universe as a big bang. Additional observations, especially measurements of the residual energy left over from the big bang (the cosmic background radiation), have convinced most cosmologists that the universe originated about 13.8 billion years ago. It is also believed that the visible matter of the universe represents perhaps only 10 percent of its actual substance.

Cosmologists and other scientists attempt to explain the forces at work within and between the elements in the universe, forces such as gravitation, electromagnetism, and the weak and strong forces within the structure of an atom. Recently cosmologists have realized that our theories about the largest-scale structures in the universe (such as the distribution of galaxies) will have to be integrated with theories about structure and forces at work in the smallest-scale elements (**quantum physics**). Some cosmologists and physicists believe that string theory (the idea that the structure of the universe is founded not on zero-dimensional points but on tiny, resonating strings some twenty orders of magnitude smaller than atoms) may hold the key to this program of integration.

Questions arise from the fact that many properties of the cosmos have to be just right in order for our universe to exist and to support life. Is the universe really fine-tuned and directed ultimately toward life (see **anthropic principle**)? Is our universe special in this regard or do we merely live in the one out of billions of universes (the so-called multi-verse theory) that just happened to get it right?

Key Points/Challenges

- The problem of the definition of cosmology is at the heart of science/religion dialogue. A purely naturalistic view of the universe is limited to models and theories about the universe as a physical system and advocates an agnosticism about a creator *beyond* the universe and about anything that might have happened before the origin of the universe or after the end of the universe's physical existence.
- Most religious people object to an a priori and total exclusion of God from the discussion of cosmology, but they do so for many different reasons and put forth very different proposals as to what should be allowed as evidence for constructing a cosmological belief system.
- Many accept that it is appropriate for a person of faith to adopt methodological **naturalism** when doing science, though they would not accept that only science can address questions about the origin of the universe and the implications of its unfolding evolution.
- Proponents of **intelligent design** contend that certain types of evidence, by the rules of science itself, appear to demand an Intelligence beyond or outside of the universe to explain phenomena within the universe. While intelligent-design theorists have focused on biological processes, one expects that theories may be forthcoming in cosmology.

Further Reading

Coles, Peter. 1999. *The Routledge Critical Dictionary of the New Cosmology*. New York: Routledge.

> An excellent and concise handbook that covers all aspects of cosmology.

Ferris, Timothy. 1997. *The Whole Shebang: A State-of-the-Universe(s) Report*. New York: Simon & Schuster.

> A popular and readable account of modern cosmology by an award-winning science writer.

Hinshaw, Gary. *Cosmology: The Study of the Universe*. National Aeronautics and Space Administration. http://map.gsfc.nasa.gov/m_uni.html.

> The most-visited Web site on the subject of cosmology.

Tyson, Neil deGrasse, and Donald Goldsmith. 2004. *Origins: Fourteen Billion Years of Cosmic Evolution*. New York and London: W. W. Norton.

> Sets forth at a popular level the current state of cosmological theories. A DVD on the book was produced by Thomas Levenson and published by WGBH Educational Foundation, Boston (2004).

Wilders, N. Max. 1982. *The Theologian and His Universe: Theology and Cosmology from the Middle Ages to the Present.* New York: Seabury.

> Examines how cosmological views have influenced Christian theology from the Middle Ages to the present.

Steve Delamarter, George Fox Evangelical Seminary

☐ Creation/Creationism

Creationism is a belief that the universe and all the things in it have been deliberately created by God and have not come into being through a chain of unplanned events. Creationism arose as a direct challenge to **Charles Darwin**'s 1859 publication of *The Origin of Species*. Proponents claim that creationism's scientific credibility is similar to, or better than, **evolution**. While it has its roots in the nineteenth century, creationism came of age after the well-publicized 1925 Monkey Trial in Dayton, Tennessee, when school teacher John Scopes fell foul of a new law that forbade anyone from teaching evolution in schools. While Scopes was found guilty of breaking the law, the trial brought the law's attack on evolution to public attention and most commentators ridiculed it.

Creationists point to the gaps that still exist in evolutionary theory and claim that these will never be filled, because a divine being made things the way they are. They point to gaps in fossil records and the apparent absence of transitional forms of organisms. They claim that any evidence for evolution is at best a misinterpretation of data and at worst a deliberate falsification of results.

Special creationism takes the argument one step further and maintains that God created everything in six twenty-four-hour days, exactly as described in the first chapters of Genesis, and that this took place about six thousand years ago. It is worth noting that most people in mainstream science say that this contradicts all geological and astronomical evidence that the universe is billions of years old.

Those who support creationism also say that if a non-literal reading of Genesis is accepted, there is nothing to stop people from interpreting all other areas of the Bible in terms of metaphor and myth, and there is nothing to stop people from choosing the parts of the Bible they like and dismissing the rest.

Creationists also say that as evolution cannot be repeated, it is therefore inaccessible to science; they then extend the argument to infer that this lack of scientific scrutiny means evolution did not occur. Mainstream scientists agree that past evolution cannot be repeated but counter by presenting the mass of evidence supporting an increasingly strong evolutionary theory of living organisms and by showing examples of evolutionary processes that are occurring in viruses, bacteria, plants, and animals that are alive today.

A few creationists carry out scientific research with the aim of collecting data that supports their view of the universe. The data they have amassed is small, but this could be because the number of people doing the research is small, and it is difficult to find funding or journals willing to publish the results. Some creationists have established the idea of *scientific concordance*, claiming that science shows that the order and process mentioned in Genesis actually occurred.

Midway between the extreme creationist view and an atheistic evolutionary position are a range of views termed *theistic evolution* or *evolutionary creationism*. These hold that while Scripture tells us about the redemption of creation, it is not a textbook that describes the structure and processes by which creation works. Proponents believe that God created and continues to act in the world, but that one of the features God created was the evolutionary processes that biologists are discovering.

A further nuance in the debate is held by the *progressive creationists* (or *old earth creationists*), who hold that the earth is old, that the flood mentioned in Genesis was local and not global, and that some life forms have evolved from others. They believe that humankind arose as a special act of God, so that humans stand unique from the other living orders.

Key Points/Challenges

- The majority of creationists are fundamentalist Christians who believe that every event recorded in the Bible took place exactly as it was written down.
- Other evangelical Christians say that the Bible is a collection of many different types of writing—laws, poetry, narrative, and so on—and that the only way to find the authors' original intentions is first to check the genre of each text. Most see the first chapters of Genesis as a form of Hebrew poetry, and as with all poetry the meaning is conveyed symbolically by the word-pictures it paints.
- A consistent fear expressed by creationists is that by buying into evolution, Western society is basing itself on increasingly materialistic views of life—views that see no intrinsic purpose in existence or that deny the ethical superiority of humanity. They therefore see creationism as a way to defeat **materialism** and defend the Christian principles they embrace.

Further Reading

Carlson, Richard. 2002. *Science and Christianity: Four Views*. Downers Grove, IL: InterVarsity.

> Presents the views of a creationist, a commentator who sees science and religion as totally separate entities, an advocate of intelligent design, and a theistic evolutionist, along with replies from each of the other positions.

Numbers, Ronald L. 1993. *The Creationists: Evolution of Scientific Creationism*. Berkeley: University of California Press.

> An examination of the North American Christians who believe that there was no life on earth before Eden (dated about 10,000 years ago), with an emphasis on the key individuals and their informal and organizational relationships with one another.

Wilkinson, David. 2002. *The Message of Creation*. Downers Grove, IL: InterVarsity.

> Unpacks the messages contained in Genesis and other creation-related passages. Wilkinson, as an astrophysicist, has great insight into the scale of the universe. As a Christian minister he sees God at work.

Pete Moore, Trinity College, Bristol

☐ Critical Realism

Critical realism affirms that objects exist independently of our thoughts about them (realism) and asserts that human knowledge of reality is a progressive dialogue between knower and known (critical). Critical realists argue that in human perception some qualities or properties accurately represent external objects while some sensory data do not accurately represent reality. Thus critical realists locate their position between direct **realism**, which takes the immediate objects of perception to be external objects, and **antirealism**, which denies that the human mind can know anything external to itself. In philosophy of science, critical realism upholds the real existence of the entities and processes that are investigated and endorses **scientific method** as a form of rationality that is appropriate for confirming theories (and thus generating knowledge) about a real world that exists independently of the human mind. In discussions of the relationship between science and religion, the term has been used by Ian Barbour (1997) and others to indicate a comprehensive conceptuality (particularly regarding epistemological and methodological issues) that would embrace both science and religion as important avenues of access to reality. For Barbour, science and religion are similar, for example, in that they both make fallible, revisable claims about the way things are through the use of theoretical terms that refer to real entities. But since our evidence for claims in science and religion is indirect, Barbour suggests four criteria for assessing their degree of correspondence with the real: agreement with data, coherence, scope, and fertility.

Key Points/Challenges

- Critical realism recognizes that knowledge must be justified by its relationship to reality, but any particular version of critical realism must be closely evaluated on the basis of how it treats the objective and subjective dimensions of perception and knowledge.

- One may be a critical realist (just as one may be a direct realist or antirealist) in different areas of human inquiry, and thus about their appropriate entities: physical sciences, **social sciences**, economics, theology, and even aesthetics.
- Empiricists and positivists criticize critical realism for positing a structured, objective reality that transcends purely empirical data, their patterns, and correlations.
- Postmodernists charge that critical realism rests on a metaphysic of a structured, objective reality without adequately appreciating the linguistically constructed nature of knowledge (see **metaphysics**).
- Direct realists charge that critical realism is a form of representationalism, which leads either to skepticism or phenomenalism and which is the reduction of the position. So the immediate objects of perception are external objects, qualities, and events.
- The extent to which critical realism identifies similarities between science and religion (affirmation of cognitive contact with independent reality, explanation of experimental results, etc.) is a fruitful question. Many argue that religious models also serve noncognitive functions (such as eliciting attitudes, personal involvement, and transformation) that are missing in science.

Further Reading

Archer, Margaret, Roy Bhaskar, Andrew Collier, Tony Lawson, and Alan Norrie. 1998. *Critical Realism: Essential Readings.* London: Routledge.

Anthologizes various directions of thought and debates that have developed within critical realism since Roy Bhaskar's 1975 *A Realist Theory of Science.* It also includes excerpts from Bhaskar and selections from other formative authors.

Barbour, Ian. 1997. *Religion and Science: Historical and Contemporary Issues.* San Francisco: HarperSanFrancisco.

Encyclopedic discussion of issues pertaining to the theological understanding of God and religious experience in relation to historical and contemporary scientific theories and findings.

Bhaskar, Roy. 1978. *A Realist Theory of Science.* Atlantic Highlands, NJ: Humanities Press.

Argues against postmodernism/constructivism (Kuhn, Feyerabend) and positivism (Carnap, Ayer) and for critical realism, which affirms that sense data accurately represent physical reality.

Lopez, Jose, and Garry Potter. 2001. *After Postmodernism: An Introduction to Critical Realism.* London: Athlone.

Interdisciplinary essays by recognized authors that illustrate connections between critical realism and important research in various disciplines, including sociology, philosophy, and literary studies.

Niiniluoto, Ilkka. 2002. *Critical Scientific Realism*. Oxford: Oxford University Press.

Defends scientific realism, which aims to make true statements about the relevant subject matter. It also offers Niiniluoto's own version of critical realism.

Polkinghorne, John. 1991. *Reason and Reality: The Relationship between Science and Theology*. London: SPCK.

Collection of essays on the nature and scope of human knowledge, the nature and limits of science, and the role of theology. The book argues that both science and theology are fundamentally rational in character and that contemporary quantum theory, as well as chaos theory, implies an open universe envisioned by a Christian understanding of reality (e.g., the relationship of contingency and necessity, freedom and law, and cooperation with the divine).

Michael L. Peterson, Asbury College

☐ Darwin, Charles (1809–82)

The English naturalist Charles Robert Darwin may be properly regarded as the thinker who has most sharply provoked controversy in the relationship between science and Christian faith in the modern era.

His voyage aboard HMS *Beagle* (1831–36) proved revolutionary for Darwin and for scientific thinking to this day. Early on the voyage Darwin read Charles Lyell's newly published *Principles of Geology* (1831) and adopted Lyell's uniformitarian picture of earth history, which posits right on the title page that the only geological forces that have ever operated throughout earth history are those "now in operation." Lyell's views empowered Darwin to not only speculate about the earth's apparently vast age but also ponder deeply the notion that a few simple and steady causes, applied constantly over vast ages, could produce complex and detailed effects in nature. Might the long history of life, he wondered, likewise be understood by the long-term action of a few basic principles?

The notion of *natural selection* as nature's analogue to the agriculturalist's artificial selection first appeared in Darwin's notes in 1837. In 1843–44 Darwin worked out the details of his theory of "descent with modification" (evolution) by means of natural selection. Aware that his naturalistic vision of nature would likely stir controversy, Darwin withheld his work from publication for nearly two decades until, alerted in 1858 to the very real risk of losing scientific priority to his younger contemporary Alfred Russel Wallace, Darwin finally completed *On the Origin of Species by Means of Natural Selection* in late 1859.

Darwin argued in *Origin* that the doctrines of divine special creation and fixity of species could not adequately account for the patterns of plant and animal geography, the similarity of fossil forms to living forms, the adaptation of organisms to their respective environments, and other natural phenomena. He proposed instead that natural forces working in an undirected but lawlike manner to shape and modify species over long ages of time accounted for these more satisfactorily.

As to the origins and nature of humankind, Darwin deftly dodged these by a brief note in *Origin* but fully developed them later in his *Descent of Man and Selection in Relation to Sex* (1871) and *The Expression of the Emotions in Man and the Animals* (1872). In these volumes Darwin extended the argument of *Origin* to humans by suggesting that not only is the physical form of the human being the product of a long process of natural selection and evolution, but that those aspects of human life traditionally considered nonphysical (emotions, thought, desires, instincts, notions of the soul or spirit) similarly have their roots in nonintentional physical processes working throughout a long evolutionary history. Darwin (and others, including Thomas Henry Huxley) also explored the indications revealed by comparative anatomy that humans may be related to today's higher primates and indeed may be descended from earlier simian primates.

Key Points/Challenges

- Darwin painted a picture of the living realm that could be viewed as devoid of intentionality, design, and purpose, both in its origins and in its ongoing operations. Such an interpretation of nature was a controversial departure from the traditional mid-nineteenth-century picture of divine design, providence, and purpose in nature, as depicted in the Bible, propounded in Christian theology and by influential figures such as **William Paley**.

- Some contemporaries, such as Presbyterian botanist Asa Gray at Harvard, contended that Darwinism was compatible with Christianity, while others believed that Darwin's essential message remained inimical to Christian theism. This reality was not lost on Darwin or his critics, such as the American Presbyterian theologian Charles Hodge, who, in *What Is Darwinism*, characterized Darwinian naturalism in 1874 as "tantamount to atheism."

- Darwin acknowledged that theological difficulties such as the problem of natural evil and the Christian doctrine of hell, rather than his own evolutionary views, led him gradually toward a posture of unbelief. Joining these convictions with his increasing commitment to naturalism and the efficacy of natural law, Darwin thought it appropriate in his autobiography to apply Huxley's neologism *agnostic* to himself. It seemed more rational to Darwin to suppose that if there was a God, such a divine being must be understood in detached, deistic terms (see **ideas of God**). Darwin's references to "Creator" in *Origin* should therefore be read in the deistic sense. A twentieth-century rumor, initiated in about 1900, that Darwin later abandoned his deism and embraced an evangelical type of Christianity under the influence of "Lady Hope" has been thoroughly discredited by recent historical work.

- While various parts of Darwin's theory have been shown to be wrong, the overarching idea that natural selection is ever shaping the living world has remained intact, influential, and as contentious as ever. Darwin's theory of natural selection has become a highly useful and powerful explanatory tool, especially in relation to the modern sciences of molecular biology and genetics.

- Despite the controversial theological implications of Darwin's views for traditional Christian faith, religious scientists, philosophers, and theologians have employed evolutionary theory as a description of how (not why) a loving God who is in enduring relationship to the creation might have created and continue to create (see, e.g., **process philosophy, kenosis, evolutionary psychology**).

Further Reading

Appleman, Philip, ed. 2000. *Darwin: A Norton Critical Edition*. 3rd ed. New York: W. W. Norton.

> A very rich resource including excerpts from Darwin and contemporaries with commentary from current scholars on the full range of Darwin's significance and the implications of his theory.

Bowler, Philip. 2003. *Evolution: The History of an Idea*. 3rd ed. Berkeley: University of California Press.

> The standard comprehensive volume on evolution theory of all kinds, prominently featuring Darwin and his influence.

Browne, Janet. 1995. *Voyaging*. Vol. 1 of *Charles Darwin: A Biography*. New York: Knopf/Random House.

———. 2002. *The Power of Place*. Vol. 2 of *Charles Darwin: A Biography*. New York: Knopf/Random House.

> A rich two-volume biography drawn from primary materials that has been called "spellbinding" and "the last word" on Darwin.

Darwin, Francis, ed. 1991. *The Autobiography of Charles Darwin and Selected Letters*. 2 vols. New York: Dover.

> A primary source, providing direct insight into Darwin's thoughts and states of mind at various times in his life.

Livingstone, David N. 1984. *Darwin's Forgotten Defenders: The Encounter between Evangelical Theology and Evolutionary Thought*. Edinburgh: T&T Clark.

> An account of the mixed reactions—some positive—to Darwin among Christian thinkers.

Ruse, Michael. 1999. *The Darwinian Revolution: Science Red in Tooth and Claw*. 2nd ed. Chicago: University of Chicago Press.

> Clearly the industry standard on the intellectual run-up to and the lively aftermath of the appearance of Darwin's *Origin*.

Rodney L. Stiling, Seattle Pacific University

☐ Descartes, René (1596–1650)

The French thinker René Descartes, author of the influential *Meditations on First Philosophy* (1641) and *Principles of Philosophy* (1644), and often called the father of modern philosophy and mathematics, played a central role in the seventeenth-century **scientific revolution** by attacking the **epistemological** and **metaphysical** underpinnings of Aristotelian natural science. Though educated in scholastic philosophy by Jesuits, as a young man Descartes became interested in the project—often associated with Galileo—of uncovering mathematical laws governing the motions of physical objects. He discovered how to solve certain geometrical problems by using algebraic equations, thus unifying the (previously disparate) studies of space and number. This mathematical insight, which he later published as an appendix to his *Discourse on Method* (1637), not only paved the way for the development of calculus but also inspired Descartes' subsequent life project: to show the fundamental unity of science by extracting from his mathematical successes a general method of inquiry for progress in all areas of knowledge.

While **Francis Bacon** criticized Aristotelian science for not being empirical enough, Descartes thought that it trusted too much in sense perception. Instead, science should rest on self-evident first principles revealed by Descartes' method of doubt. When he tried to doubt all his previous beliefs, Descartes found that he could not be absolutely certain of anything revealed by his senses, including the existence of his own body. But the very process of doubting proved that he existed as a thinking thing, as there must be someone who *does* the doubting. This shows that minds (immaterial thinking substances) are really distinct from bodies (extended material substances) and can exist without them.

Such substance dualism (see **mind/body problem**) makes room for the immortality of the soul. Using traditional cosmological and ontological arguments, Descartes established God's existence. Because God is no deceiver, we can trust the evidence of our senses, at least in part. Because God sustains the world's existence in a regular manner, there are uniform laws of nature that allow us to explain changes in objects in terms of the motions of their microscopic parts. Thus Descartes grounds mechanistic physics in a theistic metaphysics.

Key Points/Challenges

- Descartes posited causal interaction between mind and body: changes in state of bodily sense organs (e.g., the prick of a pin) cause sensations in the mind (e.g., a feeling of pain), and intentions formed by the will (e.g., to raise one's hand) lead to voluntary bodily actions (e.g., the raising of one's hand). However, critics charge that it is impossible for the thinking, unextended mind and the extended, unthinking body to interact causally, because they have nothing in common. This "problem of interaction" plagues not only Descartes, but also dualistic theories of mind and body generally.

- Descartes sees living things, including nonhuman animals and even the human body, as complicated machines. Human actions are exempt from mechanical explanation only insofar as they are caused by the soul. Critics charge that this view, coupled with Descartes' enthusiasm for using science to gain mastery over nature, encourages people to view ecosystems, animals, and even their own bodies as objects to be technologically exploited (see **environmentalism, ecofeminism, ecotheology**).

- Descartes thought that intelligent language distinguishes creatures possessing a mind (humans) from those that do not (all other animals). However, recent studies in animal language call this assumption into question.

- One of Descartes' central epistemological doctrines was that in theoretical matters we should assent only to what we "clearly and distinctly perceive." Later philosophers argued that we cannot clearly and distinctly perceive either that God exists or that the world really resembles our perceptions of it. Therefore, the enormous influence of Descartes' epistemology came to work against his theism and scientific realism.

Further Reading

Cottingham, John. 1992. *The Cambridge Companion to Descartes*. New York: Cambridge University Press.

Papers explaining key aspects of Descartes' thought, including its scholastic background and subsequent reception.

Curley, Edwin. 2006. "Descartes, René (1596–1650)." In *The Encyclopedia of Philosophy*, edited by Donald M. Borchert, 720–56. 2nd ed. Detroit: Macmillan.

An excellent brief introduction to Descartes' life and central ideas.

Gaukroger, Stephen. 1997. *Descartes: An Intellectual Biography*. Oxford: Oxford University Press.

An extensive but accessible account of Descartes' life and the development of his thought with an emphasis on his scientific ideas.

C. P. Ragland, Saint Louis University

☐ Determinism and Free Will

We say that an event (E) was causally determined to occur when the laws of nature and the complete history of the world (up until, but not including, E) made it physically impossible for E not to occur. Determinism is the thesis that all events are causally determined, so that history must unfold in a definite way with no possible "forks in the road" or alternative futures. There are no possibilities except actualities. If determinism is true, then every detail of history could be predicted by someone with a complete understanding of both the **laws of nature** and the world's initial state.

It is widely thought that we are morally responsible (deserving of praise or punishment) only for actions that we choose to perform "of our own free will." It is also widely believed that agents perform actions freely only if "free choice" is involved.

However, philosophers disagree about how free choice relates to determinism. Compatibilists claim that humans can be free and responsible even if determinism is true. They claim that choices are free when caused in the right way by the agent's character (beliefs, desires, dispositions, etc.). How the agent got her or his character—whether deterministically or not—is irrelevant. Incompatibilists insist that to be free, agents must be the "ultimate source" of their choices, so that (in some sense) they could have chosen otherwise. But if determinism is true, the causes of any choice can be traced back beyond the agent to the beginning of the world. Therefore, incompatibilists claim, determinism implies that no one is free or morally responsible. There are two kinds of incompatibilists: hard determinists believe that determinism is true and that freedom is illusory; libertarians believe that because humans are free and morally responsible, determinism must be false.

Key Points/Challenges

- Most religions presuppose that people are morally accountable (whether to God or an impersonal force, such as karma) for their actions, and many religious people take themselves to be morally responsible only because they have libertarian (or undetermined) freedom. Furthermore, popular "free will" theodicies (see **theodicy**) rely on incompatibilism in their attempt to explain why God allows evil in the world. Therefore, to the extent that modern science presents a deterministic picture of the world, it seems to conflict with many religious beliefs. However, some religious traditions (e.g., Calvinism) consider freedom to be compatible with determination of all things by God.

- Newtonian physics seemed to show that the world was deterministic, but the twentieth-century development of **quantum physics** proposed that the laws of nature governing the smallest particles of matter are probabilistic: they specify that given a certain history, one event may be more probable than another, but neither is *certain* to occur. On the one hand, it may be that the human brain, like a Geiger counter, magnifies quantum indeterminacies, realizing them as libertarian free choices. On the other hand, the brain may operate deterministically, like most other macroscopic systems. Future brain research may settle this question. However, even if the brain operates indeterministically, it is far from clear how undetermined choices would not be simply random or accidental events, for which we could not be held responsible.

- Scientific findings sometimes undermine moral responsibility. For example, a thief might not be punished because he or she is found to suffer from kleptomania. The diagnosis of psychological disease carries weight in court because it shows that the thief's action was not produced by properly functioning faculties of reason and deliberation. However, it is difficult to imagine a judge taking the general thesis of determinism as exculpatory. Compatibilists argue that in cases where our faculties are functioning properly, we know that we are free and responsible even though we do not know for sure that determinism is false. Furthermore, we are inclined to think that our moral practices of praise and blame would (justifiably) persist even if the latest scientific research proved determinism true. This suggests that the truth or falsehood of determinism in general, as opposed to particular exculpatory deterministic mechanisms, is irrelevant to moral responsibility.

Further Reading

Barbour, Ian. 1966. *Issues in Science and Religion.* New York: Harper & Row.

Chapter 10 ("Physics and Indeterminacy") contains a good introductory discussion of the implications of quantum indeterminacy for questions of freedom.

Pereboom, Derk. 1997. *Free Will.* Indianapolis: Hackett Publishing.

An anthology of writings on free will and determinism from Aristotle to the late twentieth century, representing the different philosophical positions outlined above and discussing some scientific issues.

Van Inwagen, Peter. 1993. *Metaphysics.* Boulder, CO: Westview.

Chapter 11 ("The Powers of Rational Beings: Freedom of the Will") is an excellent introduction to the philosophical positions on free will and determinism from one of the leading philosophers in that debate.

C. P. Ragland, Saint Louis University

☐ Divine Command

Defenders of divine commnd theory (DCT) contend that the commands of God serve as the best available source for moral norms. These thinkers contend that DCT best preserves the nature of religious obligation to God and not to some other competing principle (e.g., Kantian rationality, utilitarian happiness, or Thomistic natural law). Rather, the key obligation is obedience to God. Many divine command theorists (e.g., William Ockham) have argued that God cannot be bound by some principle extrinsic to God's nature and so DCT preserves God's omnipotence. Ockham's theory represents a "stronger" version of DCT since he advocates the view that God can give wildly counterintuitive commands (e.g., to hate God or to torture innocent children).

This perspective is unacceptable to most contemporary defenders of the theory, such as the philosophers Robert Adams and John Hare. They developed a "weaker" version that argues that the "good" depends on creation, but God must command humans to act in specific ways. This is because sin corrupts our knowledge of what God requires of us and our capacity to do the good we know we should do, creating a "moral gap" between our natural capacities and the demand of the moral obligation. According to this view, only the command of God can remedy our natural corruption. These latter thinkers avoid the embarrassing conclusions of Ockham's theory by claiming that we can be reasonably certain that since God is loving, God will not command a horrendous evil.

Key Points/Challenges

- A perennial problem for DCT is the idea that God could command morally horrific actions and we would be obligated to obey them. While the advocate of DCT responds that we know God is good and will not command anything evil, the problem with this defense is that the only way we have to know whether God is good is by some prior moral notion of goodness that we already possess—as given through natural law, for example—in which case God cannot command any action that violates our created nature.

- Divine command theorists John Hare and Stephen Evans see a radical contrast between "naturalistic theories" of **ethics** based on human **evolution** and their own ethical theories as based on divine revelation. Evolutionary theories fail on two counts: (1) they do not consider sin in a serious fashion, and (2) no naturalistic explanation of moral behavior can bridge the "moral gap" that exists between our nature and the demands or constraints of morality. Moreover, since evolutionary theory posits a dynamic theory of speciation, or morals based on a changing human nature, DCT seems preferable because the commands are based on God's will. If human nature changes, as the theory of evolution contends, then morality seems to be based on the arbitrary adaptations of natural and sexual selection.

- Another problem for DCT is deciding which God ought to be obeyed. Without some guiding principle that **natural law morality** proposes, how does one decide whether the God of Islam, Judaism, Christianity, or the gods of Hinduism or Norse mythology is to be obeyed? Theological provincialism threatens DCT at a most basic level.

Further Reading

Adams, Robert M. 1987. "A Modified Divine Command Theory of Ethical Wrongness." In *The Virtue of Faith and Other Essays in Philosophical Theology*, edited by Robert Merrihew Adams, 97–122. New York: Oxford University Press.

Presents the standard "modified" or "weaker" version of DCT.

Evans, C. Stephen. 2004. *Kierkegaard's Ethic of Love: Divine Commands and Moral Obligations.* Oxford: Oxford University Press.

Offers a DCT based on Kierkegaard's ethics of love; it also includes a critique of Larry Arnhart's evolutionary approach to ethics. The command to love is primary and orients the agent to God, self, and neighbor appropriately.

Hare, John. 2001. *God's Call: Moral Realism, God's Commands, and Human Autonomy.* Grand Rapids: Eerdmans.

Argues that there is a gap between descriptive accounts of human nature and the moral demands of ethics that can be bridged only by divine commands. Hare uses Duns Scotus and Kant as historic resources for his arguments.

Craig A. Boyd, Azusa Pacific University

☐ Ecofeminism

Ecofeminism is a feminist movement that draws together the concerns of environmentalism and ecology, on the one hand, and feminist issues on the other. Feminism emphasizes the vulnerability of women, and ecology points to the fragility of the ecosystem. Women have long been associated with their maternal attributes—giving birth and nurturing the young. Philosophers and theologians from the Greeks to modern times have viewed these tasks as fulfilling a purely physical and animal existence. Nature has been identified with the feminine and females with the natural. Thus in philosophical, theological, and cultural literature females have been given a status lower than that of males, who have been assigned a more rational and hence more spiritual role. Androcentrism (the adopting of masculine points of view) has given us a world in which male virtues (e.g., independence) and male constructions of reality have predominated, along with a valuing of the products of the rational mind as more spiritual than the feminine mix of body, mind, and heart. This has all led to the tendency to disregard both women and the environment.

The critique of this set of assumptions has unmasked the devaluing of the physical and natural in our cultural and religious practices and reflections. Ecofeminism thus emphasizes the need to recognize embodied existence, our mutual interdependence, the spirituality of embodiment, and the dangers of neglecting nature.

Ecofeminism and ecofeminist theology also attempt to trace the historical reasons for the loss of **nature** as a theological source and the loss of the feminine voice in theology. Ecofeminist theology and spirituality investigate the role of religion and God-language in the hierarchies, dualisms, and subjugations of the past and present, and attempt to affirm the biblical and spiritual importance of nature and of bodies to human personhood and value.

Key Points/Challenges

- Within the context of science/religion dialogue, ecofeminism is one place where feminist, scientific, and environmental concerns are integrated into one theological discourse.
- An acceptance of the solidarity between women and nature may sometimes be vulnerable to charges of essentialism and stereotyping of gender and roles. Thus it is important, while recognizing the concerns of ecofeminism, to affirm the spirituality and rationality of both genders, their shared embodied and animal nature, and the shared imperative of both men and women to protect the environment.
- Ecofeminism investigates the connection between the modernist/technological emphases on power and control, and the subjugation of both women and the natural world.
- Ecofeminism, in emphasizing the interconnections and interdependencies of the natural and social world, demands a reconstructed theology of God and of persons and creation in which the relational is emphasized over static and independent categories.
- Ecofeminism coexists with a number of new spiritualities and varieties of neo-paganism, many of which are critical of older Christian practices and teachings regarding the natural world. Christian theology under ecofeminist direction is challenged to enter into conversation with these new religious movements, which are often critical of the place of traditional religion in encouraging exploitation or disregard for the natural world.
- Ecofeminism addresses the controversies related to origins. Ecofeminism emphasizes our interconnectivity, emerging out of and dependent on our shared **evolutionary** history. It thus stands in contrast to and is critical of **creationist** or unduly supernaturalist positions, preferring to see God's hand in the natural world as immanent and slow, thus drawing on the biblical motifs of wisdom and immanence.

Further Reading

Deane-Drummond, Celia. 2004. *The Ethics of Nature*. Oxford: Blackwell.

Offers wisdom as an important theological/ecological category, and examines a feminist ethics of care with regard to the natural world. The author interacts with a number of other theologians, looking at the question of purpose in the evolutionary process, and the dialogue this produces with the Wisdom literature. See specifically chapters 8–9.

Eaton, Heather. 2005. *Introducing Ecofeminist Theologies*. London: T&T Clark.

A good, thorough, and easily readable introduction to ecofeminism in Christian theology.

Plumwood, Val. 1993. *Feminism and the Mastery of Nature*. London: Routledge.

> A classic philosophical feminist introduction to ecofeminism and to the discussion concerning control of the natural world.

Ruether, Rosemary Radford, ed. 1996. *Women Healing Earth: Third World Women on Ecology, Feminism and Religion*. Maryknoll, NY: Orbis.

> An examination of the theology of ecology by a major feminist theologian and others.

Nicola Hoggard Creegan, Laidlaw College

☐ Ecotheology

Ecotheology is the theology of the *oikos*, the household or home. The home in question is our planet. Ecological theology is concerned with earth-keeping: the attempt to rethink a religious tradition in relation to the ecological crises we face. In this sense there are Jewish, Islamic, Buddhist, Christian, and other forms of ecological theology. Christian ecological theology attempts a critical retrieval of the Christian tradition in response to the ecological crisis. Adapting a typology of Paul Santmire, Christian ecotheologies can be seen as alternative, traditional, or revisionist.

Alternative ecotheologians tend to see Christianity, or fundamental aspects of it, as part of the problem and seek to build a new approach from the ground up. A pioneering figure is Thomas Berry, who brings together elements of Christian faith, other religious traditions, and cosmology in a new story of creation. Another is Matthew Fox, who rejects what he calls the fall-redemption theology of the Christian West in favor of a theology of original blessing and the cosmic Christ. More widely there is a rejection of much of Christianity in favor of creation spiritualities that combine elements of mysticism, popular science, diverse religious traditions, feminist thought, and new age culture.

Traditional ecotheologies respond to the ecological crisis by drawing on the Christian heritage. Included in this approach are important statements made by the World Council of Churches and by individual churches and their leaders. Metropolitan John of Pergamon, an Orthodox bishop, points to the ecological significance of an authentic liturgical ethos and of the call to be priests of creation. Pope John Paul II insisted that care for creation is a moral obligation and humanity is called by God to an ecological vocation.

Revisionists seek not only to retrieve but also to re-envision and rethink the Christian tradition in light of the present context. They critically relate the practice of earth-keeping to the deepest symbols and convictions of Christian faith. Their work is critical in a two-fold sense: it challenges the Christian tradition from the perspective of ecology and it challenges contemporary attitudes, ideologies, and practices on the basis of the Christian view of God. Many seek an ecological renewal of theology involving its christological and trinitarian depths (Jurgen Moltmann, Paul Santmire, Ernst Conradie, and Celia Deane-Drummond). Some bring an explicitly ecofeminist (see **ecofeminism**) perspective (Rosemary Radford Ruether and Sallie McFague). Others work from the perspective of liberation theology (Leonardo Boff), renewed missiology (Sean McDonagh), and **process thought** (John Cobb, John Haught, and Jay McDaniel).

Key Points/Challenges

- Biblical interpretation is a key challenge and has been taken up by Norman Habel and the biblical scholars involved in the Earth Bible series, who approach biblical texts from the perspective of defined ecojustice principles in a hermeneutic of suspicion and retrieval.
- While some follow Thomas Berry in working from a general Christian theology of creation in dialogue with science and other religious traditions, others like Paul Santmire and Ernst Conradie engage the whole range of Christian theology, particularly its christological, pneumatological, soteriological, trinitarian, and eschatological center.
- Theological anthropology is crucial: Are humans called to have dominion over other creatures? Are they stewards? Are they "kin" to other creatures in a community of mutuality? What, if anything, is distinctive about human beings?
- Ecotheology tends to focus on the immanence of God, but Conradie and others insist on the transcendence and otherness of God as precisely that which enables God to be present creatively to each creature.

Further Reading

Berry, Thomas. 1988. *The Dream of the Earth*. San Francisco: Sierra Club.
>An important text from a key figure in alternative ecotheology.

Conradie, Ernest M. 2005. "Towards an Agenda for Ecological Theology: An Intercontinental Dialogue." *Ecotheology* 10:282–343.
>A helpful and thoughtful outline of the agenda for ecological theology, with responses.

Deane-Drummond, Celia. 2004. *The Ethics of Nature*. Oxford: Blackwell.
>Explores humanity's relationship with nature in a theologically grounded ethics centered on wisdom.

Edwards, Denis. 2006. *Ecology at the Heart of Faith*. Maryknoll, NY: Orbis.
>Seeks to respond to the ecological crisis by rethinking key aspects of the Christian tradition.

Haught, John. 2000. *God after Darwin: A Theology of Evolution*. Boulder, CO: Westview.

A theology of nature by a Roman Catholic ecological theologian who draws on process thought.

Hessel, Dieter, and Rosemary Radford Ruether, eds. 2000. *Christianity and Ecology: Seeking the Well-Being of Earth and Humans.* Cambridge, MA: Harvard University Press.

A useful collection of the work of ecotheologians.

McFague, Sallie. 2000. *Life Abundant: Rethinking Theology and Economy for a Planet in Peril.* Minneapolis: Fortress.

An important contribution by an ecofeminist theologian rethinking theology in light of global justice and ecology.

Santmire, H. Paul. 2000. *Nature Reborn: The Ecological and Cosmic Promise of Christian Theology.* Minneapolis: Fortress.

A Lutheran scholar's rethinking of the tradition in a fully ecological and theological way.

Denis Edwards, Flinders University

☐ Einstein, Albert (1879–1955)

The name Albert Einstein conjures up many thoughts, images, and emotions even among individuals with little background in physics. Among scientists, perhaps only **Charles Darwin** is as readily recognized as having radically changed the way we think about physical reality, humans, and the nature of God. Yet before Einstein published his papers in 1905 few would have predicted his impact. His approach to studying and solving problems was unorthodox. He considered that imagination and intuition were main ingredients to unraveling nature and reality, and many agree that these were his greatest strengths. He was a solitary thinker who instinctively avoided intimacy.

Einstein is best known for his relativity theory, which he initially called *invarianten theorie*. The *special* theory rests on two postulates: (1) the speed of light in a vacuum is independent of the motion of the observer and light source, and (2) the laws of physics are the same in every inertial reference frame. In contrast to Newtonian mechanics, space and time are no longer absolute and independent of each other. Rather, they form a four-dimensional space-time continuum. Events observed to occur simultaneously in one reference frame generally do not occur simultaneously in a different moving reference system. This theory further predicts that energy and mass are related by the famous equation $E=mc^2$, which within a few decades gave rise to the development of the atomic bomb. The *general* theory extends the special theory to noninertial reference frames. It predicts a dynamic space-time continuum with mass distorting (curving) it. Predictions from this theory include: an expanding universe, a big bang, black holes, and time travel. The observation of the bending of starlight passing close to the sun in 1919 made Einstein a celebrity.

Einstein, however, contributed much more to physics than the theory of relativity. He received the Nobel Prize in physics in 1921 for his explanation of the photoelectric effect, which was one of the key phenomena leading to the development of **quantum mechanics** (QM). Ironically Einstein could not accept key aspects of the interpretation of QM by his contemporaries, specifically as it pertained to chance and causality. On a number of occasions he stated that he did not believe that God played dice. For example, he wrote to Max Born on December 4, 1926, "*He* is not playing at dice."

Though Einstein dedicated his life to physics, he was interested and active in many other areas. From a young age he was strongly against anything military and generally seemed to rebel against authority. He was a nonconformist and somewhat of a bohemian. Einstein further had a great passion for disarmament and the abolishment of war. Later in life he called himself a "dedicated, though not an absolute, pacifist." He admired Mahatma Gandhi. Politically he was left-wing and in favor of a socialist economy. Einstein was an active Zionist and in 1952 was offered the presidency of the newly established nation of Israel, even though he was not a practicing Jew. Einstein declined because he felt he had no talent for human relations.

Key Points/Challenges

- Einstein firmly believed in the rationality and intelligibility of the world and believed that all genuine scientists must share a similar belief. In this context he said, "Science without religion is lame, religion without science is blind." He further believed in strict causality, rejecting the inherent probabilistic nature of the developing **quantum mechanics**. It was in this context that he famously remarked that "God does not play dice."

- He held on to an interactionist view of reality, that is, interaction between complicated sense-experiences and simple general theories. He did not accept Kant's concept that preconceived ideas shape reality, or that a priori categories in the mind impose order on reality.

- Einstein claimed that there is no inductive method that could lead from "data of experience" to fundamental concepts of physics; rather, the concepts and theories of science are free creations of the human imagination. To him, logical thinking is necessarily deductive.

- Nature and God were synonymous to Einstein. In his conception of God he felt akin to **Spinoza** and though some analyzed his thinking as a form of **pantheism**, he denied being a pantheist.

- Einstein believed that many common religions are a mixture of "religions of fear," which he associated with primitive humans and the presence of prophets and priests, and of "moral religions," associated with civilized peoples. He seemed to favor a third level marked by a "cosmic religious feeling," devoid of anthropomorphism. Around 1941 he wrote, "The main source of the present-day conflicts between the spheres of religion and of science lies in this concept of a personal God" (1954, 47).

Further Reading

Einstein, Albert. 1954. *Ideas and Opinions*. Edited by Carl Seelig. New York: Crown.
  Covers a wide variety of issues selected from Einstein's writings *The World as I See It* (1934), *Out of My Later Years* (1950), and *Mein Weltbild* (1953).
Holton, Gerald, and Yehuda Elkana, eds. 1982. *Albert Einstein: Historical and Cultural Perspectives*. Princeton, NJ: Princeton University Press.
  A very informative collection of papers presented at the Jerusalem Einstein Centennial Symposium held in March 1979.
Pais, Abraham. 1982. *"Subtle Is the Lord . . ." The Science and the Life of Albert Einstein*. Oxford: Oxford University Press.
  A great mixture of a personal and scientific biography, written by an accomplished physicist who knew Einstein during his last few years at Princeton.

Willem P. Van De Merwe, Indiana Wesleyan University

☐ Emergence

The sciences can now explain everything from ion channels to manic depression by showing how such entities of higher sciences, such as cell biology or psychology, are "composed" of the very different kinds of entities studied by lower-level sciences, such as biochemistry or physics. Such scientific evidence suggests that much, perhaps all, of the natural world is ultimately composed by the microscopic entities studied by fundamental physics. Reductionists therefore argue that all higher-level entities reduce down to, and are really nothing more than, their microphysical components. Various notions of emergence are offered in reaction both to such scientific evidence or reductionism.

The most commonly noted emergence occurs in cases of composition and describes a property of an individual that none of its component parts has. For example, diamonds are hard but no carbon atom is, and persons can think but their cells cannot. This phenomenon of properties developing out of a composition of parts we may term "qualitatively" or "mundanely" emergent. Qualitative emergence is often thought to refute reductionism, but reductionists actually use scientific findings about composition, and hence such mundane emergence, to drive their arguments.

Three other notions of emergence are more interesting. First, there are "ontological" or "O-emergent" properties, which are uncomposed properties of higher-level individuals. Writers such as Philip Clayton (2004) argue that, being uncomposed, such properties escape the net of the reductionist's arguments and can be used to understand human agency and other phenomena.

In contrast, "weak" or "W-emergent" properties are microphysically composed properties such that theories, statements, or explanations about these properties cannot be derived or predicted from theories, statements, or explanations about their microphysical components. The most sophisticated accounts, in Kim (1999) and others, show that W-emergence actually helps the reductionist by explaining away the apparent existence of higher-level properties.

Finally, so-called "strong" or "S-emergent" properties are basically composed properties that are claimed to be irreducible, usually because they are causally efficacious. Proponents of S-emergence, such as Peacocke (1990; 2007), Gillett (2006), and Murphy and Brown (2007), thus all take on the challenge of responding to the reductionist by attempting to show how a property can *both* be composed *and* be causally efficacious and hence irreducible.

Many researchers in science and religion, working scientists, and writers in a range of other fields defend the existence of emergence. But one must ask *which* notion of emergence are they defending, and *why* (i.e., in the service of what position)?

Key Points/Challenges

- All the substantive forms of emergentism face important ongoing challenges, and determining which notion of emergence is best supported by scientific findings is a growing topic for discussion.

- With regard to O-emergence, scientific evidence that all entities in nature are composed poses a challenge. O-emergentists need either to explain away such appearances or provide convincing evidence that some properties are not composed.

- For W-emergence, reductionists must address the evidence that composed entities, like people or glaciers, exist and act in the world.

- With regard to S-emergence, a range of arguments purport to show that a property cannot be both composed and causally efficacious. S-emergentists are presently obliged to rebut such concerns and explain how S-emergence is even possible (see **supervenience**).

- A key project in science and religion is distinguishing the different notions of emergence and associated positions offered by writers in recent debates, for example, about human or divine agency.

- A still wider task, and one we are only beginning to approach, is providing a comparative assessment of the distinct positions in science and religion, based on different kinds of emergentism, focusing on these issues: compatibility with the sciences; plausibility in understanding a range of natural phenomena, including human agency; and success in engaging a range of theological issues, such as divine agency, the incarnation, and the problem of evil (see also **theodicy**).

Further Reading

Clayton, Philip. 2004. *Mind and Emergence*. Oxford: Oxford University Press.

An extended defense of O-emergence with clear connections to scientific evidence and applications in science and religion.

Gillett, Carl. 2006. "The Hidden Battles over Emergence." In *Oxford Handbook on Religion and Science*, edited by Philip Clayton, 801–18. Oxford: Oxford University Press.

A detailed survey of the differing notions of emergence and defense of S-emergence.

Kim, Jaegwon. 1999. "Making Sense of Emergence." *Philosophical Studies* 95:3–44.

Outlines an ontological version of reductionism, critiques S-emergence, and outlines how W-emergence helps the reductionist.

Murphy, Nancey, and Warren S. Brown. 2007. *Did My Neurons Make Me Do It?* Oxford: Oxford University Press.

A detailed treatment of S-emergence and how it helps meet the reductionist challenge to human agency and freedom.

Peacocke, Arthur. 1990. *Theology for a Scientific Age*. Oxford: Blackwell.

A detailed defense of S-emergence in nature and treatment of a range of topics in science and religion.

———. 2007. *All That Is: A Naturalistic Faith for the Twenty-First Century*. Edited by Philip Clayton. Minneapolis: Fortress.

A sophisticated use of S-emergence to understand a range of important theological and philosophical issues with responses by prominent researchers in science and religion.

Carl Gillett, Northern Illinois University

☐ Enlightenment

The European Enlightenment was a period during the middle decades of the eighteenth century that saw the flourishing of secular, rationalist, and egalitarian ideals. Perhaps the best characterization of this informal international movement was provided by the German philosopher Immanuel Kant, who in his famous essay, "What Is Enlightenment?" (1784), spoke of the human race being emancipated from its "self-incurred tutelage." The motto of the Enlightenment, he declared, should be *sapere aude*—"dare to know." In the process of enlightenment, thus understood, individuals would cast off the shackles of intellectual, religious, and political oppression, and through the application of unfettered reason usher in a new progressive phase of human history.

Although pan-European in scope, the geographical center of the Enlightenment is generally thought to be France. Not only was France home to some of the more famous advocates of enlightenment—philosophers such as Voltaire, Montesquieu, Jean-

Jacques Rousseau, Denis Diderot, and Jean le Rond d'Alembert—but it also witnessed the publication of the celebrated *Encyclopédie* (1751–72), an enormous compendium of knowledge that embodied the ideal of liberation through science, technology, and learning. The editors of this iconic work acknowledged the enormous importance of the scientific advances of the previous century and specifically identified the contributions of Isaac Newton as a major inspiration for the age of Enlightenment.

Key Points/Challenges

- The Enlightenment has been regarded as a key event in the modernization of Europe and the source of such ideals as freedom, democracy, and tolerance. With the rise of postmodernism have come critiques of the so-called project of modernity, and this has led to a questioning, in some quarters, of the Enlightenment's elevation of reason and glorification of scientific progress.
- The Enlightenment is generally associated with hostility toward traditional religion. This rarely entailed atheism, however, but rather a "deism" or "natural religion" characterized by skepticism about miracles and divine revelation (see **ideas of God**).
- While some apologists for the Enlightenment appropriated scientific advances and claimed that figures such as **Bacon**, **Descartes**, and **Newton** were forerunners of the movement, it is doubtful that these earlier figures would have endorsed the secularist ideals of the Enlightenment.
- Like other schemes of historical periodization—such as the Renaissance and the **scientific revolution**—the idea of the Enlightenment has been subjected to some criticism by recent historians. Some suggest that it is more appropriate to speak of multiple Enlightenments. Others point to the importance of geographical centers outside France, such as England, Scotland, and Naples.

Further Reading

Hankins, Thomas L. 1985. *Science and Enlightenment.* Cambridge: Cambridge University Press.

> A history of eighteenth-century science that locates scientific developments within the broader context of the Enlightenment.

Horkheimer, Max, and Theodor Adorno. 2002. *Dialectic of Enlightenment.* Translated by Edmund Jephcott. Stanford, CA: Stanford University Press.

> One of the classic texts of the neo-Marxist Frankfurt School, written in 1944, that attempts to demonstrate how the ideals of the Enlightenment paradoxically gave rise to totalitarianism and authoritarianism in the twentieth century.

Israel, Jonathan. 2002. *Radical Enlightenment: Philosophy and the Making of Modernity, 1650–1750.* Oxford: Oxford University Press.

A new interpretation of the Enlightenment that argues persuasively for the importance of the radical thought of the Dutch philosopher **Spinoza**. Although a major focus is the Enlightenment critique of traditional religion, this wide-ranging and scholarly work also includes good discussions of seventeenth-century science and the influence of Newtonianism.

――――. 2006. *Enlightenment Contested: Philosophy, Modernity and the Emancipation of Man, 1670–1752.* Oxford: Oxford University Press.

A follow-up to his previous volume, in which Israel suggests that the modern West is indebted to radical Enlightenment thinkers for freedom of expression, religious toleration, and democratic institutions.

Porter, Roy. 2001. *Enlightenment.* 2nd ed. Harmondsworth, UK: Penguin.

An engaging account of the Enlightenment that stresses the importance of British contributions.

Yolton, John W. 1992. *The Blackwell Companion to the Enlightenment.* Oxford: Blackwell.

A good single-volume collection on this period.

Peter Harrison, University of Oxford

☐ Environmentalism (Ecology)

Environmentalism is both a point of view and a social movement advocating the value of nature and urging fundamental change in the human/nature relationship. Environmentalists are characterized as people who are concerned with the damage that our way of life imposes on the planet and who make the ethical claim that personal and corporate practices must change for the greater good of the planet as well as humanity. This definition of environmentalism has been contested from the outset and the movement is characterized not only by advocacy but also by controversy.

The contemporary environmental movement began with Rachel Carson's book *Silent Spring* (1962), addressing the impact of agricultural chemicals on wildlife. The range of issues grew to include air, water, and land pollution; human population growth; and wildlife conservation. Public pressure for institutional change was mobilized by nongovernmental organizations such as Greenpeace, the National Wildlife Federation, and the Sierra Club. Within a decade governments in North America and Europe, beginning at the federal level, had established new agencies, policies, and laws regulating this wide range of perceived problems.

Environmental issues include hazardous wastes, energy conservation, nuclear energy, alternative technologies, recycling, endangered species, land conservation, and indigenous peoples' rights to benefit from medicinal and food plants. The scale ranges from small urban parks, housing developments, and landfills to rivers, rain forests, oceans, and the global atmosphere.

Environmental issues often entail basic justice concerns and ethics, and the contours of a particular issue depend on the geographic, ethnic, religious, or political place one has in the movement. From the outset environmentalism has been a contested view and the movement is accused of reciting a "litany" of woes without adequate empirical support and with insufficient economic realism.

This interdisciplinary movement builds on the theoretical foundations and empirical insights of the science of ecology. Ecology is a scientific discipline investigating the structure, function, and biological interactions of species and their nonliving surroundings. However, the intellectual roots of environmentalism (see Worster 1994) run deeper than academic ecology. They are as old as the human/nature interface but most often are traced to the nineteenth-century writing of naturalist/free-thinker Henry David Thoreau and the earliest warnings of George Perkins Marsh.

Key Points/Challenges

- *Conservation* and *preservation* represent two poles on a continuum advocating different uses of nature. Conservationist and forester Gifford Pinchot claimed that he was interested in nature only insofar as it had useful human function. His goal was to conserve nature for its highest and best human use. John Muir maintained that wild, untouched nature provides the best hope for the future of humanity. This dichotomy is enshrined in numerous governmental policies, including the mandates for the US National Forest Service (multiple-use and resource extraction) and National Parks systems (preservation).

- The prefixes *eco-* or *enviro-* have been appended to myriad disciplines, movements, products, and policies (see **ecofeminism** and **ecotheology**). The emergence of "green speak" is a distinct rhetorical discourse. It represents the symbolic means by which environmental issues are constructed and communicated. Garrett Hardin suggested that *ecolacy* (i.e., ecological knowledge, insight, and sensitivity) is as essential to education as such skills as literacy and numeracy.

- Christianity has been viewed by many secular commentators as ignoring or standing in opposition to the environment (Gottlieb 2006). However, many churches have been early, strong, and continuing advocates of environmental concern (see Ellingsen 1993, Fowler 1995, and Berry 2000). The theological issues are complex and the "ecological blind spots" first pointed out in 1970 by Francis Schaeffer remain, particularly around dominion and dispensationalist doctrines (Santmire 2000). Beyond Christian activism is an academic discussion of virtue ethics as a more sufficient basis for motivating the deep changes sought by environmentalism (Bouma-Prediger 2001). The recognition of our innate tendency to orient toward living things, called *biophilia* by E. O. Wilson, suggests that loving nature is an appropriate Christian response to the environment (Wood 2001).

Further Reading

Berry, R. J., ed. 2000. *The Care of Creation: Focusing Concern and Action.* Leicester, UK: Inter-Varsity.

Articles by a variety of authors critiquing and extending "An Evangelical Declaration on the Care of Creation."

Bouma-Prediger, Stephen. 2001. *For the Beauty of the Earth: A Christian Vision for Creation Care.* Grand Rapids: Baker Academic.

An important starting place for answering the question, "What does theology have to do with ecology?"

Ellingsen, Mark. 1993. *The Cutting Edge: How Churches Speak to Social Issues.* Grand Rapids: World Council of Churches and Eerdmans.

This annotated compendium of denominational statements covers ecology and the related topics of economics, genetic engineering, and social justice.

Fowler, Robert Booth. 1995. *The Greening of Protestant Thought.* Chapel Hill: University of North Carolina Press.

A useful history of Protestant interaction with the environment in the United States.

Gottlieb, Roger S. 2006. *A Greener Faith: Religious Environmentalism and Our Planet's Future.* Oxford: Oxford University Press.

A comprehensive, sensitive, and insightful survey of the complexities of religious environmentalism.

Santmire, H. Paul. 2000. *Nature Reborn: The Ecological and Cosmic Promise of Christian Theology.* Minneapolis: Fortress.

Surveys current options in ecological theology and extends his important earlier work in the book *The Travail of Nature* (1985).

Wood, John R. 2001. "Biophilia and the Gospel: Loving Nature or Worshiping God?" In *Living in the Lamblight: Christianity and Contemporary Challenges to the Gospel,* edited by H. Boersma, 153–76. Vancouver: Regent College Publishing.

A literature-based exploration of biophilia and our love of creation.

Worster, Donald. 1994. *Nature's Economy: A History of Ecological Ideas.* 2nd ed. Cambridge: Cambridge University Press.

A comprehensive entry point into the human/nature literature.

John R. Wood, The King's University College,
The Au Sable Institute of Environmental Studies

☐ Epistemology (Empiricism, Rationalism)

Epistemology, from the Greek *episteme*, meaning "knowledge," is the study of knowledge. Epistemology attempts to answer two questions: (1) How do we know? and (2) How do we know that we know what we know (or at least claim to know)?

Two conflicting answers to the first question have dominated Western thinking and competed for preeminence since classical times: rationalism and empiricism. Empiricists claim that knowledge is attained only by way of the senses. Empiricists believe that the mind is something like a "blank slate" upon which sensory experience makes impressions, which are then organized by the mind through association and discrimination, with regularities in the relationship between impressions establishing expectations for further experiences. Before experiencing the world by means of the senses, we can know nothing. The disadvantage of empiricism is that the knowledge it provides is never certain, since it is always possible that the very next experience will contradict all our previous experiences, and the inferences we have drawn will be proven wrong.

Rationalists, who generally distrust the senses as illusory or at least misleading, hold that we can reliably know only by means of our reason. The premise here is that the mind and the world are both rationally structured, so by examining the structures of the mind we can discover the structures that hold for the world as well. Rationalism has the advantage that all of its conclusions are certain (e.g., every triangle has interior angles whose sum total is 180 degrees, and I cannot even imagine a triangle that does not, so I know a priori that every triangle I discover in the world will share this characteristic). Its disadvantage is that there is no guarantee that what is found in the mind will be found in the world at all (e.g., the fact that I can be absolutely certain that every unicorn I find will have one horn perhaps tells me nothing about the world).

Immanuel Kant famously attempted to mediate between these two positions by claiming that knowledge consists of sensory impressions being organized by categories with which the rational mind is already endowed. For Kant, we cannot know anything factual about the world until we experience it, but we can know what sorts of experiences we will be capable of having (and thus how the world will appear to us) since we can come to know the ways in which our minds will necessarily order the material provided by our senses.

The second question, of how we in fact know what we claim to know, is the project of foundationalism, the attempt to demonstrate that the foundations to our claims to knowledge are secure and that therefore our knowledge is certain. In the opposite direction, skepticism is the claim that in principle knowledge is not possible.

Key Points/Challenges

- Traditionally (beginning with Plato), knowledge has been defined as "justified true belief." According to this view, to have "knowledge" as opposed to a correct opinion, it is not enough to be right about something; we must also be able to give reasons for why we are right.

- Most contemporary science is committed to empiricism, but the admission is made that in practice some kind of selecting and organizing criteria (not derived from the data itself) must be brought to bear on the data for sense to be made of it. Thus some sort of compromise between rationalism and empiricism is common, even if the theoretical working-out of this compromise remains problematic.

- Increasingly through the twentieth century, challenges to the priority of epistemology in modern thought arose, taking knowledge not as foundational to, but as the byproduct of, other structures and forces. Prominent among these, pragmatism holds that knowledge must answer to usefulness, and postmodernism understands what counts as knowledge as *always* a parochial interpretation. Both pragmatism and postmodernism, each in its own way, reject the objective foundation for knowledge promised by the Enlightenment.

- In a religious context, revelation or illumination are often also included as legitimate means by which we come to know. See also **fideism**.

Further Reading

Barbour, Ian G. 1997. "Models and Paradigms." In *Religion and Science: Historical and Contemporary Issues*, 106–36. San Francisco: HarperSanFrancisco.

> This chapter provides a useful overview of how modern science incorporates aspects of empiricism and rationalism into its methods of theory formation, in comparison with the acquisition of knowledge in the realm of religion.

Feldman, Richard. 2003. *Epistemology*. Upper Saddle River, NJ: Prentice Hall.

> A standard among a number of good, general overviews of contemporary epistemology as practiced within the analytic philosophical tradition.

Heidegger, Martin. 2002. *The Essence of Truth*. New York: Continuum.

> An alternative approach to epistemological issues (based in a reading of Plato) from Continental philosophy, one that understands the possibility of knowing within the unfolding of a particular way of being.

Jeffrey Dudiak, The King's University College

☐ Eschatology

Eschatology is the theological study of the last things, of events beyond the fulfillment of personal and corporate history. It includes doctrines of resurrection, heaven and hell, and eternal life, relating to personal survival after death. More corporate matters relate to the end of history as space and time, "a new heaven and a new earth" (Rev. 21:1 NRSV), the second coming of Christ, the nature of judgment, together with the doctrine of the kingdom of God.

Since the time of **Augustine** in the fifth century (*City of God*), eschatology has been controversial. Although eschatology per se relates to the theological understanding of the end of history and its impact on the present, much of the scriptural writing that has been understood as relating to the End appears in the form of apocalyptic. Apocalyptic attempts to draw back the curtain between this world and the heavens; it focuses on a cataclysmic battle between good and evil, taking the form of visions with complex symbolism. Examples are found in the biblical books of Daniel, Ezekiel, and Revelation. Other Scripture references give only hints and suggestions of life after death, the redemption of the cosmos (Rom. 8:22), the last judgment (2 Cor. 5:10), and the return of Christ (Luke 21:8). Key beliefs for Christians are the promise of resurrection from the dead and the coming of the kingdom of God.

Literal readings in particular have spawned a number of positions relating to the millennium, a biblical concept coming out of Revelation's reference to the thousand-year reign of Christ. Premillennialism was made popular by dispensationalism and by Tim LaHaye's Left Behind series of blockbuster fiction. These books depict Jesus's second coming as occurring before or after a seven-year period of tribulation, in which believers will be raptured out of earth to safety, followed by the literal thousand-year reign of Christ on earth. Postmillennialists, more common in the eighteenth and nineteenth centuries, suggest that we may have already entered the millennium and that Christ will return at the end. Amillennialists, the more mainstream eschatological position, takes the thousand years less literally as referring to the whole of the period of history between Jesus's first and second comings, in which the kingdom of God will grow, even as opposition to God also exists.

Eschatology is linked to all other religious doctrines, speaking as it does of the fulfillment of personhood, history, community, and especially **Christology**. Late-twentieth-century eschatology emphasized the cosmic nature of Christ's redemption and the ongoing presence and work of the Spirit in creation. Eschatology gives direction and content to Christian practice and gives us also the virtue of hope. Eschatology is represented sacramentally in communion, which points back to the Passover and to Christ's Last Supper, but also anticipates the future "marriage supper of the Lamb" (Rev. 19:9 NRSV) at the end of history.

Key Points/Challenges

- The growing consensus that human reality is materially constituted challenges the dualism of much of the Christian tradition pertaining to eternal life (see **mind/body problem**). Models of life after death that do not require a separation of body, soul, and spirit have become more popular in recent years. These accounts are agnostic about the time after death and before the second coming, but emphasize instead the resurrection from the dead in the body. This requires less conflict with science at one level because there is no need to conceive of the person apart from embodiment. Older emphases of popular piety that give more credence to the separation of the real spiritual essence from the body continue, however. These accounts do not square well with the sensed need for human embodiment and the value of the physical, but they do separate eschatology into a realm that is off limits to the scientific.

- Others point to the limits of our scientific description of reality, especially when it addresses personal identity after death. The "new physics"—with its speculation concerning multiple universes, eleven dimensions, dark energy, and string theory—makes theological modesty and openness in this area imperative.

- Scientific descriptions of the universe—including deep time, the eventual burning up of our sun, and the scant possibility that the universe will indefinitely maintain life—affirm the existence of an end but are also in tension with the biblical promises of hope and restoration and of a new heaven and earth. Theology, however, looks for resolution from God's future, not just from the patterns of the past.

- In the last few decades environmentalists have warned that life on earth is indeed very fragile. The end of life might be closer than ever. Christians have been recalled to a sense of God's love of creation, and to a mandate to care for the earth, often requiring a rethinking of fundamentalist eschatological views that predict and even long for an abrupt ending of life. The continuities as well as discontinuities between this world and the world to come are recognized. See also **environmentalism, ecofeminism,** and **ecotheology.**

Further Reading

Grenz, Stanley J. 1992. *The Millennial Maze: Sorting Out Evangelical Options.* Downers Grove, IL: InterVarsity.

An introduction to eschatology and to the various millennial positions.

Moltmann, Jurgen. 2004. *The Coming of God: Christian Eschatology.* Minneapolis: Augsburg/Fortress.

A readable integrative and constructive theological work in dialogue with varied thinkers from the theologian of hope.

Polkinghorne, John. 2002. *The God of Hope and the End of the World.* New Haven: Yale University Press.

An introduction to much of the latest thinking in the science/eschatology dialogue, written at an accessible level.

Nicola Hoggard Creegan, Laidlaw College

□ Ethics

Ethics is a branch of philosophy concerned with theories and principles guiding moral behavior. It may be subdivided into metaethics, normative ethics, and applied ethics.

Metaethics seeks to identify the origins of our ethical principles. Do they arise from God or have humans created them? Are they universal?

Normative ethics articulates guidelines for moral behavior, standards for distinguishing right from wrong and good from bad. The major theories in normative ethics include virtue theory (developing good character habits), deontological theory (emphasizing universally applicable rules, such as "do not kill," that we have a duty to follow), **natural law** theory (acting consistently with the natural ends of human existence), and utilitarian or consequentialist theory (weighing the potential benefits and harms of an action, and engaging in only those actions in which the benefits outweigh the harm). More recently an ethic of care theory (emphasizing caring for others and self) has risen in an effort to establish a gender-equal ethics.

Applied ethics consists of analyzing contemporary, controversial moral issues. Applied ethics involving science and religion is usually subdivided most notably into medical ethics (bioethics) and environmental ethics, but also may include sexual ethics and professional ethics. Foremost normative principles in applied ethics generally include autonomy (freedom to choose), utility, and justice. Utility, in turn, consists of nonmaleficence (do not harm) and beneficence (do good). Distinctive to religious traditions are questions about how autonomy in applied ethics might be limited by normative truths revealed, for example, in Scripture, traditions, the Talmud and rabbinic teachings, papal encyclicals and teachings, and the Qur'an.

Key Points/Challenges

- In relation to science and religion, discussions of ethics are often specialized, focusing on applied ethical themes, including the following examples.
- Medical ethics addresses issues such as abortion, assisting and limiting reproduction, genetic counseling and control, animal and human experimentation, allocations of resources, euthanasia (withholding and withdrawing medical treatments, physician-assisted suicide, voluntary euthanasia), human therapeutic and reproductive cloning, bioterrorism, and biological warfare. Questions include: What does it mean to be a human and a person? What is the moral status of fertilized eggs, unimplanted embryos, and normal embryos and fetuses? What is our relationship to other animals?
- Environmental ethics explores the moral relationships of humans to nature, focusing on issues such as stewardship of resources and sustainability, human overpopulation, deforestation, land management, water quality, biodiversity, invasive species, global warming, waste management, and pollution. Questions

include: As humans, are we to dominate nature, using it for our purposes, or are we to be stewards of nature, carefully protecting and managing its vast yet limited resources? Should genetically modified organisms be released into the environment?

- Sexual ethics deals with issues such as celibacy, singleness, masturbation, dating, fidelity, marriage, divorce, and same-sex relationships. Questions include: What are appropriate expressions of human sexuality for persons who are not married? Should society permit and recognize committed, same-sex relationships?

- Professional ethics addresses issues of values in science, conflicts of interest, publication and openness, allocations of credit, errors and negligence, misconduct in science, and response to violations of ethical standards. Questions include: Should clinical scientists disclose to research subjects their potential contractual relationships with pharmaceutical firms?

- Some individuals seek to use sociobiology to derive ethics from science while critics dismiss any attempts to derive ethics from science (see **evolutionary psychology**).

Further Reading

Beauchamp, Tom L., and James F. Childress. 2001. *Principles of Biomedical Ethics*. 5th ed. Oxford: Oxford University Press.

> The foremost text on normative ethical theories and principles in biomedical ethics.

Deane-Drummond, Celia E. 2004. *The Ethics of Nature*. Oxford: Blackwell.

> A virtue ethics by a scientist and theologian, focused on wisdom and addressing humanity's relationship to nature in bioethics and environmental ethics, and their implications for social justice.

Grenz, Stanley J. 1997. *Sexual Ethics: An Evangelical Perspective*. Louisville: Westminster John Knox.

> A Christian perspective on sexual ethics from a theological ethicist.

Lammers, Stephen E., and Allen Verhey, eds. 1998. *On Moral Medicine: Theological Perspectives in Medical Ethics*. 2nd ed. Grand Rapids: Eerdmans.

> An anthology of classic and contemporary essays from Christian perspectives on issues in medical ethics.

National Academy of Engineering, Institute of Medicine, and National Academy of Science. 1995. *On Being a Scientist: Responsible Conduct in Research*. 2nd ed. Washington, DC: National Academy Press.

> The definitive work by scientists on professional ethics in the sciences.

Hessel Bouma III, Calvin College

□ Evolutionary Biology

Evolution is a theory about how species form and are modified from common ancestors. This theory was first outlined fully in **Charles Darwin**'s *On the Origin of Species* in 1859. The theory explains data from paleontology, anthropology, comparative anatomy, developmental biology, biogeography, molecular biology, and other scientific fields, and is currently the principal unifying concept in biology. There are two key aspects to evolution: (1) the fact of incremental developmental change over time, and (2) the mechanism(s) for producing this change. The main theoretical mechanism by which evolution occurs is primarily natural selection. Natural selection is based on four observations: (1) individuals within a species or population vary from one another; (2) more offspring are produced than can survive to reproduce; (3) in any given environment, some offspring will proliferate better than others because of their unique traits; (4) individuals that proliferate better will pass on their advantageous genetic modification(s) to their offspring. Another mechanism is sexual selection, which can create differences between sexes based on the manner in which one gender selects mates with certain characteristics that may be correlated with health, vigor, or fertility. These characteristics may not always be advantageous to the individual's survival, such as the bright blue color of one species of pupfish males, which attracts females but possibly also predators. However, they are advantageous to the individual's ability to reproduce and thus are passed on and even exaggerated over generations.

The synthetic theory of evolution, which emerged in the 1930s, combines Darwin's account of natural selection with knowledge of genes to explain how gene frequencies and corresponding physical or behavior traits of a population change in response to environmental conditions. Our recent ability to map genetic sequences has enabled a clearer picture of the current and historical evolutionary relationships among species (see **genomics**).

When a portion of a population is reproductively isolated from the rest of the species, it may experience different selective pressures and over decades or millennia new species can evolve (e.g., Hawaii honeycreepers). Genetic drift (smaller changes within a species) can be observed within months to decades (e.g., the Galapagos finches' beaks, and bacterial resistance to antibiotics). Genetic drift can occur through mechanisms that prevent fertilization: temporal isolation (different mating times), behavioral isolation (different courtship behaviors or reproductive signals), mechanical isolation (incompatibility of reproductive structures), and gametic isolation (incompatibility of eggs and sperm).

Evolutionary theory can be applied within a broad set of fields from paleobiology to behavior, which has generated new fields of study: sociobiology, evolutionary psychology, evolutionary anthropology, and behavioral ecology.

Key Points/Challenges

- Some biologists contrast microevolution (speciation) with macroevolution (descent from common ancestors). Others consider both processes the same, with different time scales. Support for macroevolution includes the fossil records of feathered, winged creatures with reptilian characteristics and the thecodonts, reptilian-mammal intermediates. Both are indicators of evolution beyond the level of individual species.

- The pace of evolution is debated. Gradualism is the view that evolution is a slow, step-wise, constant march with transitional forms from one species to the next. However, the fossil record shows only a few of these transitional forms. Punctuated equilibrium claims that major evolutionary changes occur in bursts of thousands to millions of years followed by periods of stasis of a few million to tens of millions of years. The incompleteness of the fossil record is explained by the short transition time precluding the likelihood of ever finding fossil intermediates.

- Brooks and Wiley (1986) see a need to improve natural selection theory to make it account better for lawlike behavior in the natural world and to reconcile it with what is known in developmental biology (e.g., the "evo-devo" field). Their modifications account better for higher groupings of species (families or phyla) and incorporate randomness as a force that determines form and function. Their modifications show that stochastic (random) events do not completely explain variation since there is no equilibrium between the creature and its environment. They propose experiments to test their ideas, but the data have not yet been developed.

- Disputes among scientists about the specific mechanisms of evolution have led some creationists to suggest that evolution is "only a theory" with little supportive evidence. However, none of these disputes challenge the basic parameters of evolutionary biology. The weight of evidence supporting evolution is such that the theory provides a framework or foundation for most biological fields.

Further Reading

Ayala, Francisco J. 1998. "Biological Evolution: An Overview." In *Evolutionary and Molecular Biology: Scientific Perspectives on Divine Action*, edited by Robert J. Russell, William Stoeger, and Francisco J. Ayala, 21–57. Vatican City: Vatican Observatory Publications; Berkeley: Center for Theology and the Natural Sciences.

Discusses evolutionary biology in the context of the science/religion dialogue.

Brooks, Daniel R., and Edward O. Wiley. 1986. *Evolution as Entropy: Toward a Unified Theory of Biology*. Chicago: University of Chicago Press.

Gives an example of testable modifications to Darwinian natural selection.

Gould, Stephen J., and Niles Eldredge. 1993. "Punctuated Equilibrium Comes of Age." *Nature* 366:223–27.

Discusses punctuated equilibrium modifications of Darwinian natural selection.

Ridley, Mark. 1985. *The Problems of Evolution*. Oxford: Oxford University Press.

A scientific critique of Darwinian natural selection.

Daniel K. Brannan, Abilene Christian University

☐ Evolutionary Psychology

Evolutionary psychology (EP) is an approach to the study of human behavior based on the principles of **evolutionary biology**. It assumes that the processes of natural and sexual selection acted on genes in a manner that ultimately influenced human behavior. EP focuses primarily on cognitive processes (perception, motivation) rather than overt behavior. This is because genes mediate behavior by altering the structure and function of the brain, which is believed to be the physical architecture of the cognitions that influence behavior.

EP assumes that the environment that primarily shaped the human species was small nomadic hunter-gatherer groups on the African savannah (referred to as the environment of evolutionary adaptedness). Although early humans migrated from Africa to populate diverse environments, most EP theorists believe this occurred too recently for significant evolutionary shifts in human cognitive processes. Thus humans share a universal set of cognitive mechanisms by which we organize our experience: "Our modern skulls house a stone-age mind" (Cosmides and Tooby 1997). This position distinguishes EP from behavior genetics, a field that examines the relationships between genetic variation and individual differences.

EP also argues that instead of a few general purpose or flexible mental mechanisms, human beings evolved a collection of very specific cognitive modules. Each module enables us to solve a particular adaptive problem, such as the detection of cheaters in a social group or the selection of a mate with genes that are both healthy and compatible. Evolutionary psychologists use a combination of fossil evidence, inference from modern-day hunter-gatherer societies, and empirical studies of modern human choices and behavior patterns to develop their theories about the origins of our behavior.

Key Points/Challenges

- With regard to science/religion dialogue, most prominent EP proponents (e.g., Richard Dawkins, Steven Pinker, Leda Cosmides) are metaphysical naturalists (see **materialism** and **naturalism**)—they believe that undirected natural processes acting over vast spans of time are fully sufficient to account for the origins and forms of life, and that there is no good scientific reason to believe in anything that transcends the material world. Other proponents argue that one can reconcile theories about the evolution of human nature with a belief in a supernatural dimension, or even more specifically, in a loving, self-giving Creator (e.g., John Haught, Ernst Benz; see **process philosophy**).

- Within EP there is a range of perspectives on how to theorize and how to gather and interpret evidence about human psychological evolution. The most prominent in the popular media (Pinker, David Buss, and others) have been criticized by other scholars for presenting an oversimplified view that is not empirically well supported (e.g., David Buller, Henry Plotkin).

- EP specifically argues for moderately extensive biological preparedness (intrinsic ways of processing information and responding to the environment) and against traditional social scientific views regarding the primary role of culture and experience in shaping human behavior. However, more recent theories have emerged that attempt to integrate evolved propensities with cultural influences.

- EP attempts to account for behaviors and thought patterns such as altruism, religion, celibacy, and morality within a naturalistic framework. Evolutionary psychologists argue that since the ultimate function of cognitive/behavioral adaptations is to maximize gene reproduction, such universal patterns must have contributed to reproductive success over evolutionary history. Thus beliefs in human sinfulness, purpose, morality, or calling are at best illusions that have facilitated our reproductive potential.

- Some scholars within science and religion (for example, John Haught, Donald Wacome, and Patricia Williams) work to show the complementarity, or at least compatibility, of an evolutionary view of human nature with theological concepts of sin, calling, and purpose.

Further Reading

Buller, David J. 2005. *Adapting Minds: Evolutionary Psychology and the Persistent Quest for Human Nature.* Cambridge, MA: MIT Press.

A persuasive and subtle critical engagement with the popularized version of EP.

Cosmides, Leda, and John Tooby. 1997. *Evolutionary Psychology: A Primer.* http://www.psych.ucsb.edu/research/cep/primer.html.

An accessible introduction to EP by two of its founding and most prominent proponents.

Haught, John F. 1995. *Science and Religion: From Conflict to Conversation.* Mahwah, NJ: Paulist Press.

A discussion of the various ways in which theistic traditions respond to evolutionary psychology, including some positive integrations. Includes a brief but helpful set of resources for further reading on these perspectives. See especially chapter 3, "Does Evolution Rule Out God's Existence?" (pp. 47–71).

Plotkin, Henry. 1998. *Evolution in Mind: An Introduction to Evolutionary Psychology*. Cambridge, MA: Harvard University Press.

A thoughtful and philosophically sound exploration of the value of evolutionary theory for psychology, aimed at an undergraduate audience.

Rose, Hilary, and Steven Rose. 2000. *Alas, Poor Darwin: Arguments against Evolutionary Psychology*. London: Random House.

A series of essays by natural and social scientists and philosophers discussing the limits and problems of EP.

Wacome, Donald H. 2003. "Evolutionary Psychology." In *Science and the Soul: Christian Faith and Psychological Research*, edited by Scott W. Vanderstoep, 183–213. Lanham, MD: University Press of America.

An accessible and sympathetic introduction to EP for Christians, with two responses by other Christian scholars.

Williams, Patricia A. 2001. *Doing without Adam and Eve: Sociobiology and Original Sin*. Minneapolis: Fortress.

Reinterprets the Genesis 2 and 3 accounts of creation and the human fall into sin in light of modern evolutionary biology, challenging traditional Christian accounts.

Heather Looy, The King's University College

☐ Fideism

Fideism is the view that accepting the truth or rationality of religious beliefs cannot depend on and should not be made to depend on any method or system of thought lying outside those beliefs. In particular, it means that religious beliefs can be known to be true independently of scientific or philosophical arguments. Some fideists argue for this independence of religious beliefs by asserting that they rest on revelation and not reason. Others argue that, although religious beliefs are characterized by rationality, they have a different rationality from the sort found in scientific proof and philosophical argumentation. Fideism is often linked to antifoundationalism, the view that there are and can be no universally acceptable standards or methods for verifying the truth of statements.

Key Points/Challenges

- Søren Kierkegaard (1813–55) represents a type of fideism that goes back to the French mathematician Blaise Pascal (1623–62), who observed that the heart has reasons of which reason is ignorant. Although faith is not irrational, it cannot be attained or verified by reason alone. For Kierkegaard, this characteristic of faith is exemplified by belief in the incarnation. For those standing outside faith, the incarnation is absurd and cannot be proved true by human reason. In order to accept the incarnation we must decide to embrace this paradox; once embraced, it is seen to be true. The idea of the incarnation, therefore, can be verified to be true only by those who stand within the situation of faith and not by those who stand outside faith.

- Another sort of fideism is represented by Karl Barth (1886–1968), who emphasized that the content of God's revelation is not the sort of universal or generalized truth that is the goal of science and philosophy. On the contrary, the content of revelation is always particular, that is, it is directed to humans in particular circumstances. This means that theology, which is the church's response to revelation, has nothing to do with science and philosophy (as least as they have been hitherto understood). That is why Barth vehemently rejected the possibility of **natural theology**. Barth was primarily concerned that we not subordinate revelation to human reason by seeing revelation as just one means of attaining universal truths that are also available by other means.

- The contemporary philosopher Alvin Plantinga (1932–) argues against the assumption that there is a universal norm of rationality. On the contrary, for those who believe in God neither science nor philosophy nor any other discipline provides grounds for such belief. This is because belief in God is not inferred from another belief but is instead "properly basic" for those who hold this belief. A belief is properly basic when it does not require rational justification and functions as a foundational belief for other beliefs. As a result, faith is methodologically independent of science, philosophy, and other disciplines.

- The main critique of fideism is expressed in the injunction, stated in classical form by William Clifford (1999), that it is always wrong to believe something on insufficient evidence. Of course, this critique assumes that there is a universal form of evidence that should govern all our beliefs, including religious beliefs. It is just this evidentialist assumption that fideists contest.

- With respect to the relationship of science to theology, fideism stands for the independence of theology from scientific inquiry. In particular, fideists argue that theology has a source of truth about the created world that is independent of the sciences even while admitting that the sciences provide important insight into the created world. Fideists are therefore suspicious of natural theology, which implies the ability to know about God and things related to God by means of human reason and universally available truths.

Further Reading

Amesbury, Richard. 2005. *Fideism*. Stanford Encyclopedia of Philosophy. http://plato.stanford.edu/entries/fideism/#2.2.2.

A good exposition of some of the main forms of fideism, with extended bibliography.

Barth, Karl. 1962. *Credo*. New York: Charles Scribner's Sons.

A readable introduction to Barth's theology, consisting of his lectures on the Apostles' Creed.

Clifford, William K. 1999. "The Ethics of Belief." In *The Ethics of Belief and Other Essays*, 70–96. New York: Prometheus Books.

The basic statement of the thesis that belief must always be warranted by evidence.

Kierkegaard, Søren. 1985. *Philosophical Fragments*. Translated by Howard V. Hong and Edna H. Hong. Princeton, NJ: Princeton University Press.

Kierkegaard's presentation of the incarnation as a paradox and of the relationship of faith to reason.

Plantinga, Alvin. 1992. "Is Belief in God Properly Basic?" In *Contemporary Perspectives on Religious Epistemology*, edited by R. Douglas Geivett and Brendan Sweetman, 133–41. New York: Oxford University Press.

Argument that belief in God is not inferred from some more fundamental belief.

Samuel M. Powell, Point Loma Nazarene University

☐ Fundamentalism

Fundamentalism describes a religious impulse that militantly resists many aspects of the modern world, including the scientific worldview, pluralism, and cultural diversity. Fundamentalism is an attempt by religious people to retain what they regard as traditional beliefs and values by rejecting those features of the modern world that threaten their religious beliefs and values. Fundamentalism is, accordingly, found in many religions today. Here, however, the focus will be on Christian fundamentalism in America. With respect to the relation of science to theology the principal importance of fundamentalism is its alliance with **creation** science. However, it is important to keep in mind that promoting creation science is part of the much larger agenda of American fundamentalists to realize their vision of a Christian America that is faithful to their understanding of the Bible. Religious fundamentalism is a worldwide phenomenon, called forth as a response to the intellectual and social pressures of Western modernism. In its militant forms, fundamentalism is expressly linked to political agendas, as in Islamic countries (where it is a response to secularizing trends), in Hinduism (where it is a part of Indian nationalism), and in American Protestantism (where it appears in the religious right).

Key Points/Challenges

- The driving force behind American fundamentalism is the collapse of the biblical worldview in American culture and in academic disciplines. Early-nineteenth-century America was a biblical culture in important respects. Biblical doctrines and ethics were both widespread and respected. Many university disciplines were accommodated to the biblical portrait of reality. In the late nineteenth century American universities began disengaging their disciplines from this culture. The result was not only the autonomy of the disciplines but the fostering of theories directly at odds with the widespread beliefs and values of America's biblical culture. In this volatile environment biological evolution (see **Darwin** and **evolutionary biology**) emerged as the great symbol of the collapse of the biblical worldview and its replacement by an alternative theory that was viewed by fundamentalists as both unscientific and atheistic. Fundamentalists sought to restore America's biblical culture. One of their main strategies was to attack the theory of evolution.

- Fundamentalist anxiety about evolution was accompanied by alarm over the application of historical criticism to the Bible. Many biblical scholars in the nineteenth century devoted themselves to the examination of the Bible using the methods applied successfully in other areas of historical inquiry. The result was that, by the early twentieth century, the traditional notion of the Bible's inspiration had been rejected by a substantial portion of the community of biblical scholars. Instead of seeing the Bible as a divinely authored book, the Bible was regarded as a collection of writings by ancient peoples. Consequently, in an era of scientific discovery, theologians saw no compelling reason to affirm that the opening chapters of Genesis described historical events. Fundamentalists consistently rejected the assumptions, methods, and results of the historical criticism of the Bible. They insisted on interpreting the Bible as a faithful and inspired narrative of historical events.

- Fundamentalism has been challenged in many ways. Since the 1930s fundamentalists have been almost completely discredited in mainline American Protestant denominations. In recent decades American evangelicals have likewise sought to distinguish themselves from fundamentalism and to present evangelicalism as an intellectually responsible approach to the Christian faith. An overt attack on creation science was offered by the National Academy of Sciences in its 1999 publication *Science and Creationism*. Perhaps the principal challenge has come from theological and sociological analyses that place fundamentalism in its historical context, present it as a mere reaction to the forces of modern culture, and thereby relativize its claims.

Further Reading

Barr, James. 1977. *Fundamentalism*. London: SCM.
     An attack on fundamentalism from a distinguished biblical scholar.

Marsden, George M. 1980. *Fundamentalism and American Culture: The Shaping of Twentieth-Century Evangelicalism: 1870–1925.* New York: Oxford University Press.

> An important historical examination of the roots of American fundamentalism. Asserts the thesis that fundamentalism is a reaction to the modern world.

———. 1991. *Understanding Fundamentalism and Evangelicalism.* Grand Rapids: Eerdmans.

> Another contribution to the portrait of fundamentalism in the context of the decline of biblical culture and the rise of evolutionary theories.

Marty, Martin, and R. Scott Appleby, eds. 1991. *Fundamentalisms Observed.* Chicago: University of Chicago Press.

> The first in a series of works that, using several methods, examine varieties of fundamentalism in the world's religions.

National Academy of Sciences, Committee on Science and Creationism. 1999. *Science and Creationism: A View from the National Academy of Sciences.* 2nd ed. Washington, DC: National Academy Press.

> A defense of the theory of biological evolution and a response to some of the questions about that theory posed by creation science.

Samuel M. Powell, Point Loma Nazarene University

☐ Galilei, Galileo (1564–1642)

Galileo taught mathematics and **natural philosophy** first at the University of Pisa and later at the University of Padua. At Padua he first turned from Aristotelian mechanics to a new sort of science of motion, mathematical in form and primarily experimental in warrant. Interrupting this work in 1609 to point his newly perfected telescope to the skies, his observations led him to support the sun-centered worldview proposed years before in Copernicus's *De revolutionibus* (1543).

The Copernican (see **Copernicus**) view had already been criticized by theologians for contradicting passages in the Old Testament that mention the motion of the sun or the immobility of the earth. Galileo was soon embroiled in controversy. He argued that the Scriptures were written with human salvation in mind, not the science of astronomy, and were clearly accommodated to the understanding of the original audience. The letter that contained this argument was forwarded to Rome by a hostile critic, where a pro-Copernican work by a reputable theologian, Paolo Foscarini, was also causing intense debate. Galileo's *Letter to the Grand Duchess* (1615), which called on the authority of St. **Augustine** in support of the exegetical (interpretive) principles on which Galileo was drawing, may not have reached Rome. In 1616 Catholic Church authorities declared the Copernican view to be contrary to Scripture. Galileo was called to appear before Cardinal Robert Bellarmine, who instructed him to "abandon" the prohibited view. Whether he also received a formal injunction not to "teach, defend, or even discuss" that view is disputed.

Some years later, when his friend Cardinal Maffeo Barberini was elected Pope Urban VIII, Galileo was permitted to return to his work on the Copernican system, provided that the system was treated as a "hypothesis" in the sense of being no more than a convenient calculating device. After a long struggle with the Catholic Church's censors, he published his *Dialogue on Two Chief World Systems* (1632). The work did not present the Copernican claims in the permitted "hypothetical" manner. The affronted pope ordered Galileo before the tribunal of the Holy Office, where he was found to be "vehemently suspect of heresy" and ordered to abjure the condemned view. After abjuring, he was condemned to permanent house arrest.

He returned to the work on mechanics he had abandoned years before and published his *Two New Sciences* (1638), the foundational work in modern mechanics. He was afflicted by progressive blindness and died in 1642.

Key Points/Challenges

- For many, the "Galileo affair" came to symbolize an inevitable antagonism between the church and the new sciences or even between religion and science generally. A mythology grew up: Galileo was tortured (he wasn't); he was imprisoned in the "dungeons of the Holy Office" (he was never placed in a dungeon); he muttered after abjuring, "And yet it moves!" (a later invention); he was condemned "for demonstrating the earth's motion" (he wasn't and he didn't).

- It is important to separate the ban on Copernican doctrine in 1616 and the trial and condemnation of Galileo in 1633. In 1616, what concerned the theologians was a perceived challenge to the integrity of Scripture. At this time the matter of biblical interpretation was bitterly argued between Reformers and defenders of the counter-Reformation. Galileo was viewed as an outsider, a mathematician defending a nonliteral interpretation of Scripture on the basis of a claim about the earth's motion that he had not demonstrated. The fact that his exegetical arguments were for the most part in accord with earlier church tradition counted for little at a time when theologians perceived support of Copernicanism as a significant threat to the authority of Scripture and of the church as its interpreter. It should be emphasized that the theologian-opponents of the Copernican position regarded the astronomical science of their day as an ally. Virtually all natural philosophers in 1616 would have viewed the Copernican position as "false in philosophy" (i.e., scientifically incorrect). Nonetheless, church authorities undoubtedly made an objective error in condemning the Copernican view as contrary to Scripture. It wasn't.

- The situation in 1633 was different. Galileo's *Dialogue* had made a far better case for the Copernican position than what had been available in 1616, but the issue was no longer the quality of the evidence in its favor. The charge that Galileo faced was whether he had violated the 1616 order to abandon the Copernican view and whether he was guilty of defending a view that had been declared contrary to Scripture. Technically, he was indeed guilty as charged, but there were many extenuating circumstances. He had been encouraged by the pope to proceed, and could claim to have misunderstood the proviso to limit himself to a "hypothetical" presentation. His book had been licensed by the censors. It was argued that he had failed to inform the censors of the formal injunction applied to him in 1616 but the validity of that injunction was debatable. The summary of evidence on which his judges proceeded was flawed in important respects. And the charge of heresy could not call on the wording of the decree of 1616; the judges at that earlier time had pointedly refused to treat Copernicanism as heresy.

- The decision in 1616 of Pope Paul V and the committee of cardinals to outlaw the Copernican worldview was, however, the crux of the Galileo affair. In 1992 the church formally, if belatedly, conceded that Galileo had indeed proved in this matter to be the better theologian.

Further Reading

Fantoli, Annibale. 2003. *For Copernicanism and for the Church.* 3rd ed. Vatican City: Vatican Observatory Publications.

   The most comprehensive history to date of the Galileo affair.

Finocchiaro, Maurice. 1989. *The Galileo Affair.* Berkeley: University of California Press.

   Compilation of the principal documents relevant to the affair, in translation.

McMullin, Ernan, ed. 2005. *The Church and Galileo.* Notre Dame, IN: University of Notre Dame Press.

   A comprehensive set of essays bearing on the role of the church in the affair.

Ernan McMullin, University of Notre Dame

☐ Genomics/Genetics

Since the early twentieth century, genetics has remained at the forefront of life science investigations. This persistent devotion among various biomedical, philosophical, religious, and agricultural constituencies evoked Evelyn Fox Keller's declaration that the twentieth century was the "century of the gene."

Genomics involves a wide array of investigations into the structure and functions of an organism's total genetic content (i.e., its genome). These investigations include determining the sequence of the biochemical units that comprise an organism's DNA and the mapping of genes in chromosomes. Genomics also explores the interplay between genetic and environmental causes of disease, personality, and behavior.

Genetic research is sometimes used to support biological **determinism**, which argues that an organism is merely the expression of its genes. Gene-level discoveries are used to explain complex activities, including behavior and life itself. Some argue that such views represent a simplified, incomplete, and irreligious overemphasis on the role of genes as the primary determinants of what it means to be human. Others have used genomic reductionism in support of religion, claiming, as Dean H. Hamer argued in *The God Gene* (2004), that faith is "hardwired into our genes."

Genetic knowledge creates the possibility of genetic manipulation, hence concern regarding its regulation. Eugenic measures in the early twentieth century to establish legal reproductive control over certain segments of populations remain a vivid reminder of one extreme type of regulation. Potential harms resulting from poor regulation are echoed in the media's frequent appellations of "Frankenstein" and "Brave New World" to genetic research. The Ethical, Legal, and Social Implications Research Program, initiated during the Human Genome Project, continues to stipulate that a specified percentage of each US federally awarded grant be allocated toward these humanitarian implications of genomic research.

Key Points/Challenges

- Christians, as stewards of God's earth, often grapple over the extent to which they can responsibly apply genomics to produce better livestock, improve crop yields, and enhance animal and crop resistance to pests, disease, and harsh environments. Genetic technology may help feed a hungry world, but some equate creating mixed gene or "transgenic" species with the Old Testament prohibition of "mixing kinds" (Deut. 22:9–11).

- Embryonic life is central to debates over applied human genomics. Fetal screening to detect genetic disease is problematic within religious frameworks that oppose abortion. Stem cell research that involves harvesting embryonic cells is arguably synonymous with abortion if the early embryo is viewed as a living entity.

- Healing is a ministry when the healer emulates God. However, "playing God" in terms of redesigning human life by "rewriting" the "code" for humanity begs moral, ethical, and religious consideration. Creating potentially patentable new genes and transgenic organisms violates the view that God is the only creator and that humanity was created in God's image.

- Selective breeding, gene therapy, and cloning will affect future generations in many ways. Beyond the genetic implications, such manipulations, as theologians frequently argue, also drive offspring toward a more standardized norm, thereby diminishing the diversity among God's creatures. Some fear that, in the words of geneticist H. J. Muller in 1959, we are headed for a "genetic Apocalypse" such that "there will be none like us to come after us."

Further Reading

Deane-Drummond, Celia, Bronislaw Szerszynski, and Robin Grove-White, eds. 2003. *Reordering of Nature: Theology, Society and the New Genetics*. London: T&T Clark.

> A recent collection from scholars in environment studies, theology, and genetics that helps us more fully appreciate how our interpretation of genetic intervention depends on our vision of humanity within the natural world.

Nelkin, Dorothy, and M. Susan Lindee. 1995. *The DNA Mystique: The Gene as a Cultural Icon*. New York: Freeman.

> An accessible work that explores the range of meanings implied by the wide use of genetic images in popular culture.

Peters, Ted. 1997. *Playing God? Genetic Determinism and Human Freedom*. New York: Routledge.

> A clearly presented theological perspective to help a general readership more closely examine the claim that "it's all in the genes."

Ridley, Matt. 2000. *Genome: The Autobiography of a Species in 23 Chapters*. New York: HarperCollins.

> An insightfully clever work in which Ridley literally turns the human genome into a book to read. The history of genes and the moral challenges of the Human Genome Project are lucidly presented.

Thistlethwaite, Susan B., ed. 2003. *Adam, Eve, and the Genome: The Human Genome Project and Theology*. Minneapolis: Augsburg/Fortress.

> A helpful primer on recent genetic research combined with ethical reflections on key questions relevant to what it means to be human.

Philip K. Wilson, Penn State University College of Medicine

☐ Gödel's Theorem

What is commonly called Gödel's theorem is actually two related incompleteness theorems in mathematical logic that were published in 1931 by Kurt Gödel. The following is a general statement of Gödel's theorem:

1. In any formal system adequate for number theory (the study of the properties of integers) there exists a formula that is not provable and whose negation is not provable.
2. A corollary of the first theorem is that the consistency of a formal system adequate for number theory cannot be proved within the system.

The result is related to the logical difficulties that can arise when self-referential statements are made. For example, the statement "All Cretans are liars," made by a Cretan, is self-referential and is neither true nor false. Similar theorems involving self-referential elements have been established by Turing, Chaitin, and others.

Key Points/Challenges

- Many people have interpreted Gödel's theorem as demolishing the epistemology of seventeenth-century rationalists such as **Descartes**, **Spinoza**, and **Leibniz**, and as being in accord with the revolt against the objectivity that characterized much twentieth-century thinking. However, Gödel himself did not agree with this interpretation of his theory. In fact, Gödel strongly empathized with Leibniz on **epistemology**.

- It is a common misconception that Gödel's theorem implies that there are non-provable mathematical propositions and that this means there are regions of the Platonic world of mathematical truths that are in principle inaccessible to us. What the theorem does say is any formal mathematical system will be necessarily incomplete because there will always be truths outside the rules. Starting from this point the mathematical physicist Roger Penrose (1994) argues that conscious awareness is a property of our brains and is something wholly different from computational-like thinking. It takes a vision of the system to create the system of rules, and this vision is never encompassed by the rules themselves. Penrose says that this is an appropriate description of the relationship between a computer, its program (system of rules), and its human programmer. The computer can never get outside its program to reflect on its own programming, but we can.

- In an address at Cambridge University in 2002 ("Gödel and the End of Physics") the mathematical physicist Stephen Hawking conceded that a rigorous "theory of everything" might not be possible, because we and our models are both part of the universe that we are describing. Thus a physical theory is self-referencing, like Gödel's theorem. One might therefore expect it to be either inconsistent or incomplete. Similar views had been expressed some thirty years earlier by theologians Thomas Torrance, Stanley Jaki, and George Murphy. The latter argued that if the universe is a representation of a mathematical pattern, then the physical universe is incomplete. This suggests that there must be something beyond physical reality. Citing Gödel for support, the physicist-theologian John Polkinghorne writes that truth always exceeds what can be proved.

• Caution is needed in extrapolating from mathematics to implications in other fields.

Further Reading

Barr, Stephen M. 2003. *Modern Physics and Ancient Faith*. Notre Dame, IN: University of Notre Dame Press.

> Discusses applications of Gödel's theorem to physics.

Franzén, Torkel. 2005. *Gödel's Theorem: An Incomplete Guide to Its Use and Abuse*. Wellesley, MA: Peters.

> Provides technical background and criticism.

Goldstein, Rebecca. 2005. *Incompleteness: The Proof and Paradox of Kurt Gödel*. New York: W. W. Norton.

> A biographical study of Gödel, providing background information about his thought.

Hofstadter, Douglas R. 1979. *Gödel, Escher, Bach: An Eternal Golden Braid*. New York: Basic Books.

> A popular introduction to Gödel's work.

Nagel, Ernest, and James R. Newman. 1968. *Gödel's Proof*. New York: New York University Press.

> A semipopular exposition that goes into some detail concerning the substance of the proof.

Penrose, Roger. 1994. *Shadows of the Mind*. Oxford: Oxford University Press.

> Extended exposition of Penrose's thesis (originally presented in his 1987 book, *The Emperor's New Mind*) with responses to critics.

Donald A. Nield, University of Auckland

☐ Handmaiden Metaphor

During the Middle Ages theology was understood to be the queen of the sciences, and classical learning, insofar as it was true, was theology's servant or "handmaiden." The metaphor described the relationship between Greek wisdom and Christian theology.

Quite early in the Christian era theologians had to come to terms with classical learning. Almost inevitably there were tensions between Christian teaching and aspects of pagan thought, with St. Paul declaring on one occasion that the Gospel was "folly" to the Greeks (1 Cor. 1:23). Subsequently, the church father Tertullian declared philosophy to be "the parent of heresy" (*The Prescription against Heretics*, chap. 7). Some early Christian writers, however, stressed the value of pagan wisdom, suggesting that it was a "preparation" for the Gospel (see, e.g., Clement of Alexandria, *Stromata*, 1.5, 1.7). Tertullian was more positive toward philosophy than some of his more extreme statements might suggest.

When Aristotelian learning (see **Aristotle**) was reintroduced in the West in the eleventh and twelfth centuries, the question of the role of Greek philosophy and its relationship to Christian theology was raised again. While there was some initial resistance to Aristotelian philosophy, by the middle of the fourteenth century it was entrenched in university curriculums. Its predominant role in the universities was justified because it was said to serve the interests of Christian theology. In this sense it served as handmaiden to the queen of the sciences, theology.

Key Points/Challenges

- The handmaiden metaphor gave to classical learning a positive, yet ultimately subservient, role in medieval learning.
- The notion that theology was the most important of the sciences was not only the position of Christian theologians, but had also been espoused by Aristotle. The Greek philosopher had distinguished three "speculative sciences": **natural philosophy** (or science), mathematics, and theology (or **metaphysics**). The last he regarded as the most elevated of the sciences.
- The sciences of natural philosophy and mathematics were thought to serve theology not only by providing information important to the interpretation of Scripture and for the articulation of doctrine. Study of natural philosophy and mathematics was also thought to be useful for inculcating the right kinds of mental habits or disciplines that would ultimately assist in the task of contemplation. The Christian philosopher was to progress by stages from the contemplation of material things (natural philosophy), to the contemplation of abstract things (mathematics), to the contemplation of the divine nature (theology).
- From the seventeenth century on with the demise of the Aristotelian view of the sciences, the handmaiden metaphor became less common. Nonetheless, various aspects of the natural sciences continue to be regarded as providing support for **natural theology**.

Further Reading

Grant, Edward. 2006. *Science and Religion: 400 BC–AD 1550*. Baltimore: Johns Hopkins University Press.

An introductory account of the relationship between science and religion in the West up to 1550. An appendix includes a selection from Roger Bacon's *Opus Majus*, which discusses the merits of Greek science.

Lindberg, David C. 1992. *The Beginnings of Western Science.* Chicago: University of Chicago Press.

The best general introduction to classical and medieval science. Covers the reception of classical ideas in the medieval West.

———. 2003. "The Medieval Church Encounters the Classical Tradition: Saint Augustine, Roger Bacon, and the Handmaiden Metaphor." In *When Science and Christianity Meet*, edited by David C. Lindberg and Ronald L. Numbers, 7–32. Chicago: University of Chicago Press.

An excellent, concise account of the relations between Greek science and Christianity in the patristic period and Middle Ages. Includes a discussion of the handmaiden metaphor.

Peter Harrison, University of Oxford

□ Hermeneutics

Hermeneutics derives from Greek *hermêneuô*, "to interpret or translate" (developed from the messenger of the Greek pantheon, Hermes). It is the theory and practice of interpretation, usually the interpretation of texts. Early Western hermeneutics can be traced from before the beginning of the common era and continuing well into the Middle Ages. Greek philosophers had some theories of interpretation; for example, **Aristotle** wrote about the processes of translation. Within the early Jewish tradition Philo of Alexandria wrote extensive treatises on the allegorical meaning of the Hebrew Bible. The nascent Christian tradition developed several strategies to interpret the Hebrew Scriptures and New Testament in an effort to understand Jesus as the Christ.

The rise of Islam prompted a boom in hermeneutics as religion scholars from the Jewish, Christian, and Muslim traditions were charged with the task of demonstrating "correct" interpretations of the Scriptures. The differing interpretations within the traditions themselves then became sources for new religious movements and conflict. Hermeneutics later expanded into two significant new directions. The first, prompted by Friedrich Schleiermacher, focused on how people understand texts. The second, advanced by Wilhelm Dilthey, advocated hermeneutic practice as a methodology for understanding the "human sciences"; that is, knowledge of humanity and human institutions was not an act of understanding but rather was a historically conditioned act of interpretation.

Interest in hermeneutics grew steadily as part of the development of Continental philosophy. For example, moving beyond Dilthey, Martin Heidegger argued that hermeneutics offered more than a formal structure for the study of linguistic communication. He expanded the hermeneutic task to the sphere of personal self-understanding. At the most basic level, hermeneutics was the study of what it means to be human. That is, hermeneutics was ontological in nature.

Hans Gadamer took Heidegger's notion of hermeneutics as **ontology** to develop a larger philosophical system in which he suggested that language is the mediator for all human understanding. Because language is the fundamental means by which people comprehend and interact with the world, people can understand themselves only as situated in a historical context mediated by language. Reality cannot be known directly. Paul Ricoeur, Jacques Derrida, and other postmodern writers developed philosophies of hermeneutics that incorporate literary criticism, linguistics, and psychoanalysis. Sensitive to the limitations of language and historical knowledge, their hermeneutic strategies stress the polyvalence of meaning (both in texts and in actions) and the instability of foundational truth claims or metanarratives. The effect of postmodern hermeneutics on Christianity has led to the development of feminist and liberation theologies in one direction and restorationist and radical orthodoxy theologies in another.

Key Points/Challenges

- Textual hermeneutics acknowledges that whenever reading occurs some act of interpretation is always involved.
- Initially hermeneutics referred to discussions about interpreting texts. Since the nineteenth century, hermeneutics has come to denote a broad range of methodologies and philosophies for understanding lived experience.
- The "hermeneutic circle" is the process by which people read a text and derive an interpretation. Perhaps a new interpretation occurs every time the text is read, or a new interpretation happens for each unique reader who brings a different set of foreknowledge and life experience with each reading.
- Reading religious texts literally is a relatively new phenomenon. Literalism is both a reaction to scientific rationalism and an application of modern under-standings about physics, biology, history, and so on to ancient texts that often did not share such concerns.
- Jürgen Habermas has raised an important challenge for postmodern hermeneu-tics. He points to what he sees as methodological contradictions and resistance to recognize individual agency in history. Moreover, he rebuffs the postmodern rejection of Enlightenment values, arguing that ethical critical theory of society must inform any hermeneutic.

Further Reading

Derrida, Jacques. 1997. *Of Grammatology*. Translated by G. Spivak. Baltimore: Johns Hopkins University Press.

> Analysis of the relationship between spoken and written word. A critical text for understanding Derrida's concept of "deconstruction."

Dilthey, Wilhelm. 1996. *Hermeneutics and the Study of History*. Edited by R. Makkreel and F. Rodi. Princeton, NJ: Princeton University Press.

> Dilthey's development of Schleiermacher's theories wherein he introduces the concept of the "hermeneutic circle."

Finlayson, Gordon. 2005. *Habermas: A Very Short Introduction*. New York: Oxford University Press.

> A brief resource on Habermas's social theory and its connections to contemporary philosophy.

Gadamer, Hans-Georg. 1989. *Truth and Method*. Translated by J. Weinsheimer and D. G. Marshall. 2nd rev. ed. (1st English ed., 1975). New York: Crossroad.

> Gadamer takes on Dilthey's hermeneutics here, putting a greater emphasis on ontology and the interpreter's historical context.

Grondin, Jean. 1994. *Introduction to Philosophical Hermeneutics*. New Haven: Yale University Press.

> Broad survey text of significant hermeneuticists from the pre- to postmodern periods.

Habermas, Jürgen. 1984–87. *The Theory of Communicative Action*. Translated by Thomas McCarthy. 2 Vols. Cambridge: Polity.

> Habermas's primary work in which he refutes modernist assumptions about the "knowing subject" stressing instead identity as developed through interpersonal communication.

Heidegger, Martin. 1962. *Being and Time*. Translated by J. Macquarrie and E. Robinson. Rev. ed. San Francisco: Harper.

> Translation of Heidegger's work on associating hermeneutics with ontology.

Peters, Edward. 1980. *Heresy and Authority in Medieval Europe: Documents in Translation*. Philadelphia: University of Pennsylvania Press.

> A source book covering several voices about hermeneutics in the Christian tradition during the premodern period.

Ricoeur, Paul. 1981. *Hermeneutics and the Human Sciences: Essays on Language, Action and Interpretation*. Edited and translated by John B. Thompson. Cambridge: Cambridge University Press.

> Collection of essays with editorial introductions that trace Ricoeur's tying together hermeneutics and phenomenology.

Schleiermacher, Friederich. 1998. *Hermeneutics and Criticism and Other Writings*. Edited and translated by Andrew Bowie. Cambridge: Cambridge University Press.

Collection of seminal pieces demonstrating Schleiermacher's theories on interpretation and translation.

Venema, Henry I. 2000. *Identifying Selfhood: Imagination, Narrative, and Hermeneutics in the Thought of Paul Ricoeur*. Albany: State University of New York Press.

Introductory survey of Ricoeur's hermeneutics.

Yarchin, William. 2004. *History of Biblical Interpretation: A Reader*. Peabody, MA: Hendrickson.

A survey of different approaches to reading the biblical sources from the start of the common era to the twentieth century.

C. Shaun Longstreet, University of Texas at Dallas

☐ Idealism

The term *idealism*, derived from the Greek word *idea* ("image," "figure," "form") and ultimately from the verb *idein* ("to see"), refers to a family of philosophical positions and schools that claim that ideas, ideals, minds, and products of the mind have a clear preeminence over the material world. At its core, any philosophical idealism is based on the notion that, in some way or other, the physical world we perceive through our senses is only a reflection, or an expression, of the activities of the mind, whether divine or human. The term *idealism* was first used in the early eighteenth century by **Gottfried Wilhelm von Leibniz**, with reference to the philosophy of **Plato** and in contrast to materialist doctrines. Plato stated (in *Phaedo* and the *Republic*, for example) that the things we see are only imperfect "copies" or "shadows" of a divine world of "ideas" or "archetypes" (ideal Forms), the only truly existent reality. Later philosophers and theologians incorporated this way of thinking into Christian theology, and the archetypes came to be seen as God's thoughts. For example, St. **Augustine** placed the archetypes in the divine Intelligence and Johannes Scottus Eriugena (800–877) claimed that all things are somehow contained in God's mind. In the footsteps of these philosophers, George Berkeley (1685–1753), probably the most prominent modern idealist (his position is often called "theistic idealism"), utterly denied the existence of matter and claimed that the world is only a visible language through which God incessantly speaks to us.

Key Points/Challenges

- After Berkeley, idealism would see a massive revival in Germany with, among others, Johann Gottlieb Fichte (1762–1814), Wilhelm Joseph Schelling (1775–1854), Immanuel Kant (1724–1804), and Georg Wilhelm Friedrich Hegel (1770–1831), the last two being the most influential. Other important idealists were Benedetto Croce (1866–1952) in Italy, Herbert Bradley

(1846–1924) and Bernard Bosanquet (1848–1923) in England, and Josiah Royce (1855–1916) in the United States.

- Depending on the philosophical context, idealism is contrasted with **materialism, realism,** empiricism, and **naturalism.** Atheism is usually contrasted with theistic idealism.

- A specific form of idealism is "ethical idealism," in which one bases one's conduct always on high moral standards and values rather than on pragmatic considerations. In the ethical sense idealism often signifies an approach to international relations, the opposite being realism.

- In the **social sciences,** an idealist approach would tend to emphasize the role of values and ideas in determining people's behavior.

- In art, idealism refers to a tendency toward representing objects as perfect, ideal types, rather than their particular instantiations. The idealist artist does not so much seek to depict something "realistically" as to embody a certain ideal of beauty.

- Idealism is sometimes dismissively equated with "utopian," "impossible," and "unrealistic." In Ingmar Bergman's film *The Seventh Seal* (1957), for example, one character remarks, "Our crusade was so stupid that only an idealist could have thought it out." Even in this pejorative sense, the term idealism, by pointing to the gap between the poor state of affairs in the real world and an ideal state toward which things should strive, still conveys something of its original Platonic flavor.

Further Reading

Bubner, Rüdiger. 2003. *The Innovations of Idealism.* Translated by Nicholas Walker. Cambridge: Cambridge University Press.

> Discusses German intellectual life between 1780 and 1830, with a special emphasis on Kant, Fichte, Schelling, and Hegel, but also discusses Rousseau, Schleiermacher, Schlegel, and Goethe.

Gersh, Stephen, and Dermot Moran, eds. 2006. *Eriugena, Berkeley, and the Idealist Tradition.* Notre Dame, IN: Notre Dame University Press.

> A collection of essays by historians, classicists, and philosophers on prominent moments of the idealist tradition: Plato, Plotinus, Roman Stoicism, St. Augustine, Eriugena, al-Kindī, Berkeley, and German classical philosophy.

Pippin, Robert B. 1997. *Idealism as Modernism: Hegelian Variations.* Cambridge: Cambridge University Press.

> A collection of essays primarily on Kant, Hegel, Nietzsche, Heidegger, and Leo Strauss. Considers idealism in relationship to the modernity problem.

Sell, Alan P. F. 1996. *Philosophical Idealism and Christian Belief.* Cardiff: University of Wales Press.

> Discusses post-Hegelian idealism (especially in Great Britain) in relation to Christian theology from an apologetic point of view.

Vesey, Godfrey, ed. 1982. *Idealism: Past and Present.* Cambridge: Cambridge University Press.

>A collection of essays approaching idealism both historically and systematically. The volume includes essays on Berkeley, Kant, Fichte, Hegel, and Bradley as idealists, as well as idealism in Marx, Schopenhauer, and Wittgenstein.

Costica Bradatan, Texas Tech University

☐ Ideas of God (Theism, Deism, Atheism)

Every aspect of the dialogue between science and religion presupposes some idea of God—or at least some sense of an absolute or ultimate reality. Even atheism makes assumptions about what kind of God is being negated. In the broadest sense the term *theism* (from the Greek *theos*, God) means belief in the existence of a God (or gods). "Classical" theism typically refers to belief in God as a person of a particular kind, one who is all-knowing and all-powerful (along with other attributes), and unaffected by the world. As the sciences of classical mechanics increasingly explained the structure and movement of bodies in the world, many natural philosophers argued for *deism*, the belief that God was the First Cause of the cosmos but does not intervene within it. Although the term *atheism* is generally used to refer to the denial of the existence of any kind of God, it is often used in a more technical sense to refer to modern "protest" atheism, which denies the existence (or even coherence) of the God of classical theism. Modern atheists wonder how the existence of such a God is consistent with the existence of evil in the world. Scientists from several disciplines (e.g., anthropology, psychology, and sociology) have suggested that the classical theistic idea of God is simply the result of extending human ideals (e.g., strength, wisdom, and kindness) and projecting them onto the divine.

Key Points/Challenges

- Many Christian participants in the science and religion dialogue maintain a classical theistic idea of God and attempt to show how this may be rendered consistent with contemporary scientific cosmology. Others explore ways in which more explicitly trinitarian views of the divine may overcome the challenges of modern atheism and provide new conceptual space for articulating the God-world relationship.

- Although the science/religion dialogue in the West has been dominated in recent decades by Christian ideas of God, other concepts of the divine have increasingly entered the discussion. Many of the issues argued in the debates on classical theism are also relevant to Jewish and Muslim ideas of God. Other religions, such as Buddhism, offer nonpersonal concepts of ultimate reality. This pluralism makes the interdisciplinary task more challenging, but also opens up opportunities for new insights.

- Rival assumptions about the nature of God are behind many of the major debates in science and religion, although these assumptions are not always brought to the surface. For example, on one hand the image of God evoked by many arguments for **intelligent design** is of a transcendent and highly rational clockmaker or engineer. Many of those who are concerned to develop an **ecotheology**, on the other hand, utilize an idea of a God who is more immanently involved in nurturing the cosmos.

Further Reading

Buckley, Michael J. 1987. *At the Origins of Modern Atheism*. New Haven: Yale University Press.

> Traces the way in which the Christian religion alienated itself from the resources of its own tradition and contributed to the rise of atheism.

Clayton, Philip. 1997. *God and Contemporary Science*. Grand Rapids: Eerdmans.

> Engages the idea of God with special attention to challenges from science and proposes a model of divine action.

McGrath, Alister. 2004. *The Twilight of Atheism: The Rise and Fall of Disbelief in the Modern World*. London: Rider Books.

> Accessible discussion on the history and modern status of atheism, from a scientist/ theologian.

Polkinghorne, John. 2006. *Science and the Trinity: The Christian Encounter with Reality*. New Haven: Yale University Press.

> Provides an overview of ways in which various contemporary scientific theories may be brought into dialogue with a trinitarian understanding of God.

Shults, F. LeRon. 2005. *Reforming the Doctrine of God*. Grand Rapids: Eerdmans.

> Outlines contemporary challenges to the early modern idea of God based on science and philosophy and offers a trinitarian model of the God-world relation.

Swinburne, Richard. 1993. *The Coherence of Theism*. Rev. ed. Oxford: Clarendon.

> Popular presentation of "classical" or modern theism.

F. LeRon Shults, University of Agder

□ *Imago Dei*

The Latin phrase *imago Dei* means "image of God." Although the phrase appears only once in the Bible (Gen. 1:26–28), it has exerted a disproportionate influence on theological anthropology. The claim that humans are created in the image and likeness of

God has been used by various theologians to assert that humans are unique beings in comparison to other creatures. Consequently the *imago Dei* grants to each human an inherent dignity that should be honored and respected by moral and legal codes. Three dominant approaches have been used to ascribe this uniqueness.

First, humans have a particular attribute that other creatures do not possess. It may be contended, for example, that only humans possess a rational soul that gives them a capacity for reason. It is essentially the life of the mind that separates humans from animals, which are driven by instinct. Although some animals have the mental capacity to learn how to perform tricks, they cannot engage in scientific inquiry or philosophical contemplation.

Second, humans perform certain tasks or functions that other creatures are incapable of performing. As Genesis 1:28 makes clear, for instance, since humans bear the *imago Dei* they have been commanded by God to subdue the earth and have dominion over its creatures. Consequently only humans can be held accountable for the stewardship of God's creation. In this respect humans are responsible for their conduct. Although ants may capture aphids and confine them to their colonies, they, unlike humans capturing and confining other humans against their will, cannot be charged with kidnapping.

Third, the *imago Dei* reflects the nature of the triune God. The love shared by the Father, Son, and Holy Spirit is both the origin and end (*telos*, see **teleology**) of creation. This relational quality is in turn imprinted upon a social human nature. People are invariably drawn toward one another to form various relationships and associations. Humans could not exist as rational and responsible beings in isolation from one another. Although some animals may live in herds, they cannot form cultures or gather together to worship.

Key Points/Challenges

- Recent scientific and technological developments challenge these traditional formulations. Darwinian **evolution** calls into question human uniqueness. The principal difference between humans and animals is one of degree rather than kind. Some primates have exhibited a limited capacity for learning rudimentary sign language, suggesting a capacity, albeit limited, for rational thought.

- Research in the neurosciences has largely discredited the notion that the soul is an entity that exists somehow within but independent from the body. Rather, the mind or will is a quality that emerges as the brain develops. If true, the very notion of responsibility as peculiarly a human function is called into question. Irresponsible or immoral behavior may be the result, at least in part, of neurological malfunctions instead of willfulness. Moreover, the human capacity for responsible conduct reflects greater evolutionary development in comparison with other species rather than any unique, God-given capacity.

- Given recent advances in artificial intelligence and robotics, some visionaries foresee a future in which machines will be built that can be said to be alive. If true, they may also exhibit a capacity for rational thought and other functions in a manner superior to humans. More speculatively, such intelligent machines may be able to form various relationships and associations not unlike those formed by humans. The possibility of virtual societies or robots gathering together for worship calls into question what exactly the *imago Dei* would mean if it were borne by inferior embodied humans (see **posthuman**).

- Although these scientific and technological challenges are substantial, they do not negate the validity of the *imago Dei* as an important theological concept. Indeed, these challenges are forcing theological reformulations that may actually prove to strengthen our understanding of what it means to be created in the image and likeness of God.

- As the preceding summaries suggest, the concept of *imago Dei* is highly complex and cannot be reduced to imagery suggested by the neurosciences or robotics, or to any single faculty such as reason. Any such reduction fails either to credit what is being compared or to describe the being bearing the image of its creator. In order to continue to embody the revealing import of the human creature the *imago Dei* must remain an opaque theological concept that is suggestive rather than descriptive or proscriptive.

Further Reading

Barth, Karl. 1958. *Church Dogmatics*. Edinburgh: T&T Clark.

> An in-depth analysis by a prominent Protestant theologian (see especially 3.1).

Herzfeld, Noreen L. 2002. *In Our Image: Artificial Intelligence and the Human Spirit*. Minneapolis: Fortress.

> A highly accessible and engaging discussion by an author trained in both computer science and theology.

Jeeves, Malcolm, ed. 2004. *From Cells to Souls—and Beyond: Changing Portraits of Human Nature*. Grand Rapids: Eerdmans.

> A readable collection of essays by scientists and theologians mainly from a nonreductive physicalist (see **mind/body problem**) perspective.

Shults, F. LeRon. 2003. *Reforming Theological Anthropology: After the Philosophical Turn to Relationality*. Grand Rapids: Eerdmans.

> Offers a theological interpretation of the *imago Dei* in light of recent scientific advances.

Waters, Brent. 2006. *From Human to Posthuman: Christian Theology and Technology in a Postmodern World*. Aldershot, UK: Ashgate.

> A reassessment of theological anthropology in response to postmodern thought.

Brent Waters, Garrett-Evangelical Theological Seminary

□ Indeterminacy

Indeterminacy is defined as a state in which an event has no causes; that is, an outcome's current state cannot be fully determined by its past state(s). Many scholars believe that true indeterminacy resides at the core of key scientific theories, particularly **quantum mechanics** and **evolutionary** processes. This is to be contrasted with a softer view of chance or **contingency**, where what appears to be indeterminable may simply reflect our epistemological ignorance (lack of knowledge) of underlying causes.

Key Points/Challenges

- Indeterminacy has been used to argue for a lack of purpose in the evolution of the universe; that is, the presence of genuine indeterminacy in the fabric of creation is necessarily anti-teleological and threatens the traditional view of God's omnipotence, omniscience, and foreknowledge, and hence God's general providence. Peacocke (1979) offers one of the most concise introductions to both the scientific and theological issues raised by ontological indeterminacy. Some evangelical theologians (e.g., John Sanders, Clark Pinnock, and Greg Boyd) have used this scientific evidence for ontological indeterminacy to bolster their case for open theism, the belief that God's foreknowledge, omnipotence, and omniscience are self-limited.

- The acceptance of ontological indeterminacy has the potential to interfere with the common understanding of divine action in the world. Whereas the natural laws in a deterministic way may restrain God from acting, a world of indeterminacy with probabilistic causation (which characterizes the relationship between cause and effect using the tools of probability theory) also has the potential to prevent God from acting in the world. Saunders (2002), Murphy and colleagues (1997), and Russell and colleagues (2000) provide a broad review of divine action in the context of modern science.

- Whether it is possible to reconcile scientific views of a universe that incorporates ontological indeterminacy with an orthodox Christian theology is being hotly contested. Some writers such as Bartholomew (1984) attempt to do just this while others (e.g., Sanders [1998], Pinnock [2001], and Boyd [2000]) argue for modifications to classical theism to account for the nature of the world revealed by science.

Further Reading

Alexander, Denis. 2001. *Rebuilding the Matrix: Science and Faith in the 21st Century.* Grand Rapids: Zondervan.

A concise overview of the various definitions of chance from both scientific and theological perspectives. See chapter 10, "The Fox and the Hedgehog: Does Evolution Have Any Religious Implications," 340–46.

Bartholomew, David J. 1984. *God of Chance.* London: SCM.

By an internationally respected statistician, a thorough introduction to the breadth of scientific and theological implications of a universe rife with indeterminacy.

Boyd, Greg A. 2000. *God of the Possible: A Biblical Introduction to the Open View of God.* Grand Rapids: Baker Academic.

Probably the best scriptural defense of open theism available.

Dowe, Phil, and Paul Noordhof, eds. 2004. *Cause and Chance: Causation in an Indeterministic World.* London: Routledge.

A compilation of a broad selection of philosophical perspectives on the implications of indeterminacy for causation.

Murphy, Nancey, Robert J. Russell, and C. J. Isham, eds. 1997. *Quantum Cosmology and the Laws of Nature: Scientific Perspectives on Divine Action.* Vatican City: Vatican Observatory Publications.

A result of a 1987 Vatican Observatory conference; a collection of research papers that explore the implications of quantum theory for philosophical and theological issues related to God's action in the world.

Peacocke, Arthur R. 1979. "Chance and the Life-Game." In *Creation and the World of Science: The Bampton Lectures, 1978,* 86–111. Oxford: Clarendon.

The most complete yet concise introduction to the scientific and theological implications of indeterminacy in the larger context of Christian theology informed by modern science.

Pinnock, Clark H. 2001. *Most Moved Mover: A Theology of God's Openness.* Grand Rapids: Baker Academic.

A less formal and more readable theology of open theism than, for example, Sanders.

Russell, Robert J., Philip Clayton, Kirk Wegter-McNelly, and John Polkinghorne, eds. 2001. *Quantum Mechanics: Scientific Perspectives on Divine Action.* Vatican City: Vatican Observatory Publications; Berkeley: Center for Theology and the Natural Sciences.

A collection of essays offering some very creative (but not prescriptive) answers to questions concerning the interaction between quantum physics and divine action.

Russell, Robert J., Nancey Murphy, and Arthur R. Peacocke, eds. 2000. *Chaos and Complexity: Scientific Perspectives on Divine Action.* 2nd ed. Vatican City: Vatican Observatory Publications.

Fifteen essays providing a diversity of thought on the interface of quantum physics, philosophy, and theology.

Sanders, John. 1998. *The God Who Risks: A Theology of Providence.* Downers Grove, IL: InterVarsity.

A rigorously developed theology for the open view of God.

Saunders, Nicholas. 2002. *Divine Action and Modern Science.* Cambridge: Cambridge University Press.

> Critiques proposed models for reconciling special divine interaction with chaos theory, quantum theory, and quantum chaos while considering the implications of indeterminism and probabilistic causation for theology.

Thomas W. Woolley, Samford University

☐ Intelligent Design

Intelligent design (ID) describes a spectrum of thought arguing that an accurate view of nature is best achieved by including a concept of agent causality. Though the word *design* by itself indicates this notion, *intelligent* design describes design as an actual phenomenon in contrast to a generic description of order seen in natural things or merely a phenomenon of appearance (apparent design), sometimes illustrated by those arguing for a denial of agency in explanations of nature (e.g., Richard Dawkins, *The Blind Watchmaker* [1986]).

ID integrates different disciplinary perspectives. For example, theologians and philosophers have addressed the phenomenon of design in nature for millennia. However, the emergence of design as ID has been driven in large part by phenomena and concepts being discovered and explored in the specialized natural sciences. Some of the discoveries concern the physical structure of the universe, such as the fine-tuning of physical constants (see **anthropic principle**), the seemingly universal behavior of physical entities and processes described by "**laws of nature**," the just-right combination of factors and positions that allow the possibility of life on earth, and the observation that these factors also enable scientific discovery.

The most frequently discussed and controversial topics in ID concern design in the biological structure of life and questions of what makes a design recognizable. Are there "fingerprints" of design? These questions are particularly challenging and intriguing since design may be of many types and occur at different levels. Intuitively it would seem that many designs familiar to (or anticipated by) the human mind may be recognized fairly readily, even in cases where little may be known of the designer or design method. To develop that intuition into a more concrete system of thought, ID-oriented scientists ask, for example, what features and characteristics of certain types of designed entities (things, processes) might distinguish them from the background order (or design) of the normal physical structure of the universe. Arguments may be presented positively as design features associated with agents (assuming we have some insight into agency via human experience), or negatively based on the limitations and adequacy of normal physical processes and mechanisms, or both together. A frequent theme in ID applied to biology could therefore be viewed as a claim that design in the physical structure of the universe is necessary but not sufficient to explain design in the biological structure of the universe. Structures at the biological level require design processes beyond design inherent at the level of physical properties alone.

Key Points/Challenges

- ID is challenged as being more of a political or theological movement than a scientific one, and some argue that the usual scientific methods do not apply to ID. Theologically, ID also raises questions regarding God's action in the world. Examples include questions such as: If God interferes in natural processes, what determines when God intervenes or refrains from intervening? How would that relate to the existence of evil in the world?
- Many of ID's leading proponents are Christian theists, but are not limited to such. ID is consistent with Christian faith in God but some features of design may correlate generally with agency.
- ID as a general concept does not entail a rejection of all evolutionary concepts, such as universal common ancestry. Neither does it require them. More specific ID ideas or hypotheses may include or reject such concepts.
- Evidence used to support (biological) ID have included examples from: *the origin of life*, such as chemical reactivity, thermodynamics, informational rules, and structures; *irreducible complexity*, the idea that biological functionality usually occurs as a multicomponent system—characteristic of many designed systems as well as negating functionality through small incremental changes via Darwinian mechanisms; and *programmatic coded biological information*, including characteristics of a type of design and a concept for which there is little theoretical context in biology.
- The notion of irreducible complexity has been challenged by co-option, the idea that subsystems may develop independently and evolve in new combinations to form new functional systems.
- Though naturalistic mechanisms as currently understood may be inadequate to account for a full evolutionary explanation, much may remain to be discovered about existing or unknown mechanisms. ID is therefore challenged as an argument from ignorance, a "God of the gaps" proposal.

Further Reading

Behe, Michael J. 1996. *Darwin's Black Box*. New York: Touchstone.
    A classic ID text discussing the notion of irreducible complexity.
Dembski, William A. 2004. *The Design Revolution*. Downers Grove, IL: InterVarsity.
    A case for ID, discussing main points and objections.
Dembski, William A., and Michael Ruse, eds. 2004. *Debating Design: From Darwin to DNA*. New York: Cambridge University Press.

Considered by many to be a valuable discussion from several perspectives—somewhat weighted toward the con side but given praise on all sides for reasonable interaction.

Gonzalez, Guillermo, and Jay W. Richards. 2004. *The Privileged Planet: How Our Place in the Cosmos Is Designed for Discovery.* Washington, DC: Regnery Publishing.

A case for design at the level of cosmology.

Sober, Elliott. 2007. "What Is Wrong with Intelligent Design?" *The Quarterly Review of Biology* 82:3–8.

A critical discussion focusing on the scientific merits of design thinking.

Trevors, J. T., and D. L. Abel. 2004. "Chance and Necessity Do Not Explain the Origin of Life." *Cell Biology International* 28:729–39.

A discussion of informational challenges in explaining the origin of life.

Paul D. Brown, Trinity Western University

☐ Kenosis

Kenosis is a theological term used to understand God's relationship with creation, especially in the context of modern science and the scientific views of evolutionary **theodicy** (or suffering). The biblical basis is Philippians 2:5–11, where Christ "emptied himself" (2:7 NRSV, *heauton ekenōsen*) of his divine status. Traditionally, Christ's self-emptying has been understood anthropocentrically, where Christ is seen as the perfect example of human nature and the fullest expression of God's intent for humanity. As a result, redemption has been understood as the repair of the divine/human relationship through Christ. The challenge of evolutionary theodicy, in which evolution intrinsically involves suffering and death for all creation, has resulted in a widening of Christ's redemptive act on the cross to include not just humanity but the whole of creation. In this context kenosis is linked to a belief in God's continuing and sustaining activity within creation, so that the incarnation of God reveals God's humble and self-emptying (kenotic) love for the whole of creation, life, and the cosmic process, and the cross of Christ shows God's sharing in creaturely suffering.

Key Points/Challenges

- Evolutionary suffering has produced a significant shift in the concept of divine suffering. Through the cross of Christ, God enters into the suffering of all life and offers the possibility of redemption. Colin Gunton (1992) warns against seeing the cross primarily as the suffering of God, which he believes would divert the focus from the suffering of Jesus as a genuinely human and representative act, and goes against the biblical view of God as the mover of history, where God through the Holy Spirit is directing creation toward perfection.

- Kenosis suggests a very different view of God's power, which has been traditionally described as "omnipotent." The Christ-event reveals that God's power is not displayed in a coercive manner but as self-emptying love on the cross. Kenosis is therefore the fulfillment of God's power, as God the Father expresses through God the Son complete love for creation through self-limitation and sharing the creaturely existence. As a result, God's love allows the world to be "other," or in other words to be autonomous and even include processes such as evolution that involve suffering and death.

- The current use of kenosis as self-emptying has been developed to include a description of God's creative act as a kenotic act of self-limitation. Gunton, however, suggests that kenosis is inappropriate as an explanation for the act of creation but appropriate in describing the point of the incarnation. In this context kenosis is understood to focus primarily on the person of Christ and not on God's relationship to creation.

- Kenosis can also be used as the basis for human action. Humanity can act as the image of God in stewardship of creation through priestly-sacrificial participation, giving and self-giving to all of creation, empowered by the Holy Spirit. Humanity as the created cocreator/coredeemer therefore participates in a much larger creative process directed by God, in anticipation of the coming new creation.

Further Reading

Evans, C. Stephen, ed. 2006. *Exploring Kenotic Christology: The Self-Emptying of God.* Oxford: Oxford University Press.

    Contributes a range of views on modern kenotic understanding focusing on the person of Christ, rather than on the more general divine disposition toward creation.

Gunton, Colin E. 1992. *Christ and Creation: The Didsbury Lectures.* Grand Rapids: Eerdmans.

    An understanding of kenosis that preserves orthodox trinitarian theology and emphasizes that kenosis in terms of evolutionary theodicy is one aspect in understanding the saving significance of the cross.

Haught, John F. 1999. *God after Darwin: A Theology of Evolution.* Boulder, CO: Westview.

———. 2005. "The Boyle Lecture 2003: Darwin, Design and the Promise of Nature." *Science and Christian Belief* 17, 1:5–20.

    In both references, Haught discusses kenosis within an evolutionary context.

Moltmann, Jürgen. 1981. *The Trinity and the Kingdom of God: The Doctrine of God.* Translated by Margaret Kohl. London: SCM.

    Emphasizes the suffering of God in the cross of Jesus.

Polkinghorne, John, ed. 2001. *The Work of Love: Creation as Kenosis.* Grand Rapids: Eerdmans.

Discusses kenosis in terms of evolutionary suffering.

Russell, Robert John. 2005. "Natural Theodicy in an Evolutionary Context: The Need for an Eschatology of New Creation." In *Theodicy and Eschatology*, edited by Bruce Barber and David Neville, 121–52. Adelaide, Australia: ATF.

An eschatological focus on kenosis, sharing Gunton's caution about linking kenosis and creation.

Graham J. O'Brien, Anglican Diocese of Nelson, Adelaide, Australia: ATF

☐ Kepler, Johannes (1571–1630)

The astronomical and cosmological accomplishments of German mathematician-mystic Johannes Kepler represent a critical turn in the so-called **scientific revolution**. After a troubled childhood Kepler matriculated in the Lutheran University at Tübingen in 1587, where he studied astronomy under mathematician Michael Maestlin (1550–1631). Maestlin introduced Kepler to Copernican (see **Copernicus**) cosmology, which Kepler soon adopted. After distinguishing himself in mathematics he went on to graduate study in the Faculty of Theology.

Kepler exhibited deep Christian faith and deep appreciation for the philosophy of **Plato**, especially mathematical harmonies; **Aristotle**, especially his etiology, or analysis of **causation**; and neo-Platonism with its conception of forces of nature. While Kepler ultimately relinquished his dream of theological studies at Tübingen in 1594, he found an appointment at a Protestant secondary school in Graz, Austria, teaching mathematics, where he continued to reflect on the implications of Copernican cosmology.

If the Copernican cosmological model were true, Kepler noted, then the number of planets in the system would be six, rather than the long-established and accepted number seven. Convinced that some divine rationale must exist for this unlikely number of planets, Kepler discovered his answer in the five regular "Platonic solids." By interleaving regular solids with the nested spheres representing the orbits of the planets, the result stands precisely at six. Kepler published these findings in 1596 as the *Prodromus Dissertationum Cosmographicarum continens Mysterium Cosmographicum* (*The Cosmographic Mystery*).

This volume attracted the attention of Danish astronomer Tycho Brahe (1546–1601), recently appointed Imperial Mathematician for Holy Roman Emperor Rudolph II in Prague. Tycho invited Kepler to join him in Prague, which Kepler did in 1600. As Tycho's associate, Kepler began to work with Tycho's famously precise observational data on the heavens. When Tycho unexpectedly died in 1601, Kepler succeeded him as Imperial Mathematician.

Convinced of the divinely purposeful geometrical rationality of the Copernican system, Kepler applied Tycho's mathematical data and discovered that planetary paths are not circular but elliptical, and that the planets sweep out equal areas (as measured from the orbital focus to the orbital path) in equal times. He later discovered that the square of the orbital period of a planet bears precisely the same relation to the cube of that planet's radius ($T^2 \alpha\ R^3$; or $T^2 / R^3 = K$) for every single planet (the so-called planetary constant). Since the time of **Newton** these three principles have been known as Kepler's three laws of planetary motion.

These findings were published in Kepler's masterwork, *Astronomia Nova* (*The New Astronomy*), in 1609, and effectively ended the reign of the circle as the key to all insights into the heavens. His further discoveries were published in *Harmonice Mundi* (*The Harmony of the World*) in 1619 and *Epitome Astronomiae Copernicanae* (*Epitome of Copernican Astronomy*) of 1618–21.

In the years that followed, Kepler continued his duties as a royal mathematician, developed a telescope of his own (after hearing of Galileo's), and furthered his work on Tycho's celestial data, resulting in the *Tabulae Rudolphinae* (*Rudolphine Tables*) in 1627, named in honor of their late patron. Kepler died November 15, 1630.

Key Points/Challenges

- Kepler's success rests in the fact that he invested so much in the concepts of divine purpose, design, archetypes, final causation, and, in short, **teleology**. For example, Kepler suggested that God had created the universe in order to "express divine aesthetics" (Martens 2000, 4) in the form of archetypes, patterns, and laws that were discoverable by humankind. "Those laws are within the grasp of the human mind," Kepler wrote to a friend in 1599. "God wanted us to recognize them by creating us after his own image so that we could share in his own thoughts" (Kepler to Johann Georg Herwart von Hohenburg, in Carola Baumgardt, *Johannes Kepler: Life and Letters*, 1951, 50).

- Kepler interpreted the human endeavor to understand the cosmos as "a right, yes a duty" to search for the "norms of everything He has created" (quoted in Caspar 1993, 381). In short, God, "who wishes to be recognized from the book of nature," (quoted in Baumgardt, *Johannes Kepler*, 1951, 31) had created a discoverable universe whose features reflect God's character, and God endowed humankind with the capacity to discover those features.

- Kepler's work raises several key questions, including: Is the observed orderliness of the universe merely apparent, or does the structure of the universe reveal actual order, as Kepler believed? If the universe exhibits actual order and that order is attributable to some ordering principle or agency that is external to it, can that ordering principle or agency be identified by human capacity and effort? In other words, is the universe created by the deliberate action of a Creator who desires that humankind know and understand this? And to that end, are humans intentionally equipped with the capacity to discover these things?

Further Reading

Caspar, Max. 1993. *Kepler.* Edited and translated by C. Doris Hellman. New York: Dover.

> The biographical standard since 1948 (German original; ET 1959). This edition features invaluable added bibliographic resources and a new introduction by historian and astrophysicist Owen Gingerich.

Field, J. V. 1988. *Kepler's Geometrical Cosmology.* Chicago: University of Chicago Press.

> A helpful elucidation of Kepler's mathematical methodology and use of geometrical paradigms.

Kozhamthadam, Job, S J. 1994. *The Discovery of Kepler's Laws: The Interaction of Science, Philosophy, and Religion.* Notre Dame, IN: University of Notre Dame Press.

> An overview of the philosophical and religious issues but with less sophistication than the Martens volume.

Martens, Rhonda. 2000. *Kepler's Philosophy and the New Astronomy.* Princeton, NJ: Princeton University Press.

> A very valuable interpretation of Kepler's methodology and philosophical interests.

Methuen, Charlotte. 1998. *Kepler's Tübingen: Stimulus to a Theological Mathematics.* Aldershot, UK: Ashgate.

> Solid background on the development of Kepler's theological thought.

Stephenson, Bruce. 1994. *Kepler's Physical Astronomy.* Princeton, NJ: Princeton University Press.

> Discusses all aspects of Kepler's work, with emphasis on his examination of physics and forces, rather than the "mere" beauty of the geometrical relationships.

Rodney L. Stiling, Seattle Pacific University

☐ Laws of Nature (Scientific Laws)

The laws of nature are those factual principles (as opposed to logical principles) that govern or describe the natural world. They are generally accepted to be universal (they apply to all time and space), absolute (they do not depend on the observer), and complete (nothing lies outside their scope). Scientific laws are human attempts to articulate the laws of nature. Scientific laws are inductive and falsifiable statements that emerge from a series of observations. For example, the second law of thermodynamics states that the entropy of the universe increases for all spontaneous processes. No exception to this law has ever been observed.

Much of the discussion regarding the laws of nature centers on whether they are prescriptive or descriptive. In the prescriptive view (sometimes called the necessitarian view), the laws of nature prescribe the way that nature *must* run. The world "obeys" the laws of nature, and the laws are viewed as necessary truths. In the descriptive view, the laws of nature describe the way that nature *does* run. According to this view (often associated with Hume), the laws of nature are not really laws at all, but simply principles that describe the regularities in the physical world. Therefore, the laws are viewed as **contingent** truths.

Key Points/Challenges

- The nature of the laws of nature is related to the issue of divine action. How does God act in a world governed by the laws of nature? Does God momentarily suspend the laws, or does God somehow act through them? Or are the laws themselves simply statements of God's normal modes of action (see **divine command**)?

- The nature of the laws of nature is also related to human free will (see **determinism**). How do human minds act freely in a world governed by laws? The view that the laws of nature are simply descriptive is perhaps more consistent with human free will than the prescriptive view. For example, if one decides to do B and not A, then, since the laws of nature simply describe what happens in nature, that decision is part of the laws themselves.

- The existence of the laws of nature has often been used as an argument for the existence of God. The regularities and order in the universe are presented as evidence for a divine being that created the regularity and order. This argument is part of the long tradition of **natural theology**, the study of God through the study of natural order. Some have argued that the development of modern science itself grew out of the Christian concept of an orderly creation designed by a Creator.

- The fundamental laws of nature can be expressed mathematically, making precise quantitative predictions possible. Mathematics has been said (by Eugene Wigner) to be "unreasonably effective" in describing the natural world. It is not clear why this should be so and some have used this as further evidence of a divine being.

Further Reading

Armstrong, David M. 1983. *What Is a Law of Nature?* Cambridge: Cambridge University Press.

    Articulates the prescriptive or necessitarian view of the laws of nature.

Carroll, John W. 2006. *Laws of Nature*. Stanford Encyclopedia of Philosophy, edited by Edward N. Zalta. http://plato.stanford.edu/archives/fall2006/entries/laws-of-nature/.

> An overview of the current philosophical debates concerning the laws of nature.

Pannenberg, Wolfhart. 1988. "The Doctrine of Creation and Modern Science." *Zygon* 23:3–21.

> Explores the connections between the existence of natural laws and the Christian doctrine of creation.

Peacocke, Arthur R. 1979. *Creation and the World of Science*. Oxford: Oxford University Press.

> Also explores the connections between the existence of natural laws and the Christian doctrine of creation.

Nivaldo J. Tro, Westmont College

□ Leibniz, Gottfried Wilhelm von (1646–1716)

Leibniz was a German mathematician and philosopher who introduced the infinitesimal calculus independently of **Newton** and made pioneering contributions to the study of binary numbers and mathematical logic. He also made major contributions to physics and technology and wrote on a vast array of subjects. He formulated traditional proofs (ontological, cosmological, and one based on preestablished harmony) for the existence of God. He also introduced the word **theodicy** in a 1710 book of that name, where he maintained that suffering is a necessary evil that is a part of the greater divine good. Because of this, he believed that God created "the best of all possible worlds." Although this was the subject of a satire by Voltaire (*Candide*), its rationalistic optimism was later an influence on Enlightenment religious thought. In *Monadology* (1720), he developed the idea that all things are composed of an infinite number of "monads," simple units containing spiritual energy that exist on a scale of increasing complexity, the highest being God.

Key Points/Challenges

- For Leibniz, the best of all possible worlds follows as a consequence of God, the perfect Creator of the world. His optimism does not deny that there are evils in the world but suggests that it is credible that they are a necessary part of the best possible world. What is involved in the nature of perfection? Leibniz admitted metaphysical imperfection as well as pain and moral evil, so for him the best possible world would be the most harmonious in spite of the existence of those things.

- Today Leibnizian optimism is being accorded more respect in the light of recent scientific developments associated with the idea of fine-tuning and expressed in books by John Barrow and Frank Tipler (*The Anthropic Cosmological Principle*, 1988), Michael Denton (*Nature's Destiny*, 2002), Peter Ward and Donald Brownlee (*Rare Earth*, 2003), Simon Conway Morris (*Life's Solution*, 2003), and Guillermo Gonzalez and Jay Richards (*The Privileged Planet*, 2004). The 3 + 1 dimensional structure of space-time (where there are three spatial or bidirectional dimensions and one temporal-unidirectional dimension), may be ideal for the fruitfulness of the universe. The Earth, solar system, and Milky Way possess a number of unusual characteristics that permit intelligent life to exist. The numerical values of fundamental physical constants are in a small range that allows the universe to contain complex structures (see **anthropic principle**).

- With the discovery of **quantum mechanics**, many of Leibniz's speculative ideas about aspects of phenomena not reducible to statics and dynamics now make more sense. He anticipated **Einstein** in arguing, against Newton, that space, time, and motion are relative, not absolute. Allan F. Randall ("Quantum Superposition, Necessity and the Identity of Indiscernibles") has shown how the so-called paradox of quantum superposition can be considered as the consequence of Leibniz's rationalist assumptions such as the principle of sufficient reason and the identity of indiscernibles (since there must be a sufficient reason for any truth, there must be sufficient reason for two things to be considered different objects).

Further Reading

Jolley, Nicholas, ed. 1995. *The Cambridge Companion to Leibniz*. Cambridge: Cambridge University Press.
   Multi-authored work providing an account of the range of Leibniz's thought.
———. 2005. *Leibniz*. New York: Routledge.
   An introduction to the whole of Leibniz's philosophy.

Donald A. Nield, University of Auckland

☐ Materialism

Materialism is a philosophical system that regards matter as the only reality in the world. It attempts to explain every event in the universe as resulting from the conditions and activity of matter, and thus denies the existence of God and the immaterial soul.

Materialism undertakes to answer the fundamental question of philosophy by asserting the primacy of the material world; in short, matter precedes thought. It maintains that: reality is basically material; all phenomena in the universe consist of matter in motion, wherein all things are interdependent and interconnected and develop in accordance with natural law; the world exists outside us and independently of our perception of it; thought is a reflection of the material world in the brain; and the world is in principle knowable. So Karl Marx could assert, in the afterword to the second German edition of *Capital*, "The ideal is nothing else than the material world reflected by the human mind, and translated into forms of thought."

Materialism is a set of related theories that hold that all entities and processes are composed of—and so are reducible to—matter, material forces, or physical processes. All events and facts are explainable, actually or in principle, in terms of body, material objects, or changes or movements. In general, the metaphysical theory of materialism entails the denial of the reality of spiritual beings, consciousness, and mental or psychic states or processes, as ontologically distinct from or independent of material changes or processes. Since it denies the existence of spiritual beings or forces, materialism typically is allied with atheism or agnosticism.

Key Points/Challenges

- Historical materialism is the application of Marxist science to historical development. The fundamental proposition of historical materialism can be summed up in a sentence: human **consciousness** does not determine our existence, but our social existence determines our consciousness (Marx, *Preface to a Contribution to the Critique of Political Economy*, Chicago: Kerr, 1913).

- Dialectical materialism is the philosophical basis of Marxism as defined by later communists. Using Hegel's concepts of thesis, antithesis, and synthesis, it tries to explain the growth and development of human history dialectically (through logical arguments) and not necessarily progressively.

- Eliminative materialism is the radical claim that our ordinary, commonsense understanding of the mind is deeply wrong and that some or all of the mental states posited by common sense do not actually exist. **Descartes** challenged much of what we take for granted, but insisted that we can generally be confident about the content of our own minds. Eliminative materialists go further, challenging the existence of various mental states that Descartes took for granted. It has roots in the writings of the mid-twentieth-century philosophers Wilfred Sellars, W. V. O. Quine, Paul Feyerabend, and Richard Rorty.

- Nonreductive materialism (physicalism), advocated by Nancey Murphy, Philip Clayton, and colleagues claims "rationality, emotion, morality, free will, and, most importantly, the capacity to be in relationship with God" (Brown, Murphy, and Malony 1998, 2) without postulating the distinct ontological entity, soul. Murphy and Clayton bring in the notion of **supervenience** in order to give a nonreducible account of morality, mental events, and spiritual faculties without postulating a superior entity (soul) (Clayton and Davies 2006; Murphy 1998).

- Historically, materialism and Christianity have been at odds. This is due both to antimaterialist passages in Christian Scripture, and to the denial, by most materialist thinkers, of the existence of the kinds of spiritual realities that were fundamental to the traditional scholastic philosophy and the Catholic traditions. Despite these apparent discrepancies the two beliefs are not always viewed as being in opposition. Pierre Teilhard de Chardin (1881–1955), a French Jesuit and paleontologist, was a pioneer of Christian materialism, which respects the world and sees spiritual realities as integrally related to the material. Without denying the spiritual entities, de Chardin along with Karl Rahner (1904–84), Joseph Marechal (1878–1944), Emerich Coreth (1919–2006), and liberation theologians, attempt to refocus on the material dimension of Christian life (incarnation, resurrection).

- Basic to all nuances of materialism is some sort of **reductionism**. Posing against dualism of all sorts, materialism attempts to reduce all phenomena to the material realm. Reductionism (methodological reductionism) is the essential (methodological if not ontological) presupposition of contemporary natural science.

Further Reading

Armstrong, Dave M. 1968. *A Materialist Theory of the Mind*. London: Routledge.

> A classic, readable presentation of materialism. Though dated, the essential ideas are found in this book.

Brown, Warren S., Nancey C. Murphy, and H. Newton Malony, eds. 1998. *Whatever Happened to the Soul? Scientific and Theological Portraits of Human Nature*. Minneapolis: Fortress.

> A provocative and insightful contemporary appraisal of Christian and spiritual concerns.

Clayton, Philip, and Paul Davies, eds. 2006. *The Re-Emergence of Emergence: The Emergentist Hypothesis from Science to Religion*. Oxford: Oxford University Press.

> A readable, provocative, and controversial approach to **emergence**.

Dennett, Daniel C. 1978. *Brainstorms: Philosophical Essays in Mind and Psychology*. London: Bradford Books.

> A contemporary approach that is relevant for today.

Murphy, Nancey. 1998. "Supervenience and the Nonreducibility of Ethics to Biology."
    In *Evolution and Molecular Biology: Scientific Perspectives on Divine Action*, edited
    by Robert John Russell, William R. Stoeger, SJ, and Francisco J. Ayala, 463–89.
    Vatican City: Vatican Observatory Publications; Berkeley: The Center for Theology
    and the Natural Sciences.

    A rather technical and scholarly account of supervenience and human causation.

Teilhard de Chardin, Pierre. 1976. *The Phenomenon of Man*. New York: Harper
    Perennial.

    A classic, indirect critique of reductionism based on progressive Christian ideas.

Kuruvilla Pandikattu, Jnana-Deepa Vidyapeeth (Papal Seminary)

☐ Merton Thesis

This thesis, proposed by the sociologist Robert K. Merton (1910–2003), is also known
as the Puritanism and science thesis. It suggests a link between Puritanism and the
burgeoning of scientific advance and achievement in seventeenth-century England.
Merton viewed this as a special case of the connection between "the Protestant ethic
and the spirit of capitalism," which had been proposed in 1904 by Max Weber (one
of the founders of sociology), in his book of that title. Implicit in Merton's Weberian
approach was the belief that modern science was seen by its promoters as pragmatically
useful for the benefit of humankind, a perspective exemplified in the philosophy of
Francis Bacon. Although remaining controversial, this thesis has received influential
support from the eminent historian of the *Puritan Revolution*, Christopher Hill, and
from a leading historian of science, Charles Webster.

Key Points/Challenges

- A major challenge to the Merton thesis hinged on the designation *Puritan*. *Puritan*
  was used by historians as a loose way to refer to broadly Calvinistic groups in
  England opposed to the policy of the Stuarts. This in turn led historians to refer
  to the increasing opposition to the crown as the Puritan revolution. Merton's
  use of the term *Puritan* was vague but it fit perfectly within contemporary usage
  of the word among historians. Subsequent generations of historians, however,
  have taken issue with the term and criticized Merton for an opportunistic use
  of *Puritan*.
- Merton's evidence for the claim that Puritans contributed to the flowering of
  the natural sciences in seventeenth-century England depended to a large extent
  on "counting heads" and making claims about the religious orientation of contributors to scientific advance. Such claims were all too often open to criticism.

Robert Boyle, for example, was an important case because he was the leading scientist of the day and known to be highly devout. Merton presented him as a Puritan, but the historical evidence makes it clear he was always a committed Anglican.

- The thesis looks like a claim about cause and effect: Puritanism was a cause of the burgeoning of science in seventeenth-century England. But this cannot be sustained without qualification because other Puritan cultures, such as those in Scotland or Geneva, did not enjoy a similar flowering of scientific thought and practice. Furthermore, it is difficult to see any specific reasons why Puritanism should favor science more than, say, Catholicism.

- Merton himself denied that the thesis was a claim about cause and effect. It was more a matter of understanding the prevailing ethos. The dominant means of cultural expression in the early modern period was through religious values. Inevitably, therefore, study of the natural world would tend to be directed by and justified in terms of religious beliefs. This has been dismissed by subsequent generations as far too vague. The thesis first appeared, however, at a time when the predominant view was that science and religion were necessarily in conflict— inimical worldviews, perpetually at war with each other. It was, therefore, the first serious claim that science might actually have been influenced in a positive way by the religious culture from which it emerged. It initiated a much more historically accurate understanding of the relationship between science and religion.

- Qualifications of the thesis raise a new problem—perhaps the qualifying factors were really responsible for the rise of science, not the Puritan background itself. Some historians have argued, for example, that many thinkers turned to the study of nature during the Interregnum (1642–59), the period from the outbreak of the Civil War to the Restoration of the monarchy, simply because they could not exercise their minds in governance of either church or state, as they would have done in normal circumstances. This argument goes hand in hand with claims that the real burgeoning of science took place after the restoration of the monarchy in 1660 and is more closely affiliated with Anglicanism than Puritanism.

Further Reading

Cohen, I. Bernard, ed. 1990. *Puritanism and the Rise of Modern Science: The Merton Thesis*. New Brunswick, NJ: Rutgers University Press.
> Anthology of articles by various scholars writing both for and against the Merton thesis. Includes an extensive bibliography.

Hill, Christopher. 1965. *Intellectual Origins of the English Revolution*. Oxford: Clarendon.
> A historically informed restatement of the Merton thesis.

Merton, Robert K. 1970. *Science, Technology and Society in Seventeenth Century England*. New York: Howard Fertig.

> Merton's influential doctoral thesis, first published in 1938, reprinted with additional reflections from the author.

Webster, Charles, ed. 1974. *The Intellectual Revolution of the Seventeenth Century*. London: Routledge & Kegan Paul.

> Collection of essays by various scholars, both for and against Merton and Hill.

———. 1975. *The Great Instauration: Science, Medicine and Reform, 1626–1660*. London: Duckworth.

> Major study of the sciences in England in the early seventeenth-century that concludes with the most forceful defense of the Merton thesis.

John Henry, University of Edinburgh

☐ Metaphysics (*see also* Ontology)

Metaphysics is the most foundational area of philosophical inquiry. Essentially and most generally, metaphysics asks, "What is there?" That is, what things exist in the universe and what is the nature of these things? In this sense, all other areas of philosophy depend on or presuppose metaphysical claims. Do all things ultimately consist of tiny material particles? Are there such things as souls or angels? Is time an objective reality? These are questions of metaphysics, and the answers that are given have significant consequences for what is claimed in other areas of philosophy.

Inquiry into metaphysical topics has sometimes proceeded on purely speculative grounds. Merely by reflecting carefully on their own conscious experience or on the concept of God, rationalist philosophers confidently concluded that humans possess minds distinct from their bodies and that God exists. Empiricist reactions to such methods ultimately led their twentieth-century heirs, the positivists (see **verification principle**), to assert that metaphysics is meaningless since its claims cannot be verified in experience. Today, however, it is generally accepted that even claims like the positivists' involve metaphysical presuppositions about reality. Sometimes, then, *metaphysics* is used to refer to the background or worldview-defining beliefs without which any organized thought would be impossible.

It would be a mistake to characterize metaphysical beliefs as untestable. Metaphysics involves not only the foundation of other areas of inquiry, it can also be the fruit of such inquiries. Our theories about what there is in the world have been greatly influenced by scientific discoveries; for example, by careful astronomical observations the Copernican revolution eradicated the widely held belief that the universe was composed of concentric crystalline spheres centered on the earth. Religions offer answers to metaphysical questions as well; for example, monotheistic religions have traditionally held the revelation that God is omniscient. Thus metaphysics is found both in the premises and the conclusions of any systematic inquiry.

Key Points/Challenges

- In the science/religion dialogue the foremost challenge in metaphysics concerns the existence and nature of God. The traditional Judeo-Christian understanding of the nature of God raises interesting questions in many of the areas of metaphysics: God's relationship to time, God's foreknowledge and the possibility of human freedom, and God's interaction with the causal structure of the natural world.
- In the past two decades, the philosophy of mind has become the predominant subdiscipline in philosophy. Ultimately, this is a metaphysical question: What is the nature of humans and their conscious experience? Science contributes to this dialogue through recent findings in neuroscience; religion contributes through its understanding of the soul and its relationship to the person.
- **Emergence** is a concept invoked by some metaphysicians to explain how something could be more than the sum of its parts. Typically proponents describe reality as a hierarchy of levels in which higher-level entities emerge from lower-level entities without being able to be reduced to the lower levels. For example, an emergentist claims that while there are no additional metaphysical ingredients beyond the matter that makes up a person, that emergent person is not just a material composite, but a higher-level reality that emerges from the matter.
- There is no general agreement on the proper methodology for metaphysics. Some claim that science is the only proper way to go about answering metaphysical questions; others insist that there are other legitimate ways to gain knowledge about the world—revelation, for example. The methods allowed will affect the answers that are given to metaphysical questions.

Further Reading

Burtt, Edwin A. 1932. *The Metaphysical Foundations of Modern Science.* Rev. ed. Atlantic Highlands, NJ: Humanities Press.

> A classic in the history of science revealing the metaphysical presuppositions and commitments of the scientific revolution.

Hasker, William. 1983. *Metaphysics: Constructing a Worldview.* Downers Grove, IL: InterVarsity.

> An accessible introduction to some of the major topics in metaphysics, including God and the natural world.

Kim, Jaegwon, and Ernest Sosa, eds. 1995. *A Companion to Metaphysics*. Oxford: Blackwell.

> More than two hundred encyclopedia-style entries on all the major topics and important historical figures in traditional metaphysics.

Loux, Michael, and Dean Zimmerman, eds. 2004. *Oxford Handbook of Metaphysics*. Oxford: Oxford University Press.

> A recent collection of essays on cutting-edge metaphysical research with extensive bibliographic information.

James B. Stump, Bethel College

☐ Mind/Body Problem (Dualism, Monism, Physicalism)

How the mind and the body relate to each other has been a controversial topic in philosophy for millennia. Today this controversy focuses primarily on the mind and the brain, and has implications for important theological and religious beliefs. Several views of this relationship have been proposed. Dualisms see human nature as consisting of two or more substances—*substance* meaning a thing that has certain properties without which the thing would cease to exist. Perhaps the oldest of the perspectives is substance dualism, which holds that while the brain is clearly a physical or material substance, the mind is an immaterial substance that can exist independently of, and act causally on, the brain.

Monisms hold that there is only one kind of substance, either matter or nonmatter. Material monisms can assume a number of forms, including eliminative monism (or reductive physicalism), which holds that because there is only matter (the brain), we can eliminate any discussion of the mind. All so-called mental functions are nothing more than physical brain activity. Other monisms, while acknowledging that there is only one kind of substance, nevertheless allow for the emergence of other powers or qualities. Nonreductive physicalism represents this view of mind/brain interaction. The mind emerges from the physical brain in the form of new powers and abilities that cannot be understood by reducing the brain to its component parts (see **emergence**).

A middle ground between substance dualism and nonreductive physicalism is emergent dualism, which agrees that mind emerges from brain but insists that what emerges (mind) is not new powers or qualities but actual substance, a thing that is distinct from and can exist without the physical body. A final perspective on the mind/body relationship, the constitution view, suggests that the mind is constituted of the physical brain (as a statue might be constituted of marble), but is not identical with the brain (as a marble statue is not identical with the marble itself).

Key Points/Challenges

- Views of the mind/body problem are important for the science/religion dialogue because each represents different views of human nature (identity, consciousness, the self, and the soul).

- Substance dualism has been widely held in the Christian tradition since the early church and is thought by many to be necessary for any belief in life after death, because the immaterial soul survives the death of the material body. The philosophers **Plato** and **René Descartes** were substance dualists. Contemporary philosophers and theologians who advocate some form of dualism include Stewart Goetz, John Cooper, Charles Taliaferro, and William Hasker (emergent dualism), and the late neuroscientist Sir John Eccles.

- Other Christian thinkers argue that a dualistic view of human personhood is not necessary for a belief in life after death, and furthermore it is not a biblical view of human nature. The Old and the New Testaments, as well as the sciences of psychology and neuroscience, teach a holistic view of humanity in which the individual is a biological-psychological-social-relational unity. These individuals include philosophers (e.g., Nancey Murphy), theologians (e.g., Joel B. Green, Lawson Stone, and Alan Torrance), and scientists (e.g., Malcolm Jeeves, Gareth Jones, and Warren Brown).

- Individuals holding a reductive or eliminative monism include philosophers (e.g., Patricia and Paul Churchland and Daniel Dennett) and scientists (e.g., the late Francis Crick).

Further Reading

Brown, Warren S., Nancey Murphy, and H. Newton Malony, eds. 1998. *Whatever Happened to the Soul? Scientific and Theological Portraits of Human Nature.* Minneapolis: Fortress.

> Reviews how current nondualistic accounts of human nature coming from genetics, neuroscience, and the cognitive sciences can be integrated with biblical teaching and Christian tradition.

Corcoran, Kevin, ed. 2001. *Soul, Body, and Survival: Essays on the Metaphysics of Human Persons.* Ithaca, NY: Cornell University Press.

> A book of essays considering various perspectives on how the soul and body are related as well as the implications of these perspectives for life after death.

Green, Joel B., ed. 2004. *What about the Soul? Neuroscience and Christian Anthropology.* Nashville: Abingdon.

> Contains chapters written by scientists, theologians, and philosophers on the theoretical and practical implications of recent biblical scholarship and psychological/ neuroscientific research on personhood.

Green, Joel B., and Stuart L. Palmer, eds. 2005. *In Search of the Soul: Four Views of the Mind-Body Problem*. Downers Grove, IL: InterVarsity.

A good and effective summary of the substance dualism, emergent dualism, nonreductive physicalism, and constitution views of persons.

Gregersen, Niels Henrik, Willem B. Drees, and Ulf Görman, eds. 2000. *The Human Person in Science and Theology*. Grand Rapids: Eerdmans.

Chapters from theologians and scientists develop a biological and relational view of human personhood.

Jeeves, Malcolm, ed. 2004. *From Cells to Souls—and Beyond: Changing Portraits of Human Nature*. Grand Rapids: Eerdmans.

Scientists, theologians, and philosophers discussing the nature of spirituality and personhood as well as how these qualities and characteristics of our humanity can be affected by neurological illness.

Seybold, Kevin. 2007. *Explorations in Neuroscience, Psychology, and Religion*. Hampshire, UK: Ashgate.

An overview of neuroscientific research, especially in relation to human nature, the self, and religious experience.

Kevin Seybold, Grove City College

☐ Miracles

David Hume famously defined a miracle as "a transgression of a law of nature by a particular volition of the Deity, or by the interposition of some invisible agent" ([1748] 1988, 149) and went on to argue that belief in miracles is never justified. Many philosophers take Hume's discussion as their starting point but often get bogged down in disagreements about how to interpret him. According to some interpreters, Hume was arguing that miracles are conceptually incoherent because they involve the violation of natural laws and this is an impossibility. According to others, Hume thought that there could never be evidence strong enough to justify belief in a miracle report, on the grounds that miracle reports stand in opposition to evidence for laws of nature. Against the first of these interpretations of Hume it can be argued (Clarke 1997) that laws of nature should not be understood as governing the behavior of natural occurrences that are the result of supernatural intervention, so miracles are not incompatible with there being laws governing nature, properly understood. It can be further argued (Clarke 1997), against the second interpretation, that the occurrence of supernatural intervention can be part of the best explanation of some possible events and so we can potentially be justified in believing that miracles have occurred, under some circumstances.

Conceptions of the miraculous that predate Hume and the rise of the seventeenth-century mechanistic worldview are various and unsatisfyingly imprecise. A "miracle" was sometimes understood to be an event evoking wonder, a use that sometimes continues in our time. Before the seventeenth century it was very difficult to give a clear meaning to the idea of supernatural intervention in the natural world. The supernatural stands in relation to the natural; it is literally "above nature." So a clear understanding of what a miracle is requires a clear understanding of what the limits of the natural are. However, this was not achieved before the rise of the mechanistic worldview.

Key Points/Challenges

- Many writers on miracles, including Hume, have been especially concerned about the possibility of reliable testimony about the miraculous.

- Most writers on the miraculous hold that a miracle is the result of an intervention in the natural world that is intended by a supernatural agent. However, Stephen Mumford (2001) has defended the view that all natural events that have a supernatural cause are understood as miracles, whether they are intended by a supernatural agent or not. Others understand natural events that have a supernatural cause, but are not intended by a supernatural agent, as magical rather than miraculous acts.

- A minority of philosophers, including R. F. Holland, adhere to a "contingency conception" of miracles. In such a view a miracle is an event that has the capacity to inspire feelings of religious awe but need not involve supernatural intervention. Someone who claimed that the birth of a baby was miraculous, even though it involved no supernatural intervention in the natural world, would be utilizing the contingency conception.

- Is the creation of the universe a miracle? Some say so on the grounds that it is caused by a supernatural agent. Others argue that it is not as the creation of the natural world is not, properly speaking, an intervention in the natural world.

- Historically, theologians have been divided over the role of the miraculous in justifying belief in God. While some welcome miracles as potential evidence of the existence of God, others are uncomfortable with any conception that involves supernatural intervention in the natural world.

Further Reading

Clarke, Steve. 1997. "When to Believe in Miracles." *American Philosophical Quarterly* 34:95–102.

> A defense of the view that the miraculous is conceptually coherent and that it can sometimes be rational to believe that a miracle has taken place.

Holland, Robert F. 1965. "The Miraculous." *American Philosophical Quarterly* 2:43–51.

> Classic statement of the "contingency conception" of miracles.

Hume, David. [1748] 1988. *An Enquiry Concerning Human Understanding.* Edited by Antony Flew. La Salle, IL: Open Court.

> Contains (in chapter 10, "Of Miracles") Hume's famous and influential argument for the conclusion that one is never justified in believing in miracles.

Levine, Murray. 2002. *Miracles.* Stanford Encyclopedia of Philosophy. http://plato .stanford.edu/entries/miracles/.

> A reasonably comprehensive survey of recent philosophical discussion of the miraculous.

Mumford, Stephen. 2001. "Miracles: Metaphysics and Modality." *Religious Studies* 37:191–202.

> Articulates the view that miracles need not involve supernatural agency.

Steve Clarke, Charles Sturt University and University of Oxford

☐ Naturalism

Naturalism has been used in many different senses in the past hundred years. Metaphysical naturalism is the philosophical theory that all that exists is the natural world (whether one universe or many; see also **materialism**). Some commentators on contemporary science (e.g., Richard Dawkins, Daniel Dennett) have argued that contemporary science, especially the neo-Darwinian synthesis and the cognitive neurosciences, establishes metaphysical naturalism as the worldview with the most intellectual plausibility. This has been criticized by many philosophers and people of faith. Philosophical naturalism holds that the sciences are of primary importance for philosophical method and reflection. Science sets the agenda for philosophy. Some see philosophy as a branch of science; others view philosophy as an independent discipline, the task of which is to sort out the findings of the various special sciences. While this view may easily be associated with metaphysical naturalism, it is also consistent with a number of traditional faith perspectives (see Leiter 2007). However, philosophers investigating the supernatural, or who take theological principles as salient in philosophical inquiry find this methodological perspective unhelpful as a guiding light (see Plantinga 1997).

Methodological naturalism (MN) primarily concerns a set of norms for how one should pursue the scientific study of nature (including humans as part of nature). It may be defined as follows: (1) in the study of nature one should investigate those entities, processes, and events that are internal to nature; and (2) within science, theological assumptions are not appropriate elements in the evaluation of arguments, observations, models, hypotheses, and so on. A corollary to this is that supernatural agents should not be invoked to explain scientific hypotheses.

Key Points/Challenges

- This definition focuses mainly on the context of justification, not the context of discovery. Because of the limits set by methodological naturalism as an explicit norm, religious commitments have no place within the explicit, public evaluation of scientific claims qua (in the character of) scientific claims.

- This does not mean that scientists must explicitly suspend religious belief while pursuing scientific questions. It means rather that beliefs peculiar to religious faith are not relevant to the evaluation of evidence, the examination of an experiment, or the evaluation of a theory in light of evidence. That is, they will not function in the explicit discussions of the scientific community as they might inform one's own personal, philosophical, and theological evaluation of scientific claims and research programs.

- It should be noted that this is a distinct point of view from metaphysical naturalism. Clearly methodological naturalism can guide scientific practice without entailing metaphysical naturalism (see McMullin 1991, Pennock 2001).

Further Reading

De Caro, Mario, and David Macarthur, eds. 2004. *Naturalism in Question*. Cambridge, MA: Harvard University Press.

    A helpful range of articles representing the contemporary debate regarding various sorts of naturalism, but especially philosophical and metaphysical naturalism.

Leiter, Brian. [2002] 2007. *Naturalism in Legal Philosophy*. Stanford Encyclopedia of Philosophy, edited by Edward N. Zalta. http://plato.stanford.edu/entries/lawphil-naturalism/.

    Though this article focuses primarily on questions peculiar to the philosophy of law, Leiter nicely describes the distinct meanings and uses of "naturalism" in contemporary philosophical discussions.

McMullin, Ernan. 1991. "Plantinga's Defense of Special Creation." *Christian Scholar's Review* 21 (1): 55–79.

    A response to an article in the same volume by Alvin Plantinga, making the case that a Christian view of evolution and the science of natural history is consistent with methodological naturalism.

Numbers, Ronald L. 2003. "Science without God: Natural Laws and Christian Beliefs." In *When Science and Christianity Meet*, edited by David C. Lindberg and Ronald L. Numbers, 265–85. Chicago: University of Chicago Press.

    A brief but helpful overview of Christian contributions to methodological naturalism over a broad sweep in the history of science.

Pennock, Robert T. 2001. "Naturalism, Evidence, and Creationism." In *Intelligent Design Creationism and Its Critics*, edited by Robert T. Pennock, 77–97. Cambridge, MA: MIT Press.

A response to the criticisms of naturalism (of various kinds) by the Berkeley law professor Phillip Johnson. This article provides a helpful overview of the current debate and how it applies to evolutionary theory.

Plantinga, Alvin. 1997. "Methodological Naturalism." *Perspectives on Science and Christian Faith* 49 (3):339–61.

A careful and thoughtful critique of many of the standard sorts of arguments in defense of methodological naturalism. Plantinga argues for a view of science that respects methodological naturalism where appropriate but also leaves room for the possibility of a "theistic" science whereby commitments of theism or sacred texts can play a role as background beliefs in the evaluation of scientific claims.

Patrick McDonald, Seattle Pacific University

☐ Natural Law Morality

Defenders of natural law morality (NLM) are moral realists who believe that the normative principles of **ethics** can be discovered in human nature. The classic articulation of NLM is found in the work of the thirteenth-century philosopher/theologian **Thomas Aquinas**. In this view, God created humans with a nature that is both animal and rational. Since all animals have a desire to preserve themselves, there is a prohibition on suicide. And since there is a drive toward sexual reproduction among the higher animals, and since children need a stable family environment, there is a prohibition on adultery. But humans also possess reason and have desires appropriate to their rational nature, including the desires for truth, virtue, and God. NLM, therefore, posits a natural **teleology** to all human activity wherein the natural desires we have, as reflected on by reason, point us to the human good. These normative precepts apply universally to all humans in all cultures. Humans know these precepts not as innate ideas but by rational reflection on the desires and behaviors that make human existence possible.

Key Points/Challenges

- Since NLM appeals to human nature as a means to understand human morality, it is one of the few ethical theories that has an affinity for (or with) the biological and psychological sciences. As a result NLM sees the human urges for self-preservation, sexual reproduction, and nurturing the young as morally relevant aspects of human nature. Thus the sciences may shed light on morality in ways that may run counter to much of twentieth-century analytic ethics.
- Many analytic ethicists believe that NLM is guilty of the "is-ought" (naturalistic) fallacy (i.e., the idea that we cannot move from descriptions of human nature

to prescriptions). However, arguments on the validity of this fallacy are highly contentious. Some defenders of NLM, such as John Finnis (*Natural Law and Natural Rights* [1980]), accept the validity of the is-ought fallacy and attempt to reformulate NLM in light of the challenges of analytic philosophy. Others, such as William Frankena (*Ethics* [1973]) and Ralph McInerny (*Ethica Thomistica: The Moral Philosophy of Thomas Aquinas* [1989]) reject the validity of the is-ought fallacy and contend that it is possible to move from descriptive statements to normative judgments.

• Some theologians charge NLM with "methodological atheism" that is, an autonomous approach to ethics that requires no special appeal to God since the basic precepts of ethics can be known without an appeal to God. Yet most defenders of NLM argue that God plays two roles in ethics: as the ultimate *telos* of all human activity and as the Creator of human nature.

• Existential philosophers, such as Sartre and Nietzsche, have held that there is no such thing as human nature. If this is the case, then the attempt to derive normative principles from human nature is doomed to failure since human nature is a fiction. Yet these existential relativists have an extraordinarily difficult time accounting for the phenomenal successes of the sciences, which rather compellingly suggest that humans have a nature and are subject to the same physical laws and processes as the rest of the world.

Further Reading

Arnhart, Larry. 2001. "Thomistic Natural Law as Darwinian Natural Right." *Social Philosophy and Policy* 18:1–29.

> Contends that traditional NLM (e.g., David Hume) is compatible with a Darwinian account of human nature.

Boyd, Craig A. 2007. *A Shared Morality: A Narrative Defense of Natural Law Ethics.* Grand Rapids: Brazos.

> Develops a sustained argument for natural law ethics that incorporates evolutionary biology into the description of "nature" while retaining the insights of traditional NLM.

Porter, Jean. 1999. *Natural and Divine Law: Reclaiming the Tradition for Christian Ethics.* Grand Rapids: Eerdmans.

> A mediating position between traditional theories of natural law and divine command theory.

Simon, Yves. 1992. *The Tradition of Natural Law: A Philosopher's Reflections.* New York: Fordham University Press.

> The standard twentieth-century neo-Thomist interpretation of natural law as both a moral and political theory.

Craig A. Boyd, Azusa Pacific University

□ Natural Philosophy

In the sixteenth and seventeenth centuries, many studies now classified as **science** were classified as "natural philosophy." To describe these studies as science makes the past misleadingly similar to the present and overlooks what is unfamiliar about seventeenth-century beliefs and practices. The labels "science" and "scientist" are anachronisms for the activities and people of early modern Europe.

There is no straightforward correspondence between modern science and early modern natural philosophy. There were specialist technical disciplines, distinct from natural philosophy, that look similar to modern science (mathematical specialties such as astronomy, optics, and mechanics), and disciplines related to medicine such as anatomy and *materia medica*. These specialist studies described the natural world. Natural philosophy was superior to these in status because philosophy, in the **Aristotelian** tradition, was explanatory, and explanation was superior to description. Natural philosophy offered causal explanations for the chief features of the natural world.

There were competing natural philosophies in early modern Europe. Mechanical, corpuscular, and chemical philosophies were proposed in opposition to the previously dominant Christianized Aristotelian philosophy. All offered causal explanations for why the world behaved in the way it did. The proponents of competing natural philosophies usually claimed that their system was consistent with true Christian belief. **Isaac Newton** was not making an unusual claim when he asserted that God was a proper topic of discussion within natural philosophy: "To discourse of God from the nature of things does certainly belong to natural philosophy" (*Principia Mathematica*, General Scholium). Historians of science have argued that assumptions about creation and discussions about God were fundamental to natural philosophy. Hence the relationship of modern science to early modern natural philosophy is a significant issue if historical precedents are used when discussing the relationship of science and religion (see **natural theology**).

Key Points/Challenges

- Some (especially Cunningham 1988 and 1991) assert that natural philosophy was always about God's creation and therefore about God. Others (e.g., Dear 2001a and Osler 1997) argue that although beliefs about God and theological concepts were significant in the development of all varieties of natural philosophy, natural philosophy did not have to be about God.
- Either way, beliefs about God were both assumed and debated in the early modern discussions of the natural world. Natural philosophers discussing atoms, gravity, momentum, or the size of the universe, that is, topics usually viewed as moving toward modern science, made regular reference to God's nature and powers.

- The implications for the relationship of religion and modern science vary. According to Cunningham, science, unlike natural philosophy, is by definition not about God. Dear, however, argues that there is not a clear-cut distinction between natural philosophy and science, and that the shifting place of God in natural philosophy demands close historical analysis. He suggests that God was gradually replaced by a reified nature as the ultimate point of reference in much eighteenth-century natural philosophy but emphasizes that some nineteenth-century science was still about God.

Further Reading

Cunningham, Andrew. 1988. "Getting the Game Right: Some Plain Words on the Identity and Invention of Science." *Studies in History and Philosophy of Science* 19:365–89.

> A major and extreme statement of the thesis that natural philosophy and science are different enterprises, in large part because natural philosophy was about God.

———. 1991. "How the *Principia* Got Its Name; Or, Taking Natural Philosophy Seriously." *History of Science* 29:377–92.

> A more readable and shorter version of Cunningham's argument that natural philosophy was quite different from modern science.

Dear, Peter. 2001a. "Religion, Science and Natural Philosophy: Thoughts on Cunningham's Thesis." *Studies in History and Philosophy of Science Part A* 32:377–86.

> Argues against Cunningham that although natural philosophies were usually about God, this characteristic cannot be used to distinguish natural philosophy from science.

———. 2001b. *Revolutionizing the Sciences: European Knowledge and Its Ambitions, 1500–1700.* Princeton, NJ: Princeton University Press.

> Useful history of science text that begins with Greek traditions and the relationship of natural philosophy to the Aristotelian conception of philosophy as explanation.

Henry, John. 1997. *The Scientific Revolution and the Origins of Modern Science.* New York: St. Martin's Press.

> An excellent introductory text that discusses natural philosophy, religion, magic, and science with reference to how these categories changed through the sixteenth and seventeenth centuries.

Osler, Margaret J. 1997. "Mixing Metaphors: Science and Religion or Natural Philosophy and Theology in Early Modern Europe." *History of Science* 35:91–113.

> Argues that many of the historical discussions of science and religion should be recategorized as being about the relationships of natural philosophy and theology.

Ruth Barton, University of Auckland

☐ Natural Theology

Natural theology refers to the attempt to learn about God by applying human reason to the natural world, rather than through divine revelation. The Bible hints at a form of natural theology: Romans 1:20 suggests that God's eternal power and divine nature are seen "through the things he has made" (NRSV). Systematic natural theology developed in the thirteenth century with **Thomas Aquinas**, who believed that some knowledge of God, such as God's existence and some of God's attributes, could be gained through reason, while other doctrines, for example the incarnation and the **Trinity**, could be known only through revelation.

Reformation theologians emphasized the corruption of human knowledge after the fall, leading to skepticism toward natural theology. Notably, John Calvin argued that knowledge of God could be gained from creation only once a believer has the "spectacles of faith" (*Institutes*). Despite this criticism natural theology remained popular into the nineteenth century. One of the most famous and popular examples was **William Paley**'s *Natural Theology*, a collection of evidence for divine design in nature. Critiques of natural theology continued in the twentieth century. In the tradition of John Calvin, theologian Karl Barth declared that natural theology compromised the sovereignty of God. Knowing God, he argued, is not something we can achieve on our own (Barth and Brunner, *Natural Theology* [1934]).

John Ray (1627–1705) was an English naturalist and clergyman. He was elected a fellow of the Royal Society of London in 1667 and contributed accounts of his botanical studies to the society's journal, *Philosophical Transactions*. Ray is best known for his 1691 work *The Wisdom of God Manifested in the Works of Creation*, in which he argued that evidence from the natural world demonstrated God's providence. The most distinctive feature of Ray's natural theology is the exhaustive collection of evidence drawn from detailed research of the natural world. These were no armchair theologians; rather, people like Ray were active in studying, describing, and cataloging nature. Ray also saw the study of nature as an act of divine worship, as did other seventeenth-century "priests of nature" such as **Johannes Kepler** and **Robert Boyle**.

Key Points/Challenges

- Natural theology is difficult to define, as there have been many uses of the term. Additional terms such as *physico-theology* and *natural religion* cause further complications, since they can be either synonyms for natural theology or refer to different concepts.
- English natural theology is often linked to the rise of Newtonian (see **Newton**) science in the late seventeenth century. However, the tradition of natural theology dates back to the early church fathers, and a variety of natural philosophical and theological concepts have been employed.

- Historians have long considered natural theology as opposed to revealed theology, but this appears to be a consequence of the rise of deism (see **ideas of God**) and concomitant or accompanying rejection of revelation during the Enlightenment. Before this time many natural theologians viewed their arguments as complementing or supporting Scripture.

- The value of natural theology in modern times is disputed. The traditional arguments offered for the existence of God are widely viewed as so flawed that they discourage, rather than encourage, religious belief. The "argument from design," made famous by **William Paley** (*Natural Theology* [1802]), has been challenged, if not refuted, by Darwinian evolution and natural selection, despite attempts by the **intelligent design** movement to revive it. Philosopher Alvin Plantinga suggests that natural theological arguments may still have a role, not in convincing someone of the existence of God, but in providing supporting evidence for a pre-existing belief.

- So called fine-tuning arguments represent one of the more interesting survivals of natural theology in the twenty-first century. These arguments suggest that the fundamental physical constants of the universe seem to have been designed to produce life and intelligence (see **anthropic principle**).

Further Reading

Brooke, John Hedley. 2000. "'Wise Men Nowadays Think Otherwise': John Ray, Natural Theology and the Meanings of Anthropomorphism." *Notes and Records of the Royal Society of London* 54:199–213.

   Discusses the perceived anthropocentrism of John Ray's natural theology.

Harrison, Peter. 2004. "'Priests of the Most High God, With Respect to the Book of Nature': The Vocational Identity of the Early Modern Naturalist." In *Reading God's World: The Scientific Vocation*, edited by Angus J. L. Menuge, 59–84. St. Louis: Concordia.

   A key study of the concepts of physico-theology and the "priest of nature."

Olson, Richard. 1987. "On the Nature of God's Existence, Wisdom and Power: The Interplay between Organic and Mechanistic Imagery in Anglican Natural Theology—1640–1740." In *Approaches to Organic Form*, edited by Frederick Burwick, 1–48. Dordrecht: D. Reidel.

   Identifies Anglican natural theology as part of a long-running tradition. Discusses the use of both organic and mechanistic imagery.

Pailin, David A. 1994. "The Confused and Confusing Story of Natural Religion." *Religion* 24:199–212.

   A useful discussion of the numerous uses of the term *natural religion* in seventeenth- and eighteenth-century England.

Plantinga, Alvin. 1991. "The Prospects for Natural Theology." *Philosophical Perspectives* 5:297–315.

Suggests a role for natural theology as supporting a pre-existing belief in theism.

Larissa Johnson-Aldridge, University of New South Wales

□ Nature

The concept of "nature" has played a major role in the development of the natural sciences, and remains a significant concept for religion. The Greek term *physis* was used at a relatively early stage in the classical period to designate the objective realm of reality lying outside the human mind, on which ideas and values might ultimately be based. Although many have an intuitive idea of what *nature* designates, it has proved to be a remarkably difficult notion to define. In scientific works, the term *nature* is often used to mean "the forces and processes that produce and control all the phenomena of the material world," which are open to scientific study. Many philosophers of science use a slightly circular definition of nature, understanding it as "that which can be investigated using the scientific method." In religious works the term is often used to refer to the realm of reality apart from God. Although many religions use the term *creation* to designate this reality, the term *nature* is increasingly used, particularly in science/religion dialogues. In Christian theology *nature* is often used to refer to the natural state of humanity, as distinguished from the state of grace.

Key Points/Challenges

- The concept of nature plays a critical role in the dialogue between the natural sciences and religion, in that it is often viewed as the "common ground" to which both may appeal during conversations.
- In recent years, discussion has tended to focus on the origins and explanation of nature. Is nature a self-originating entity, something that came into existence on its own accord? Or is it to be viewed as something that was created—that is to say, brought into being and given its distinct identity by a creator? This debate has been given fresh impetus in recent years through the rise of the big bang theory of the origins of the universe, and increasing interest in anthropic issues, particularly in relation to the fine constants of nature (see also **anthropic principle**).
- The debate is particularly heated in relation to biological accounts of the origins and development of life, with neo-Darwinism, evolutionary theism, **intelligent design**, and various forms of **creationism** offering rival accounts.
- A further issue of debate is the extent to which nature is able to function as a gateway to the transcendent. Writers such as Richard Dawkins argue that nature

itself points toward atheism; others, such as Arthur Peacocke, hold that nature is capable of revealing God when viewed and interpreted in the correct manner.

Further Reading

Cornwell, John, ed. 1995. *Nature's Imagination: The Frontiers of Scientific Vision*. Oxford: Oxford University Press.

> An excellent survey of the development of concepts of nature from the classical period to the present day, particularly in the sciences.

Dawkins, Richard. 1986. *The Blind Watchmaker: Why the Evidence of Evolution Reveals a Universe without Design*. New York: W. W. Norton.

> A widely-cited and influential argument that natural selection can explain the complex adaptations of organisms without reference to a designer.

Gregersen, Niels H., Michael W. S. Parsons, and Christoph Wassermann, eds. 1997. *The Concept of Nature in Science and Theology*. Geneva: Labor et Fides.

> A slightly uneven collection of essays considering the theological and scientific interpretation of the concept of nature.

Lindberg, David C., and Ronald L. Numbers, eds. 1986. *God and Nature: Historical Essays on the Encounter between Christianity and Science*. Berkeley: University of California Press.

> A series of helpful essays from a variety of contributors exploring how the idea of nature has been understood by scientific and religious writers.

McGrath, Alister E. 2001. *A Scientific Theology*. Vol. 1, *Nature*. Edinburgh: T&T Clark.

> A detailed analysis of how the concept of nature has been understood in Western thought, and a proposal for developing a specifically Christian theology of nature.

Peacocke, Arthur R. 2001. *Paths from Science towards God: The End of All Our Exploring*. Oxford: Oneworld.

> An important account of how nature can be interpreted as a pointer toward the divine.

Alister McGrath, University of Oxford

☐ Newton, Isaac (1642–1727)

Isaac Newton's standing in the history of science is unparalleled both with respect to the breadth of his accomplishments and their revolutionary nature. His ground-breaking work on mathematics, optics, and physics began in earnest shortly after receiving his BA at Cambridge University in 1665. He was appointed Lucasian Professor of Mathematics there at the age of twenty-six and in 1703 was elected president of the Royal

Society of London. Newton's 1672 paper on colors revealed the heterogeneous nature of white light. His *Principia* (1687) introduced not only a powerful new mathematical physics with which natural philosophers could describe both terrestrial and celestial mechanics with unprecedented precision, but also demonstrated the lawlike nature of the cosmos. The *Opticks* (1704) elaborated in spectacular and comprehensive ways the principles of optics. Newton also co-invented calculus and, through his publications, made lasting contributions to the inductive and experimental methods in science. Partly because of these achievements in the sciences, in the eighteenth century Newton was transformed into a "saint" of the Age of Reason and his physics came to be interpreted in increasingly secular ways. However, the recent availability of his unpublished theological papers reveals a Newton radically different from the icon of popular imagination.

Justly celebrated for his achievements in science, Newton published virtually nothing on religion in his lifetime. Yet the single greatest area of growth in Newtonian studies during the past decades has been Newton's theology. Even in the *Principia* and the *Opticks* it was clear that Newton believed that natural philosophy points to the existence of the Creator through the inductive study of nature. Newton's firm commitments to **natural theology** are brought out in the General Scholium that he added to the *Principia*. "This most beautiful system of the sun, planets, and comets," he wrote, "could only proceed from the counsel and dominion of an intelligent and powerful Being" (General Scholium, in Cohen and Smith 2002, 340). Newton also asserts that discussions about God are a part of **natural philosophy**. Newton's private theological papers help confirm that he was attempting to construct a science that would be meaningless if the world were not a creation, and if a sovereign, all-powerful God did not constantly uphold its laws and operations. Newton's private manuscripts have deepened our understanding of Newton's belief in the design argument and have revealed his animus toward atheism. It is also now clear that Newton's concept of absolute space was based partially on his powerful biblical belief in God's omnipresence, just as his understanding of absolute time owed much to his belief in God's eternal duration.

Newton's theological manuscripts also reveal much about the relationship between his science and religion that would not have been clear to his contemporaries. In a treatise on the Apocalypse he composed in the 1670s, Newton lays out inductive principles for prophetic interpretation that closely resemble the Rules of Reasoning he later developed for the *Principia*. This same manuscript demonstrates that Newton was not only committed to the doctrine of the two books—that God revealed himself in nature and Scripture—but that he believed similar (inductive) methods could be used in the interpretation of both books. His study of ancient philosophy and religion also led him to conclude that the original religion involved both the worship of one God and the study of nature, a conclusion that was likely prescriptive for Newton.

Newton can also be studied as a theologian in his own right. His vast studies of Daniel and Revelation point to his passion for deciphering apocalyptic symbols, which he took to be one of the highest intellectual endeavors for a Christian scholar. Newton's biblical research led him to conclude that the Trinity is a post-New Testament corruption of monotheism that owed much to the unwarranted intrusion of Greek philosophy into Christianity. While this belief that the one God was the Father alone would render Newton a heretic in the eyes of mainstream Christianity, it must be stressed that his theological views were not the product of deism or any incipient rationalism. Newton remained a traditional theist as well as a passionate biblicist.

Key Points/Challenges

- Recent research has begun to correct the Enlightenment portrayal of Newton, the dominant view today among scientists and in popular culture. The new understanding of Newton rejects the vision of a rational scientist who separated science from religion to create a clockwork universe in which God is superfluous.
- Although still a point of contention among Newtonian scholars, it is now accepted that there was some sort of relationship between Newton's science and religion.
- Newton's unorthodox theology has provided insight into his natural philosophy, compounding its importance to Newtonian studies. While Newton's religious nonconformity may have helped reinforce his willingness to take new paths in the sciences, it is clear that Newton linked purity in religion with purity in natural philosophy, and that he thought both Christianity and natural philosophy (particularly Cartesianism) were in need of dramatic and thorough reform.

Further Reading

Cohen, I. Bernard, and George E. Smith, eds. 2002. *The Cambridge Companion to Newton.* Cambridge: Cambridge University Press.

    Introductory essays on Newton's natural philosophical, theological, and alchemical thought.

Force, James E., and Sarah Hutton. 2004. *Newton and Newtonianism: New Studies.* Dordrecht: Kluwer.

    A collection of essays on aspects of Newton's religious thought written by leading scholars.

Newton, Isaac. 1995. *Newton: Texts, Backgrounds, Commentaries.* Edited by I. Bernard Cohen and Richard S. Westfall. New York: W. W. Norton.

    A selection of Newton's writings on natural philosophy, theology, and alchemy, with helpful overviews by two respected Newtonian scholars.

The Newton Project. www.newtonproject.sussex.ac.uk.

    Online repository of Newton's theological and natural philosophical writings.

Stephen D. Snobelen, University of King's College, Halifax

☐ Nominalism

Nominalism refers to an austere (or strict) view about the metaphysical (see **metaphysics**) status of universal terms. Only names (or linguistic terms) are universal. It stands opposed to Platonism and moderate **realism**. Platonism holds that universal terms like "red" or "human" refer to entities or "Forms" independent of the mind and of their instances (that is, the actual thing or Idea the term is referring to, such as red fire engine). In other words, human nature is an *existing* universal Form by virtue of which any human person is in fact human. Moderate realists reject that Forms exist independently of their instances but do hold that the content of universal terms has some sort of existence independent of the mind.

Nominalists by contrast hold that particular objects are the only things that exist. Universals are, instead, names that apply to many instances (*red* is merely a term that applies to all things red) but the universality is a property of language, and in no way is a real thing with existence independent of the mind. Conceptual nominalists hold that the mental concepts signified by the linguistic terms are the universals in question. More radical nominalists hold that only the names are the universal terms "predicable of many." That is, "red fire engine" is, on the radical nominalist construal, nothing but a name that picks out those individuals that count as red fire engines.

William of Ockham is among the most famous and philosophically astute of the medieval nominalists. Ockham's razor is often summarized, "What can be accounted for by fewer things is needlessly dealt with by more" (also known as "the principle of parsimony"; see Loux [1998] 2004). In the case of universals, the razor says that if one can account for all of the uses and meanings of linguistic terms for classifying objects without postulating any entities beyond linguistic expressions, mental concepts, and mind-independent concrete particulars, then one need not postulate anything else such as real universals or abstract entities.

Wilfrid Sellars and Hartry Field have contributed to a more modern nominalist discussion of abstract objects or concepts such as relationships (e.g., maternity), sets, and propositions.

Key Points/Challenges

- Nominalism should not be seen as opposed to theism or religious conviction and was associated in the late Middle Ages (fourteenth and fifteenth centuries) with a heightened view of divine freedom and sovereignty. That is, God was viewed by some as having more control over events and moral commands if these did not follow from universal kinds, but rather straight from God's immediate will (contrast the **divine command theory** of morality with **natural law theory**).

- One of the first chapters in the history of nominalism is Aristotle's criticism of Plato's doctrine of Forms. In medieval discussions of universals, Peter Abelard moved the debate forward in a trenchant critique of extreme forms of **realism** and nominalism. Abelard and Ockham argued that talk of universals is talk about certain linguistic expressions. Ockham's reflections on logic and language offered one of the most sophisticated discussions on the status of universal terms of the medieval period (see Freddoso's introduction to William of Ockham 1998 and Loux [1998] 2004).

Further Reading

Field, Hartry. 1980. *Science without Numbers: A Defense of Nominalism*. Princeton, NJ: Princeton University Press.

A recent defense of nominalism in the context of a discussion of modern physics.

Gilson, Etienne. 1955. *History of Christian Philosophy in the Middle Ages*. New York: Random House.

A classic source for a magisterial survey of medieval thought.

Loux, Michael J. [1998] 2004. *Nominalism*. Routledge Encyclopedia of Philosophy. London: Routledge. http://0-www.rep.routledge.com.deborah.spu.edu:80/article/N038.

An excellent and concise survey of the varieties of nominalism in history and their contemporary philosophical significance.

Oberman, Heiko. 1967. *The Harvest of Medieval Theology: Gabriel Biel and Late Medieval Nominalism*. 2nd ed. Grand Rapids: Eerdmans.

A detailed and sensitive study of the theological significance of nominalism in the fourteenth and fifteenth centuries.

Sellars, Wilfrid. 1967. "Abstract Entities." In *Philosophical Perspectives*, 229–69. Springfield, IL: Charles C. Thomas.

One of the most sophisticated recent defenses of a nominalist view in contemporary Anglo-American philosophy.

William of Ockham. 1998. "Quodlibetal questions: Volume 1 and 2, quodlibets 1–7." In *The Yale Library of Medieval Philosophy*, edited by Norman Kretzmann, Eleonore Stump, and John Wippel, translated by Alfred J. Freddoso and Francis E. Kelley, xxviii and 391. New Haven: Yale University Press.

An excellent source for Ockham's view and a most helpful introduction by Freddoso.

Patrick McDonald, Seattle Pacific University

□ Ontology (*see also* Metaphysics)

Ontology relates to the question of *what* there is to reality. Philosophers use it to describe "a theory of being" (from the Greek *ontos*, "being"). Ontology involves talking about the basic categories and relationships between entities, and the types of entities that exist. An ontology, therefore, has something in common with a worldview. It differs from the latter, however, in that it has a theoretical rather than a concrete or commonsense nature.

All sciences have a theoretical character. However, while this statement appears simple enough on the surface, this apparent simplicity tends to hide many issues of ontological controversy, including the very meaning of the term *theory* itself. Karl Popper described three ways in which scientific theories might be considered to have ontological validity. The first he described as essentialism. Such theories involve ultimate essences deemed to be embedded in real things so that their form accounts for their properties and behavior. The second view is conventionalism or instrumentalism. The entities and the relationships espoused by a theory are of a "conventional" character, meaning that the human mind, via a scientific theory, organizes reality with a view toward increasing our ability to manage and control it. While the theories of science are not arbitrary, they are deemed to be "instruments" whose "meaning exhausts itself in the permission or license that they give us to draw inferences or to argue from some matters of fact to other matters of fact" (Popper 1963, 109). The issue is well-illustrated by the Ptolemaic system of astronomy, especially as this philosophical view was imputed to Galileo's *Two World Systems* in the preface by Osiander (see, for example, **Ptolemaic system**). Thus the entities and relations in theories do not necessarily correspond to the world that is there. In one way, this view can be said to be exemplified in Thomas Kuhn's influential book, *The Structure of Scientific Revolutions*. In another, it was exemplified by the philosophical views of such thinkers as Berkeley and Mach.

Popper's third view was realism. Both essentialism and realism consider the theoretical entities of science to be ontologically real, at least in some sense. However, realism considers the postulated entities of scientific theories as tentative formulations that do not claim ultimate validity. It recognizes that the history of science is littered with conjectural real entities that have had to be abandoned, such as the phlogiston (a substance released during combustion) and the ether (a medium that filled all space) of eighteenth-century science.

The main option today is between realism and conventionalism. Realism asserts that the hypothesized entities of science may really have an existence as proposed by the theory. Conventionalism asserts that the theory, as a construction of the human mind, imposes its categories on reality and, in that sense, is not ontologically real (see also **realism/antirealism**).

Key Points/Challenges

- Marx's view of history and the Darwinism promoted by people like Richard Dawkins have an essentialist quality. This accounts for their dogmatic character. Not only are their basic categories deemed to be real and ultimate but they are also thereby deemed, in effect, to be immune from criticism. Many such theories hold to a mechanistic or physicalist ontology, reducing the concrete common-sense world of our everyday experience to a lowest common denominator (see **naturalism** and **reductionism**).

- When scientists speak of "**laws of nature**" they may unwittingly be making an ontological assertion to the effect that the cosmos is a system of self-generated order, in some form, deemed to have existed forever.

- The Bible speaks of the divine as the Creator, Sustainer, and Redeemer of all things. If the existence of this God is deemed ontologically false, then nature and its laws, rather than God, are deemed to be ultimately ontologically real, having existed forever.

- From a biblically oriented ontology, the sciences are a theoretical investigation into the ways in which God both originates and sustains all the order and meaning of the cosmos.

- The word *ontology* can also connote the interrelatedness of things. In the modern university system this functions both sociologically and bibliographically. The university is divided into faculties, schools, and departments; a library classifies books by subject matter. However, the worlds of learning in the modern *uni*versity system present us with something deserving the name *multi*versity. The task of a philosophical ontology is to give an account of just how the foci of the diverse sciences fit together in the world as God's creation, bringing together a picture of ourselves, the nonhuman world, and the human task of developing the resources of the earth while caring for their integrity. A significant twentieth-century contribution to this enterprise was made by the Dutchmen Hermann Dooyeweerd (1953) and Dirk Vollenhoven (2005) in their development of what has become known as "Reformational philosophy."

Further Reading

Burtt, Edwin A. 1924. *The Metaphysical Foundations of Modern Physical Science*. London: Routledge & Kegan Paul.

> Not an easy book, but clearly sets out the way in which the early development of the modern scientific movement, from the sixteenth century, set the ontological foundations for a mechanistic worldview.

Clouser, Roy A. 2005. *The Myth of Religious Neutrality*. Notre Dame, IN: University of Notre Dame Press.

> Because of its attempt to deal with clear views of the nature of "religion" and "theory," this book gives both an interesting and provocative view of the relationship of religion to science.

Dooyeweerd, Hermann. 1953. *A New Critique of Theoretical Thought*. 4 vols. Philadelphia: Presbyterian and Reformed.

This is a major piece of philosophical work that is too little known. It has profound implications for the work of the special sciences, both natural and cultural.

Jaki, Stanley. 1966. "The Chief World Models of Physics." In *The Relevance of Physics*, 2–137. Chicago: University of Chicago Press.

Gives a valuable historical survey of the way physics has been influenced by three ontologically oriented worldviews: biologism, mechanism, and mathematicism.

Popper, Karl R. 1963. "Three Views Concerning Human Knowledge." In *Conjectures and Refutations*, 97–119. London: Routledge & Kegan Paul.

A good place to start with respect to the basic ontological issues involved in scientific theories.

Vollenhoven, Dirk. 2005. *Introduction to Philosophy*. Translated by John Kok. Sioux Center, IA: Dordt College Press.

This book provides probably the best available initial insight into the way the ontological theories of Dooyeweerd and Vollenhoven relate to the scientific enterprise.

Duncan L. Roper, University of Western Sydney

☐ Paley, William (1743–1805)

Natural Theology (1802), William Paley's best-known book, was one of the great publishing successes of the nineteenth century, admired by **Charles Darwin**. The book opens with a famous passage about coming across a watch. Seeing how all the intricate parts fit together to tell the time, no one could doubt that the watch had a maker. Paley argues that we, animals, and indeed the solar system are likewise products of design and contrivance. God has made a clockwork universe, which moreover produces the greatest happiness for the greatest number of people. God is both almighty and good. There is pain, but it is minimized: predators bring euthanasia to elderly herbivores. Richard Dawkins admires the book, and his *Blind Watchmaker* (1986) picks up Paley's theme. But for Dawkins, Darwin's *Origin of Species* (1859) showed how apparent design is really the product of natural selection and the struggle for existence. In contrast to Paley, Dawkins's world is the outcome of blind forces and laws, and has no maker.

Darwin's and Paley's styles of argument were akin. The existence of God (or of evolution) cannot be proved logically from evidence of real or apparent design in the universe. Thus the argument cannot be a chain of reasoning, as in geometry, where each link depends on the one before, and the deduction is watertight. Instead, theirs is like a cumulative legal argument making a case certain beyond reasonable doubt— a rope rather than a chain of evidence, where many strands of varying strength will together support the conclusion.

Paley had, in fact, contemplated becoming a lawyer. Instead, he was ordained in the Church of England and after a spell as a parish priest was appointed archdeacon of Carlisle. Subsequently, he moved to the very well-endowed parish of Monkwearmouth, in Sunderland, and also became sub-dean of the cathedral at Lincoln. He was prominent and successful but never became a dean or bishop. *Natural Theology* was his last book, written after others on ethics, on the harmony between the Epistles and the Acts of the Apostles, and on the evidences for Christianity from miracles and prophecies. He recommended that his books be read in the reverse order, because natural theology only brings us to the threshold of church teaching and Christian behavior.

Key Points/Challenges

- Paley demonstrated forcefully and effectively **Francis Bacon**'s idea that there were two books, nature and Scripture, that told us about God. Though not an original scientist, he built on the writings of John Ray (*Wisdom of God Manifested in the Works of Creation* [1691]) and William Derham (*Physico-Theology* [1712]), stayed up to date, and ensured that **natural theology** remained part of the scientific worldview for a generation.

- David Hume, in *Dialogues Concerning Natural Religion* (1779), had argued that pain, disease, and death are such prominent features of the world that it could not be created by a loving God. Subsequently, Paley's utilitarian argument failed to satisfy all critics—or console widows and orphans.

- Evangelicals such as Thomas Gisborne were suspicious that natural theology meant natural religion, a form of deism (see **ideas of God**) acknowledging a First Cause but not a personal God. They also saw the world as imperfect, fallen, a place of punishment from which we need to be redeemed through grace. Arguments about God's existence miss the point.

- The existence of fossils (from which it could be concluded that innumerable kinds of creatures had flourished and become extinct), the discovery of many species of distinct but similar living creatures, and animals curiously adapted to very specific ecological niches were difficult to reconcile with the view that all creatures were one-off designs by an omniscient God. These were, however, explicable by development over time.

Further Reading

Eddy, Matthew D. 2004. "The Science and Rhetoric of Paley's Natural Theology." *Literature and Theology* 18:1–22.

> Investigates Paley's use of rhetorical devices to get his message across in his famously clear and persuasive style.

Fyfe, Aileen. 1997. "The Reception of William Paley's *Natural Theology* in the University of Cambridge." *British Journal for the History of Science* 30:321–35.

> Explores the use made of Paley's text in Charles Darwin's Cambridge.

Paley, William. 2006. *Natural Theology*. Edited by Matthew D. Eddy and David Knight. Oxford: Oxford University Press.

> Reprints Paley's text with introduction, commentary, and bibliography in the World's Classics series.

David M. Knight, Durham University

☐ Pantheism, Panentheism

Derived from the Greek words *pan* (all) and *theos* (God), pantheism identifies the universe or nature with the divine: God is neither externally transcendent to the world (as in classical theism) nor immanently present but identical with the world. It has close counterparts in Taoism, Advaita Vedanta, and some schools of Buddhism and can also be used as an umbrella term for diverse concepts of all-unity and holism (e.g., the anthroposophy of Rudolf Steiner; new age of Frietjof Capra; Gaia hypothesis of James Lovelock; mystical ideas affiliated with Goethe's contemplation of nature). Its roots date back to philosophies in the ancient world (e.g., Parmenides), the philosophies of Stoicism and Neoplatonism, and the mystical Jewish and Islamic traditions of kabbalah and Sufism, respectively. As a philosophical concept it is nevertheless a modern phenomenon, coined in the eighteenth century during the debates about Spinozism. **Spinoza**'s notion that God equals nature became a kind of signal term for pantheism.

For Friedrich Schleiermacher, pantheistic thinking was a necessary complement to the personification of God and an expression of personal piety. Nevertheless, pantheism has often been identified with religious criticism, even atheism, because of its nontraditional perspective on the relationship between God and nature—which it certainly is not. Compared to an excessive emphasis on God's transcendence, as found in some forms of classical theism, pantheism's lasting and important theological contribution is stressing the necessity to think anew about God's presence in the world; to maintain respect, reverence, and awe over against nature; and to develop anew human self-understanding in relation to this *all is God*.

The line between pantheistic (*all is God*) and panentheistic (*all is in God*) positions is often difficult to draw. But whereas pantheism tends toward a materialist (see **materialism**) understanding of God, panentheism still maintains clear distinctions between God and nature: God is all-encompassing with respect to being, and certain properties of divinity (e.g., self-existence, omnipotence) still apply to God only. Thus panentheism seeks to to mediate between *deism* and traditional *theism* (see **ideas of God**), on one hand, and pantheism, on the other. Process theology (see **process philosophy/theology**) could be considered panentheistic in nature.

Key Points/Challenges

- As supernaturalism or theism becomes less prominent among scientifically educated people, pantheism offers a way to express one's piety without surrendering to atheism or religious indifference. Pantheism does not carry any subversive character with respect to science and theology as does, for example, the **intelligent design** movement, which seeks to replace science with a *theistic science*.
- In pantheism the living God replaces the personal God but the uniqueness of God is beyond question. Nevertheless, in a secularist view the questions arise: Why call nature God? Is God only a superfluous synonym for the word *world*?
- By criticizing theism and the notion of a personal and self-conscious God, pantheism creates difficulties in determining criteria for good or bad—"it is as it is." However, a strength of pantheism is its stress on the ambiguity and contextual nature of the ordering of values.
- Whereas philosophical pantheism is correlated with an empirical-scientific redirection of our understanding of the world, pantheism in a theological framework led to relativism of classical properties of God, especially with respect to God's freedom and perfection. The "creation out of nothing" loses its importance, and the notion of sin takes on new meaning. However, a liberal pantheistic theology has yet to be written.

Further Reading

Clayton, Philip, and Arthur Peacocke. 2004. *In Whom We Live and Move and Have Our Being: Panentheistic Reflections on God's Presence in a Scientific World*. Grand Rapids: Eerdmans.

> A collection of articles by leading theologians, philosophers, and scientists, and thus a helpful resource exploring appreciatively and critically various forms of panentheism.

Levine, Michael P. 1994. *Pantheism: A Non-Theistic Concept of Deity*. London: Routledge.

> A comprehensive study of pantheism as a philosophical position, offering definitions and their distinctions, history, relation to theism, and religious implications in terms of practice.

McFague, Sallie. 1993. *The Body of God: An Ecological Theology*. Minneapolis: Fortress.

> McFague develops a feminist ecotheology by using the model of the universe as the body of God, addressed to creation, theology, Christology, ecology, and more.

Hubert Meisinger, Center for Social Responsibility,
Mainz, and Protestant Academy, Arnoldshain

☐ Person

Although it had its forerunners in ancient philosophy, the concept of a person is essential to Christianity. In Stoic philosophy a person was mainly understood by the role one played in society, and the word derived from the Greek *prosopon*, meaning the mask used in a dramatic performance. In Christian theology the concept of a human person was deepened through development of the doctrines of the **Trinity** and **Christology**. Persons were described in terms of rationality, individuality, and responsibility. Thus according to St. **Augustine**'s treatise *De trinitate* human persons, as the *imago Dei*, mirror the trinitarian structure of the divine person in their *vestigia trinitatis* (trace of the Trinity in the created order), which consists of memory, intelligence, and will. The divine persons are also constituted by their relationship to each other. Thus Augustine created a relational understanding of the concept of a person. Later, Boethius introduced a substantial understanding of a person modeled on the Christology of Chalcedon. He defined a person, according to Aristotelian metaphysics, as "an individual substance of a rational nature," that is a being or body with the characteristic of rationality (*Theological Treatises*, V:III).

These religious connotations of the concept of the human person made this notion normative (how persons ought to be), rather than descriptive (how persons are), as they were the rationale for inalienable human dignity. The relational concept of a human person was further elaborated in the Middle Ages by Richard of St. Victor. The notion of a substance defining a person was abolished by David Hume (1711–76). For him a person is "a bundle or collection of different perceptions" (*Treatise*). This normative character of the human person in terms of liberty and dignity was preserved in the secularized natural law of Samuel Pufendorf (1632–94), who identified the moral character as being essential for personhood (*ens morale*) in his *De officio hominis et civis iuxta legem naturalem* (1673).

In contrast to this normative religious heritage and the tradition of natural law, modern concepts of a human person focus in a reductionist, naturalist, and even a functionalist manner on certain properties, such as consciousness (Descartes, Locke), action and will (Hobbes, B. Williams, H. G. Frankfurt), liberty, responsibility, intentionality, autonomy and decision making, and memory and expectation. All these properties highlight the subjective process of becoming a person (N. Rescher), including the problem of identity (D. C. Dennett). Some philosophers have developed lists of the necessary properties of a person (P. Singer, M. Tooley). The notion of a person was further discussed in American personalism (Bonne, Brightman, Hocking, Flewelling), and in analytical philosophy (G. Ryle, P. F. Strawson). Today in theology, the relational understanding of the human person is predominant and draws on the theological and philosophical traditions as well as on the insights of psychology (LeRon Shults). Another tradition, beginning with Kierkegaard, relates personhood to the self. According to MacIntyre the unity and identity of the person as a self is guaranteed by the person's social role, virtues, and history. Here the human person is viewed as a "story-telling animal" (1984, 216).

Key Points/Challenges

- Understanding a person in a reductionist, naturalist, and functionalist way according to certain properties, which are developing and ending in the course of the life story of a person, conflicts with the religious understanding of the inalienable dignity of a person. This dignity is independent of certain properties that are said to constitute a person. This conflict occurs in the debates about embryonic stem cell research, abortion, and active and passive euthanasia.

- One debate that concerns how *person* is defined is whether personhood can be attributed to higher mammals such as primates. Some scientists, and philosophers like Peter Singer, claim that certain traits, such as intentionality, qualify primates as persons, whereas the lack of such traits in some human beings (as humans with dementia) disqualifies them as persons. To distinguish human persons from animals or robots creates a dilemma. A distinction must be made, but as soon as it is made, some humans may no longer be regarded as persons.

- As robots develop more and more characteristics of human beings, can they be called persons ("fictitious persons") and be permitted human rights?

- The ongoing process of merging electronic devices with biological substrates (implants, cyborgs) challenges the concept of a human person as relates to carbon-based life (see **posthuman**).

- Is the moral character of a person accidental (functionalism) or essential (personalism)?

- Genetic, electronic, and technological engineering, as well as nanotechnology, may enhance naturally given abilities, again raising questions of personhood.

Further Reading

Baier, Annette C. 1994. "A Naturalist View of Persons." In *Moral Prejudices: Essays on Ethics*, 313–26. Cambridge, MA: Harvard University Press.

> Perspectives on the person, based on naturalism and physicalism, as opposed to the moral character tradition based on metaphysical dignity or indispensable uniqueness of the person according to his or her life story.

MacIntyre, Alasdair. 1984. *After Virtue. A Study in Moral Theory*. Notre Dame, IN: University of Notre Dame Press.

> Examines the moral disaster of modernity caused by rule-based abstract morals. The author seeks to cure the moral shortcomings of modernity by recovering virtue-based ethics, which are indispensable properties of a concept of a person that has a stable self as a result of an ongoing story directed by virtues.

Pollock, John L. 1989. *How to Build a Person: A Prolegomenon*. Cambridge, MA: MIT Press.

> Based on the philosophical functionalism of cybernetics. Pollock equates constructing a person with creating a computer model with a human rational architecture.

Singer, Peter. 1979. *Practical Ethics*. Cambridge: Cambridge University Press.

> In the context of the bioethical debate, discusses certain properties as essential for the human person.

Warwick, Kevin. 2004. *I, Cyborg*. London: Century.

> Warwick claims that merging the human body with technological devices will create a new species (cyborgs) with enhanced intellectual capabilities.

Wolfgang Achtner, Justus Liebig University, Giessen, Germany

☐ Plato (422–347 BC)

Plato is one of the most famous and influential philosophers in the Western world. He was a student of Socrates and studied and taught in Athens, Greece, where he started the first Western academic institution, the Academy. Plato's writings treat many topics, such as virtue, justice, piety, and immortality of the soul. Plato highly valued mathematics, which through him became the paradigm for truth in Western philosophy. He was profoundly influenced by the Pythagoreans, for whom geometry held the key to a physical and spiritual understanding of the universe. Most significant for the science/religion debate are his strict distinctions between soul and body and between temporal appearances and ultimate reality, which arose out of his study of the changeable nature of politics and the natural environment. Philosophy, he argued, should be the practice of separating from the body and all other temporal, worldly connections to focus on the soul and ultimate truth.

Plato portrayed philosophy as a journey out of a cave of shadows into the realm of light and truth (the *Republic*). Ultimate truth is expressed in the Forms (eternal principles or Ideas, of which the true, the good, and the beautiful are the highest): realities of another realm of which ours is merely a poor imitation. In this process astronomy, geometry, and arithmetic play an important role. Philosophers have an obligation not only to cultivate their own souls but also to guide others toward truth (personally and politically). Plato also wrote a mythical account of creation (the *Timaeus*), in which he described the material world as the rational and organized product of a demiurge (a semi-divine being) who gave Form to "fallen" matter. This creation story profoundly influenced Plotinus (founder of Neoplatonism) and much of medieval thinking about the universe.

Key Points/Challenges

- Plato has so profoundly shaped Western thinking as a whole that it is difficult to isolate specific instances of his impact. One of the most significant influences, however, is his "divided line," (the *Republic*) which proposes distinctions among various levels of reality and of corresponding knowledge. Reality and truth are located in another (spiritual) realm, which is eternal and unchanging. This material world is one of appearance or opinion only.

- Human persons and society may be divided into three parts: reason (the highest and the one that ought to be in control), spirit, and emotion/desire. This often leads to condemnation of our passions and emotions as irrelevant or even evil, rejection of the body (and sexuality) as a hindrance to finding truth, and elevation of reason or science as a disconnected, disembodied exercise that reaches pure truth (and is superior to other kinds of endeavors, such as those based on emotion or on mythology/religion) (the *Republic*).

- Many of these implications are spelled out much more explicitly by Plato's followers, such as Plotinus. The *Timaeus* was the main Platonic text available to scholars in the Middle Ages and thus was the authoritative source for Platonic thought.

- Plato profoundly shaped Western religious thought—especially Christianity—in both its heretical and orthodox versions. Many early Christian heresies were gnostic in character, carrying Plato's dualism (separation between soul and body, this world and the divine) to an extreme. But mainstream Christian thinking was also shaped by his thought, especially the tendency to focus on the immortality of the soul over resurrection of the body. Soul and body were thus seen as two separate entities, and there was a strong focus on the afterlife rather than on our present condition.

- Through **Augustine** and later medieval thinkers (and a recovery of Plato's thought during the Renaissance, e.g., in Marcilio Ficino), Plato's ideas also influenced scientific thinkers such as **Copernicus**, **Kepler**, and **Newton**. Copernicus, for example, argued that the heliocentric theory is superior to the **Ptolemaic system**, not because it fits the data better, or because he had any proof for it, but because it is more beautiful for the sun to be at the center—since the sun is the source of light and a much worthier body than the earth.

Further Reading

Bowen, Alan C., ed. 1991. *Science and Philosophy in Classical Greece.* New York: Garland.

> Papers originally presented at a 1986 conference on the interaction of science and philosophy during the fifth and fourth centuries BC. See especially the article by A. O. D. Mourelatos, "Plato's Science—His View and Ours of His," 11–30.

Lindberg, David C. 1992. *The Beginnings of Western Science: The European Scientific Tradition in Philosophical, Religious, and Institutional Context, 600 BC to AD 1450.* Chicago: University of Chicago Press.

> An accessible survey of the history of ancient and medieval science, including a discussion of Plato's contribution (chapter 2, "The Greeks and the Cosmos," 21–45).

Pelikan, Jaroslav. 1997. *What Has Athens to Do with Jerusalem? Timaeus and Genesis in Counterpoint*. Ann Arbor: University of Michigan Press.

> An award-winning examination of the influence of Plato's *Timaeus* on cosmology, with particular relevance for the modern creation/evolution debate.

Christina M. Gschwandtner, University of Scranton

☐ Polanyi, Michael (1891–1976)

Michael Polanyi, a pioneer of the science/religion dialogue, briefly practiced medicine, pursued a career in chemistry, and made influential contributions in economics and philosophy. Against the objectivism, empiricism, and Marxist-influenced thinking of his time, he argued for the importance of transcendent ideals in science and society. He developed a sharp criticism of the modern Western philosophical tradition and articulated a constructive alternative that included a persuasive account of how science is actually practiced and how new discoveries are made. Among the numerous thinkers influenced by Polanyi are John Haught, John Polkinghorne, Langdon Gilkey, Bernard Lonergan, and Thomas Torrance.

Born into a liberal, highly educated Jewish family in Budapest, Polanyi left Hungary after World War I and pursued scientific interests in Germany, eventually at the renowned Kaiser Wilhelm Institutes. After the Nazis took power, Polanyi accepted a physical chemistry chair in 1933 at Manchester University in England, where he also pursued his interests in economics and social philosophy. In 1944, in recognition of his outstanding accomplishments in physical chemistry, Polanyi was made a Fellow of the Royal Society. In 1948, he exchanged his chair in chemistry for a chair in social science. His Gifford Lectures of 1951–52 were later published as *Personal Knowledge: Towards a Post-Critical Philosophy*. This work, arguably his magnum opus, has attained classic status as a result of its fertile reflections on science, society, and religion.

Polanyi clarified and defended the values underlying institutions of Western civilization; he saw civilization as an "embodiment of the human mind." Believing that "men need a purpose which bears on eternity" (*The Tacit Dimension* [1966]), he contended institutions can progress by continuously pursuing and submitting to the truth upon which and for which they came into being. While many religious thinkers have found a rich source in Polanyi's philosophy, his own religious ideas were never clearly or systematically developed.

Polanyi attacked the nihilism that he saw manifest in fascism and Marxism. Totalitarian governments, Polanyi argued, fail to promote the public liberty that undergirds the operation of science, law, and other "dynamic orders" that are the foundation of modern society. He criticized Marxism's "dynamo-objective coupling" and "moral inversion," his shorthand terms for how Marxism hides its moral passion in allegedly scientific objectivity.

Key Points/Challenges

- From the sense of *fides* (Latin for "faith" or "trust"), Polanyi argued for the "fiduciary" structure of all knowledge. For him faith is more basic than doubt for those seeking and holding knowledge. The belief that some things are real and others are not is the basis of scientific and religious knowing. The devotion, energy expended, and passion of the scientist who pursues discovery indicates great faith that something is there to be discovered.

- Polanyi's epistemological stance can be summarized as "personal knowledge." Against the prevailing empiricism (logical positivism) of his time, he contended that knowing is neither purely objective nor whimsically subjective, but rather, a skillful act that requires both responsibility and commitment. Personal knowledge is more than subjective because a responsible knower submits to reality and is committed to a truth that has universality.

- For Polanyi human life involves a "dwelling in and breaking out." All life and knowing begins in community and with the community's way of seeing things—with "dwelling in." But we "dwell in" in order to "break out" into more encompassing knowledge, as we pursue the unknown in the human vocation of exploring the cosmos.

- There is more to knowing than what is conscious, explicit, and clearly before the mind's eye. Tacit elements of knowing include things such as the unnoticed glasses we see through or the very beginnings of a hunch that often lead to the discovery of solutions to problems. In Polanyi's view, every act of learning is a skillful integration of tacitly known elements that produces a more comprehensive whole. By creatively demonstrating how tacit knowing and explicit knowing are interrelated, Polanyi recast many of the problems of science, religion, and their interaction.

- Polanyi resisted reductionistic explanations, including those of neo-Darwinism. He argued that just as lower levels such as physics and chemistry cannot exhaustively explain the operation of higher-level biological operations, so, too, the higher level of human behavior cannot be fully explained in biological terms. Polanyi was one of the first thinkers to argue for the "emergent" qualities of living forms, and he linked the quest for knowledge by humans and the development of more complex living forms (see **emergence**).

Further Reading

Gelwick, Richard. [1977] 2004. *The Way of Discovery: An Introduction to the Thought of Michael Polanyi*. Eugene, OR: Wipf and Stock.

    An outstanding older introduction (recently reprinted) to Polanyi's ideas, organized around Polanyi's central interest in discovery.

Grene, Marjorie. 1977. "Tacit Knowing: Grounds for a Revolution in Philosophy." *Journal of the British Society for Phenomenology* 8 (3):164–71.

> An incisive interpretative account of Polanyi's postcritical philosophical innovations by an influential philosopher who worked with Polanyi on many of his publications.

Mitchell, Mark T. 2006. *Michael Polanyi: The Art of Knowing.* Wilmington, DE: ISI Books.

> A very readable, concise, and competent new introduction to Polanyi's thought.

http://www.missouriwestern.edu/orgs/polanyi/.

> Polanyi Society Web site with current issue and archives of *Tradition and Discovery: The Polanyi Society Periodical,* links to the *Guide to the Papers of Michael Polanyi* and to many short Polanyi articles, as well as audio files of Polanyi conversations and lectures.

Polanyi, Michael. [1958] 1974. *Personal Knowledge: Towards a Post-Critical Philosophy.* Chicago: University of Chicago Press.

> Polanyi's most comprehensive philosophical statement.

Scott, William Taussig, and Martin X. Moleski, SJ. 2005. *Michael Polanyi: Scientist and Philosopher.* Oxford: Oxford University Press.

> A biography showing how Polanyi's ideas emerged from his life experiences. Includes a bibliography of all Polanyi's writing.

Phil Mullins, Missouri Western State University, and Philip A. Rolnick, University of St. Thomas

☐ Positivism (Logical and Neo-Positivism)

This nineteenth-century philosophy of science gained favor through the writing of the French philosopher Auguste Comte (1798–1857), especially in his *Cours de Philosophie Positive.* "Things positive" were those phenomena that are observable by the senses, testable by experiment, and correlated by order, sequence, and empirical associations. In Comte's "law of three stages," humanity progressively gained knowledge of observed natural events, first through theology (explained by acts of supernatural beings), then **metaphysics** (attributed to abstract essences or powers), and finally positivism (acquired through the scientific method of **Francis Bacon**). At any point in history, some branches of human knowledge functioned at a more naive stage while others had progressed to the full sophistication of positivism. By the mid-nineteenth century Comte felt that mathematics, astronomy, physics, chemistry, and biology had fully adopted positive explanations of observed phenomena and that sociology (a science "fathered" by Comte) and moral ethics (including **altruism**, also coined by Comte) could begin the same developmental transition in the advancement of humanity.

Positivist philosophy arose with the work of Francis Bacon (*Novum Organon* [1620]) and progressed well into the twentieth century, adopted, promoted, and embellished by the support, both intellectual and financial, of Descartes, Galileo, John

Stuart Mill, Nietzsche, T. H. Huxley, and many other philosophers throughout Europe (prominently those in the Vienna Circle) and in North and South America. From the Vienna Circle a philosophy of logical positivism distinct from Comte's positivism grew to espouse a "verifiability criteria of meaning" where all statements that cannot be verified by sense perception are meaningless nonsense, including all metaphysical statements (see **verification principle**).

Key Points/Challenges

- Comte's positivism did not attempt to discard theology and metaphysics as senseless, but instead saw them as inaccessible by positivist methods—it is not possible to label metaphysical claims as either true or false.

- Positivism lost intellectual favor in the later 1800s as Comte established a cultlike religion where humanity itself could progress when followers "studied it (science and education), loved it (religion), beautified it (fine arts), and enriched it (industry)," leading to a new sociocracy founded on science. Comte's Religion of Humanity had doctrines, a Catechism of Positive Religion, a motto of Love-Order-Progress, and a new Positivist Calendar (to replace the Gregorian calendar) with a discipline ascribed to each month and a saint for each day— described by T. H. Huxley as "Catholicism minus Christianity," while Richard Congreve, a positivist, preferred "Catholicism plus science."

- The Vienna Circle advanced a neopositivist tradition after Comte's death, when the University of Vienna appointed Ernst Mach (1895) as professor of inductive sciences, then his successor Moritz Schlick (1922), and the Circle, led forward by Rudolf Carnap, established a very empirical, logic-based, anti-metaphysical form of logical positivism.

- In assessing the history of logical positivism, Passmore develops the growing dilemma, "Throw metaphysics in the fire, and science goes with it, preserve science from the flames and metaphysics comes creeping back" (1957, 392). This statement describes what happened when the **verification principle** grew to require the support of significant metaphysical arguments.

- The legacy of positivism remains evident in Comte's predicted hierarchy of scientific disciplines, autonomous in their epistemologies, and also in the science/religion dialogue, especially in the areas of scientism (see **science**), mind/body dualism (see **mind/body problem**), methodological and metaphysical **naturalism**, humanism, **critical realism**, and **intelligent design**.

- Revisiting positivism may prove useful when responding to critics who choose to conflate metaphysical naturalism and evolution, and to intelligent design theorists (with claims of logical access to the detection of the "designed").

Further Reading

Passmore, John. 1957. *A Hundred Years of Philosophy*. London: Duckworth.

>Links the positivism of Comte with the early work of John Stuart Mill and the development of logical positivism in the Vienna Circle.

Scharff, Robert C. 1995. *Comte after Positivism*. Cambridge: Cambridge University Press.

>The key contemporary, historico-critical study, clearly integrating Comte's three-stage law with theology, metaphysics, and science.

Singer, Michael. 2005. *The Legacy of Positivism*. Houndmills, UK: Palgrave Mac-Millan.

>A short, detailed text by a mathematician and lawyer, returning to Comte's original French works and providing a very useful treatment of the structure and legacy of positive science.

Sokoloff, Boris. 1975. *The "Mad" Philosopher, Auguste Comte*. Westport, CT: Greenwood.

>An accessible, historical novel portraying the intellectually tortured life of Auguste Comte and revealing his "morally pure," yearlong affair with the ailing and ineligible Madam Clotilde de Vaux.

Henry S. Tillinghast, Ottawa University

☐ Posthuman

The term *posthuman* refers to a particular view of humanity that assumes that the human condition is simply a stage in our evolution as we push toward becoming beings that are more biologically and psychologically advanced. Posthumanism advocates the gradual overturning of the humanistic notion of a human-centered world by challenging traditional understandings of the body and what it means to be human in order to make room for new forms of being created or facilitated through emerging technologies. It has become an important topic of discussion for those exploring and debating the impact of new technologies on ideas of being and personhood (see **person**) within the intersection of science and religion. Posthuman discourse explores and reflects on how technologies may enable us to enhance our human limitations or weaknesses (e.g., through gene therapy and regenerative medicines), or to eliminate natural boundaries and extend our abilities (through artificial intelligence, nanotechnologies, or even brain downloading). *Posthuman* as a term can be used to describe an experimental quest advanced through technology, or an expected outcome of human evolution.

Key Points/Challenges

- In many respects posthuman discourse is not a new conversation but begins with issues raised in Mary Shelley's *Frankenstein*. Ideas of posthuman bodies have been explored in science fiction and cyberpunk literature such as William Gibson's *Necromancer* and Neil Stephenson's *Snow Crash*. They also surfaced in popular movies such as *Bicentennial Man*, *AI*, and the *Terminator* trilogy.

- From the late twentieth century to the present, posthuman discourse has been of interest to philosophers, artists, technologists, and scientists involved in conversations and research about biotechnological (see **biotechnology**) enhancements that challenge traditional boundaries of embodiment, gender, sexuality, and species.

- Posthuman discourse intersects with transhumanism, a philosophical movement that believes in the moral right to extend life and mental and physical capabilities, and to embrace new technologies that enable these advancements. The term *transhuman* derives from "transitional human" and is viewed as a "way station" between humanity and the posthuman. The World Transhumanist Association is one organization representing these views.

- Many claims and proposals related to a posthuman existence are futuristic and are not currently scientifically feasible (i.e., brain downloading). However, emerging technologies and innovations may open possibilities for new forms of existence through explorations in gene therapy, neuroscience-based interventions in the brain, and models of interaction offered though social networking via the Internet.

- The idea of the posthuman is important in ethical debates related to human nature, personal rights or freedom, and technological access.

Further Reading

Bostrom, Nick. 2005. "In Defense of Posthuman Dignity." *Bioethics* 19 (3):202–14. www.nickbostrom.com/ethics/dignity.html.

> Argument for the acceptance of human enhancement technologies, which the author sees as offering recognition and dignity to both humans and posthumans.

Graham, Elaine L. 2002. *Representations of the Post/Human*. Manchester, UK: Manchester University Press.

> Explores the roots of the posthuman in literature and offers a first attempt at theological reflection on technological being.

Hayles, N. Katherine. 1999. *How We Became Posthuman*. Chicago: University of Chicago Press.

> Foundational book addressing the changing conceptions of the body and embodiment in a technological age.

Moore, Vincent. 1999. "Bibliography of Posthuman Theory and Critical Resources." *Bulletin of Bibliographies* 56 (3):127–36.

A helpful resource highlighting and summarizing sources related to the posthuman discourse in the humanities.

Waters, Brent. 2006. *From Human to Posthuman: Christian Theology and Technology in a Postmodern World*. London: Ashgate.

Examines the religious foundations and implications of the posthuman worldview and suggests a Christian theological framework for constructively evaluating biotechnological developments.

World Transhumanist Association. 2002. *The Transhumanist Declaration*. http://www .transhumanism.org/declaration.htm.

Declaration of the WTA summarizing shared visions and aims of the transhumanist movement.

Heidi A. Campbell, Texas A&M University

☐ Process Philosophy/Theology

Process thought considers all existing things and individuals to be events of experience. Each event is influenced by previous events, freely develops in response to others, and influences what occurs thereafter. Process thought is often called a relational way of thinking, because it supposes that things come to be through relationship with others. Process philosophy in general and process theology in particular play a leading role in the contemporary science and religion dialogue.

Alfred North Whitehead (1861–1947) is often regarded as the seminal process thinker. Whitehead believed that the future course of world history depends on our decisions about the relationship between science and religion. He believed that an adequate understanding of reality required that we take both domains as offering essential information about existence. Whitehead's solution to conflicts between science and religion was to suggest modifications in the typical understandings of the two.

Following Whitehead and others, process theologians are known for their belief that God is the best and most moved mover. By this they mean that God influences all others but is also influenced by all others. God is relational. Although God's experience is affected by others, God's eternal nature remains the same.

Most process thinkers believe that God is unable to withdraw or override creaturely freedom. This belief solves the problem of evil, because harmful creaturely actions generate evil. Because this loving God cannot prevent the evil that free creatures cause, God is not culpable for failing to prevent genuine evil.

Christian process theologians affirm basic Christian convictions about Jesus's life, death, and resurrection. But they use process metaphysics to describe these convictions instead of the metaphysics presupposed in many early Christian creeds.

Prominent early (nineteenth- and twentieth-century) process thinkers include Samuel Alexander, Charles Hartshorne, William James, Pierre Teilhard de Chardin, Alfred North

Whitehead, and Daniel Day Williams. Contemporary contributors include John Cobb, Lewis Ford, David Griffin, Catherine Keller, Schubert Ogden, and Marjorie Suchocki. Prominent contemporary process thinkers whose work most often directly engages the science and religion dialogue include Ian Barbour, Charles Birch, and Nancy Howell. Philip Clayton and John Haught also make use of the insights of process thought.

Key Points/Challenges

- Process thought is widely regarded as congenial with the general theory of **evolution**. Process theology rejects the claim that creatures are entirely determined by the laws of nature, their genes, the environment, or God, although each factor influences their evolution. Process thinkers believe that God is involved in evolution in a noncontrolling manner. For this reason process thinkers typically embrace a position on the emergence of life called theistic evolution (see **creation/creationism**).

- Process thinkers believe that God is intimately related to all things and yet not to be equated with all things. This belief, often called **panentheism** (also theocosmocentrism), states that God indwells all of creation and yet is more than creation.

- Most process thinkers believe that God created this universe from the chaos of a previous universe. Affirming the opening lines of Genesis, process thinkers speculate that God created from chaos. They deny that the universe was created from absolutely nothing (creation ex nihilo).

- Many process thinkers believe that all existing things are best understood as serially ordered experiences. This belief is part of the broad doctrine often called panexperientialism. This theory suggests that all entities possess interiority, which is to say that all individuals have some degree of subjectivity. Panexperientialism helps to solve the problem of how the body relates to the mind, because it suggests that the parts of the body and the mind are mutually influencing experiences of the same general ontological kind.

- Process thought escapes the "God of the gaps" charge (that gaps in scientific explanations of nature can be explained only as God's action), because process thinkers deny that the causal processes of the universe are occasionally overpowered or interrupted by divine acts. Instead, process theism supposes that God persuades rather than coerces all creatures all the time.

Further Reading

Barbour, Ian G. 1990. *Religion in an Age of Science: The Gifford Lectures 1989–1991*. Vol. 1. San Francisco: HarperSanFrancisco.
> Benchmark university-level introduction to the science and religion dialogue, with special focus on process thought in later chapters.

———. 2002. *Nature, Human Nature, and God*. Minneapolis: Fortress.

> Clearest and most complete exposition of Barbour's process-influenced views.

Griffin, David R. 2000. *Religion and Scientific Naturalism: Overcoming the Conflicts*. Albany: State University Press of New York.

> A sophisticated analysis of key questions in philosophy of science, such as methodological naturalism, and a detailed explanation of theistic evolution.

Haught, John F. 2000. *God after Darwin: A Theology of Evolution*. Boulder, CO: Westview.

> Process-oriented reconciliation of theology and evolution.

Keller, Catherine. 2003. *Face of the Deep: A Theology of Becoming*. London: Routledge.

> Theology of creation that combines process thought with other theological ideas and traditions.

Whitehead, Alfred N. 1925. *Science and the Modern World*. New York: Macmillan.

> Accessible introduction to key ideas in process thinking about science and religion

Thomas Jay Oord, Northwest Nazarene University

☐ Ptolemy, Claudius (AD 90–168), (Ptolemaic System)

For nearly fifteen hundred years, from AD 150 to the time of **Galileo**, one book and one name defined astronomy. The book was the *Almagest* and the author was Claudius Ptolemy. In the *Almagest*, Ptolemy develops the most sophisticated and successful mathematical theory of solar and planetary motion developed up to the time of **Kepler** and **Newton**. It was the essential book of astronomy, a subject that made up part of the *quadrivium* (or "four ways") to a liberal arts education.

When viewed through modern eyes it is tempting to see the Ptolemaic system as hopelessly wrong. Such a view, however, fails to understand Ptolemaic astronomy on at least three fronts.

1. Ptolemaic astronomy was deeply influenced by **Plato** and **Aristotle**. From Plato, Ptolemy inherited the belief that, since the circle was considered a perfect shape, all heavenly motions must conform to circular paths. Furthermore, this motion should be uniform.

2. From Aristotle, Ptolemy derived a comprehensive and hierarchical worldview that provided an explanation for motion, including heavenly motion, as a consequence of "natural place." The earth, being "heavy," must occupy the centermost position in the hierarchy. Hence all heavenly motion must be earth-centered.

Given these constraints, it is a testament to Ptolemy's ingenuity that his system worked as well as it did.

3. Modern readers unacquainted with observational astronomy often underestimate the difficulty of creating a comprehensive theory of planetary motion based solely on the most basic of naked-eye astronomical tools at Ptolemy's disposal.

Historically, astronomy fulfilled two important functions. The principal function was the construction of calendars and the accurate prediction of key dates such as the equinoxes and solstices and the positions of the sun, moon, and planets. A secondary task concerned the creation of astrological charts. Both tasks are deeply influenced by errors, either in observations or in the mathematical theory upon which predictions would be made. Many of these errors are cumulative in nature and, by the time of Ptolemy, the predictions made by geocentric astronomical systems were obviously wrong. In attempting to "save the appearances" Ptolemy faced three significant problems.

1. *Motion of the sun and the unequal length of the seasons.* Greek astronomers realized that the length of the seasons was not constant. To account for this, Ptolemy proposed that the sun moved in a circular path, called the deferent, whose center was off-set from the observer on earth. By this "sleight of hand," Ptolemy maintained circular motion and saved the appearance. This introduction of the eccentric did however challenge the notion of geocentrism, a problem not lost on some critics of his day.

2. *Retrograde motion.* The superior planets (Mercury, Jupiter, and Saturn) reverse the direction of their paths in the sky during the course of a season. To explain this Ptolemy introduced the epicycle, which was a small circular motion made by the planet as it moved along the eccentric described above.

3. *Nonuniformity of retrograde motion.* Finally, to account for subtle variations in observed motions of the planets Ptolemy introduced the equant, which was halfway between the earth and the center of the eccentric. This was the point around which a planet's motion would be truly uniform and circular.

In its finished form the Ptolemaic system was a remarkable achievement with an intricate web of numerous circles within circles, carrying out the complex choreography of the heavens. It represents the culmination of early Greek astronomical models and, for several centuries, was able to make accurate predictions before needing to be "tweaked."

Key Points/Challenges

- Ptolemy inherited, likely from **Plato**, a deep-seated ambivalence toward interpretations drawn from observational science. The burden of astronomy was to make correct mathematical predictions and not to comment on the nature of reality behind the appearances. Thus it is crucial to make a distinction between the Ptolemaic system as a mathematical description and the Ptolemaic system as a physical explanation. The *Almagest* is purely mathematical and even though Ptolemy may have made explanatory claims in other writings, his magnum opus makes no attempt to explain a reality behind the appearances.

- Contrary to popular belief, the Ptolemaic system was not overthrown by the Copernican (see **Copernicus**) system in the sixteenth century because of the latter's superior predictive power. In fact, the Ptolemaic system was superior in predictive ability to the early heliocentric model of Copernicus. However, to borrow from **Michael Polanyi**, as an explanatory model it was the incipient "claim of rationality" within Copernicanism that ultimately triumphed.

Further Reading

Dijksterhuis, Eduard J. 1986. *The Mechanization of the World Picture: Pythagoras to Newton*. Princeton, NJ: Princeton University Press.

A classic and very thorough discussion of issues relating to the development and entrenchment of a mechanical worldview.

Stafleu, Marinus D. 1987. *Theories at Work*. New York: University Press of America.

An excellent treatment of the shift from Ptolemy to Copernicanism.

Brian Martin, The King's University College

☐ Quantum Theory (Mechanics, Physics)

Quantum theory, also known as quantum mechanics and quantum physics, is the postclassical development of physics that began in the early twentieth century and significantly advanced our understanding of matter and energy on the small scale of atoms and subatomic particles, and in the process explained larger-scale puzzles as well, such as the periodic table of the elements, the stability of matter, and the thermal electromagnetic radiation spectrum. The theory recognized that light is not a continuous beam but a stream of discrete photons, and that energies of electrons in atoms are quantized in levels instead of having a continuous range of possible values. A key idea in the theory is Heisenberg's Uncertainty Principle: the more one knows about where something is, the less one can know about its speed (an effect not noticeable for larger particles). Another key observation is that systems prepared identically give a distribution of results (where an electron hits a screen, or when a radioactive nucleus decays, for example) rather than the same predictable result each time. The probability of each result can be calculated from the "wave-function," a solution of the Schrödinger wave equation (a fundamental equation of physics describing quantum mechanical behavior). Most physicists believe that the uncertainties and probabilities are intrinsic instead of simply a limit to human knowledge; thus, a system is not in a particular state unless and until measured by a conscious observer (or, for some, a large, nonquantum recording device) in which case one says the wave-function has "collapsed" from representing a spread-out set of possibilities to giving a single definite result.

Quantum theory describes the wave-particle duality of matter and energy: photons (particles of light) and electrons each display either wave aspects or particle aspects, but not both simultaneously, depending on the type of observation made. This feature of the world is called "complementarity."

Quantum field theory incorporates quantum mechanics into Einstein's special theory of relativity, which had revised our understanding of high-speed motion and space-time interrelationships. Quantum field theory shows how each fundamental force involves particle exchange instead of simply acting across a distance; it also predicted the existence of antimatter before its discovery in 1932. The subfields of nuclear and particle physics use quantum mechanics as a basic tool, but there remains significant doubt as to whether quantum mechanics can successfully incorporate Einstein's general relativity to produce a "grand unified theory."

Quantum mechanics has contributed, in varying degrees, to a number of shifts in worldview, including continuum to quantum, certainty to uncertainty, dualism (each entity is either a particle or a wave) to duality (each entity exhibits both a particle and a wave nature), predictability to probability, determinism to indeterminism, objectivity to subjectivity, reductionism to holism, naive to critical realism. These worldview shifts are relevant to many areas, most notably philosophy of science, theological reflections on the nature of reality, and psychology. Furthermore, quantum physics led to many of the technological advances of the twentieth century, such as the transistor and the laser.

Key Points/Challenges

- Primary among its philosophical ramifications is quantum theory's challenge to a classical objective realist (see **realism**) position as well as classical determinism, both of which have connections with theological positions in the Christian doctrines of creation and providence.

- The wave-particle duality has been used in **Christology** as a fruitful analogy for the divine-human nature of Jesus. In addition, several writers have used this analogy to compare the historical development of the methods of Christian theology with those of modern physics.

- The involvement of the observer in the collapse of the wave function raises questions of the role of **consciousness** in the cosmos. Some quantum cosmologists regard the universe as having a single wave function, which collapsed only on the arrival of human consciousness. Perhaps more popular are many-worlds theories, which postulate that at every quantum event each possible result actually occurs in a spontaneously created parallel universe.

- Quantum theory is suggested by some as a means of divine or human free action in the world, in which true **indeterminacy** allows for selection of particular results with wide-ranging consequences. There is, however, much disagreement regarding the control, number, scale, and impact of quantum events.

Further Reading

Polkinghorne, John. 1994. *The Faith of a Physicist: Reflections of a Bottom-Up Thinker*. Princeton, NJ: Princeton University Press.

> An appreciative walk through the Nicene Creed, particularly its Christology, from the point of view of a quantum physicist.

———. 2002. *Quantum Theory: A Very Short Introduction*. Oxford: Oxford University Press.

> A clear, concise, comprehensive, and conceptual guide to the basic features of quantum theory, with a mathematical appendix.

Russell, Robert J., et al., eds. 2001. *Quantum Mechanics: Scientific Perspectives on Divine Action*. Vatican City: Vatican Observatory; Berkeley: Center for Theology and the Natural Sciences.

> A substantial volume presenting a range of scholarly opinion by leading thinkers on how quantum theory, particularly because of its probabilistic outlook on the future, might help to understand God's interaction with creation.

Arnold E. Sikkema, Trinity Western University

☐ Quine-Duhem Thesis

In the late nineteenth and early twentieth centuries, the French physicist/philosopher Pierre Duhem (1861–1916) argued that scientific ideas involving theoretical and unobservable matters cannot be evaluated and tested separately and in isolation, but only in conjunction with other principles. For example, if a theory about meson decay (a type of unstable subatomic particle) is to be tested via linear accelerator events, then both generating the experimental prediction and interpreting the results will involve electronics theories, particle theories, **quantum theory**, relativity theory, and others. In general, more than one theory factors into making predictions, designing experiments, and interpreting what the experimental results mean. As Duhem put it, "The physicist can never subject an isolated hypothesis to experimental test, but only a whole group of hypotheses" (1954, 187). In an influential 1951 article the American philosopher W. V. O. Quine (1908–2000) advanced a closely associated idea: "Our statements about the external world face the tribunal of sense experience not individually but only as a corporate body" (1953, 41).

Duhem and Quine saw science as an integrated system. Its component theories, hypotheses, and so forth were not self-contained, isolatable chunks that could be considered and evaluated independently of one another. For example, Quine employed an analogy of a web, where pulling on one strand could propagate effects to the far reaches of the web.

The Quine-Duhem thesis (QDT) is an interconnected triad of views highlighting different facets of each philosopher's thought presented above. There are different (and disputed) versions, but the basics include variant forms of these components:

1. Scientific theories or hypotheses typically cannot be tested in isolation, but only in "bundles" with other hypotheses, presuppositions, and so on.
2. Scientific theories or hypotheses typically cannot be conclusively falsified or refuted by empirical data alone.
3. There can be no such thing as an empirically conclusive "crucial experiment."

A fourth principle (underdetermination) is also widely associated:

4. It is in principle possible for there to be multiple competing theories consistent with any set of empirical data whatever.

In the past (but now less frequently) a fifth principle was often associated with the first three:

5. No specific set of empirical data can be uniquely linked to specific theoretical terms in a scientific theory or hypothesis.

Philosophers disagree over how principles 1–3 relate to one another, their status, their substance, and their ramifications for science. Some argue that Bayesianism provides an adequate solution to whatever problems QDT might appear to pose for science. Bayes's Theorem is intended to provide a way to distribute probabilistic confirmation or disconfirmation among interacting components. There are also disputes over what form of principles 1–5 either Duhem or Quine themselves actually held.

Key Points/Challenges

- Given principle 1, when experimental data contradict predictions, scientists face a choice of abandoning or modifying the theory or abandoning or modifying some other assumption in the context.
- Given principle 2, not only scientific confirmation but scientific refutation is always tentative. Some (e.g., Quine) argue that any theory can be held no matter what.

- Given principle 3, there is typically no logically decisive resolution of competition between alternative theories.

- Given principle 4, empirical data alone never point exclusively to just one theory. If scientists select one theory as *the* right, true, or rational theory, they must do so on grounds going beyond empirical data and reason, that is, on extra-empirical grounds.

- Given principle 5, the meaning of a theoretical term cannot be uniquely defined in terms of some specified set of empirical data.

- Philosophers of science now acknowledge that metaphysical principles, values, and other extra-empirical factors play legitimate, crucial, and inevitable roles within science itself—that science cannot even in principle function without them.

- The way is thus opened for the possibility of even theologically shaped conceptual resources playing legitimate roles in science—something not uncommon historically in science although often considered inadmissible today. Much contemporary science/religion discussion turns ultimately on just this point: whether such resources can have any legitimate role, can support fundamental scientific presuppositions (e.g., the intelligibility of nature), can provide conceptual shapes and boundaries (along the lines of Nicholas Wolterstorff's "control belief" suggestion), can function among evaluative criteria for theories, or can even provide legitimate data for scientific explanation.

- While QDT does imply that there can be no *logically conclusive purely empirical* procedure for choosing among competing theories, it does not imply that there can be no *rational* grounds for such choices. Nor does QDT remove the distinction between science and nonscience, or imply that science is subjective choice, social construction, or anything of the like.

Further Reading

DeWitt, Richard. 2004. *Worldviews*. Malden, MA: Blackwell.

  Includes an accessible overview of QDT and its implications (see chapter 5, "The Quine-Duhem Thesis and Implications for Scientific Method," 45–56).

Duhem, Pierre. 1954. *The Aim and Structure of Physical Theory*. Princeton, NJ: Princeton University Press.

  A classical source of Duhem's position, originally published in 1906.

Harding, Sandra G. 1976. *Can Theories Be Refuted? Essays on the Duhem-Quine Thesis*. Dordrecht: Kluwer.

  A collection of seminal essays by major figures in the discussion.

Quine, Willard V. O. 1953. "Two Dogmas of Empiricism." In *From a Logical Point of View*, 20–43. Cambridge, MA: Harvard University Press.

  A reprint of Quine's influential 1951 paper.

Wolterstorff, Nicholas. 1984. *Reason within the Bounds of Religion*. 2nd ed. Grand
  Rapids: Eerdmans.

> A short, readable discussion of a religiously shaped general "theory of theorizing,"
> which has been influential among religious believers and others.

Del Ratzsch, Calvin College

☐ Realism, Antirealism

Realists argue that we are justified in believing that the world exists independently of
our ideas about it. Antirealists disagree, and they argue that it is reasonable to believe
that the way the world is depends, at least in part, on our thinking about it. As well as
the question of the interdependence of the world as a *whole* with our minds, there are
questions about the mind's dependence on particular *aspects* of reality. Questions of
realism about observable entities, such as tables and chairs, are conceptually distinct
from questions of realism about the unobservable entities postulated by science, such as
atoms and electrons, and all of these questions are conceptually distinct from questions
about the truth of scientific theories. The "constructive empiricist" Bas van Fraassen
argues for realism about observable entities alongside antirealism about the unobservable entities postulated by science. Entity realists argue for realism in the unobservable
entities of science, but are skeptical about the truth of scientific theories.

Key Points/Challenges

- The majority of realists are scientific realists. They believe that the success of
  science justifies the belief that the theories of science are true and that the unobservable entities that science postulates exist.
- Antirealists include **idealists** (who believe that reality is generally mind-
  dependent), constructive empiricists (who believe that we do not have a
  compelling reason to believe in the existence of postulated entities that cannot
  be observed), social constructivists (who believe that reality is collectively
  constructed by the members of particular societies), and entity realists (who
  believe in the reality of the unobservable entities of science without accepting
  the truth of scientific theories).
- While realism/antirealism is a key divide in **metaphysics**, it is also an issue
  in debates in ethics (moral realists believe in objective moral facts), aesthetics
  (aesthetic realists believe that beauty is not "in the eye of the beholder"), and
  other areas.
- If God is understood as a discrete being, then it is relatively easy for scientific
  realists, who already accept the existence of discrete beings, to accept that God

may exist. Pantheist and panentheist (see **pantheism, panentheism**) conceptions of God as lacking distinctness from the world are conceptually problematic
for scientific realists, even though they pose no special conceptual difficulties
for many other sorts of realists (Peacocke) and for many antirealists.

Further Reading

Clarke, Steve. 2001. "Defensible Territory for Entity Realism." *British Journal for the Philosophy of Science* 52:701–22.

A recent defense of entity realism.

Devitt, Michael. 1997. *Realism and Truth.* 2nd ed. Princeton, NJ: Princeton University Press.

Examines, and takes issue with, all the significant philosophical arguments against realism, including arguments stemming from Davidson, Putnam, Rorty, and van Fraassen.

Kukla, Andre. 1998. *Studies in Scientific Realism.* Oxford: Oxford University Press.

A recent defense of scientific realism.

Peacocke, Arthur. 1984. *Intimations of Reality: Critical Realism in Science and Religion.* Notre Dame, IN: University of Notre Dame Press.

A short, readable introduction to the way realist debates influence understanding of the relation between science and religion.

Psillos, Stathis. 2003. "The Present State of the Scientific Realism Debate." In *Philosophy of Science Today*, edited by Peter Clark and Katherine Hawley, 59–82. Oxford: Oxford University Press.

A recent summary of contemporary debates about scientific realism.

van Fraassen, Bas. 1980. *The Scientific Image.* Oxford: Oxford University Press.

The classic articulation of "constructive empiricism."

Steve Clarke, Charles Sturt University and University of Oxford

☐ Reductionism

Reductionism is a philosophical position maintaining that a more complex whole
can always be explained by, reduced to, or predicted from simpler, more fundamental
components. For example, the boiling point of water is explainable from the properties
of its component hydrogen and oxygen molecules. Reductionists frequently hold that
reduction is possible in principle even if the relationships among parts and wholes
are too complex for us to elucidate or comprehend. This distinction is important
because we have at present very few successful reductions in the sciences other than

trivial ones. Nevertheless, science/religion discussions have been at the forefront of renewed interest in reductionism.

Reduction is used in a variety of senses. Reduction schemes typically are organized hierarchically, where different levels are related to one another. For instance, water in a glass can be considered as at a higher level while the molecules composing the water represent a lower level, and the subatomic particles composing the molecules represent an even lower level. We also distinguish between epistemic and ontological frameworks for reduction. Broadly speaking, levels of description belong to epistemic frameworks, while levels of reality belong to ontological frameworks (see **epistemology** and **ontology**).

There are three main categories of relationships between levels. (1) Theory reduction refers to the relations between theories. A standard example of theory reduction is the relationship between special relativity and classical mechanics. Some have argued that theology will eventually be explained away in terms of biological and physical theories. (2) Property reduction refers to the relation of properties at one level to other properties at a different level. A much-discussed example of ontological property reduction is explaining the temperature of a gas as the mean kinetic energy of its molecules. Some have argued that religious belief will be explained in terms of neural states in the brain. (3) Mereological reduction refers to the relationships between wholes and parts. The relationship between wholes and parts is primarily conceived ontologically insofar as it refers to elements of reality rather than their description. A typical example of a part/whole relationship is one between molecules and their constituent nuclei and electrons. Some have argued that if mereological reduction is true, there is no room for God's action in physical reality.

Debates about reductionism feature prominently in science/religion discussions and have important implications. For example, if reductionism's picture of the world is true, what form could divine action take? Is the conscious awareness of divine presence that many people experience merely the result of neural and chemical activity in the brain? Would the truth of reductionism disprove God's existence?

Key Points/Challenges

- A major source of confusion about reduction is a naïve understanding of the implications of scientific methodology (see the essay by Atkins in Cornwell 1995 for an example of this confusion). As a mode of analysis, scientific methodology typically breaks things down into their smallest parts. Methodical analysis is not equivalent to reductionism, however. The latter is a metaphysical view about the relationship between parts and wholes going far beyond scientific methodology. Scientific analysis does not imply that wholes are merely reducible to their parts, as the parts alone are often insufficient to fully explain the properties and behavior of the whole (see Bishop 2005 and Bishop and Atmanspacher 2006).

- Many authors make reference to the supposed reductions of chemical properties like acidity to electrons, protons, and neutrons, or of thermodynamic properties like temperature to mechanical properties of molecules as successful examples of reduction. However, these examples are highly problematic as the lower levels (e.g., electrons, protons, and neutrons, or mean momentum and kinetic energy of molecules) typically are insufficient to produce the chemical and thermodynamic properties in question (see Bishop 2005 and Bishop and Atmanspacher 2006).

- Reductionism also appears in philosophy of mind, where a key question is whether the mind or consciousness is reducible to or explainable by the body (see **mind/body problem**). Typically these examples involve naive reductionism, mistaking a methodological form of scientific analysis for a metaphysical statement about the relationship between minds and bodies.

- The chief alternative to reduction is **emergence**, often characterized as "the whole is greater than the sum of its parts." This philosophical position denies that complex wholes are explainable by, reducible to, or predictable from their simpler, more fundamental components.

- Some have thought that religious sentiments, beliefs, and practices can be reduced to or explained in terms of neurophysiology or biology. These tend to be examples of theory or property reductions. Others have wondered if various biological developments or neural properties are actually affordances given to humans to facilitate our connection with God, which are not well described by reductionism.

Further Reading

Bishop, Robert C. 2005. "Patching Physics and Chemistry Together." *Philosophy of Science* 72:710–22.
> Discusses problems for the received view of reduction and standard accounts of emergence within the context of chemistry's relationship to physics. An alternate framework to reduction and emergence is sketched.

Bishop, Robert C., and Harald Atmanspacher. 2006. "Contextual Emergence in the Description of Properties." *Foundations of Physics* 36:1753–77.
> A detailed discussion of problems in reducing molecular structure to physics and thermodynamic properties to mechanical or statistical mechanical properties.

Cornwell, John. 1995. *Nature's Imagination: The Frontiers of Scientific Vision.* New York: Oxford University Press.
> Collected essays on reductionism in physical and neural sciences and mathematics.

Dawkins, Richard. 2006. *The God Delusion.* Boston: Houghton Mifflin.
> Argues for atheism and against religious belief based on developments in biology and evolution, where all beliefs and behaviors—even evolution itself—are ultimately explained in terms of the laws of physics and chemistry.

McGrath, Alister. 2006. *Dawkins' God: Genes, Memes, and the Meaning of Life*. Oxford: Blackwell.

> Response to Dawkins's *The God Delusion*, arguing in part that science doesn't support a reductionist picture of humanity and the world.

Polkinghorne, John. 2003. *Belief in God in an Age of Science*. New Haven: Yale University Press.

> Discusses differences between "bottom-up" reductionism versus a "top-down" view of the world in the context of science/religion debates.

Robert C. Bishop, Wheaton College

☐ Relationship between Science and Religion

Science in the early Abrahamic civilizations was deeply influenced by ancient Greek **natural philosophy**. Centuries later, Christian culture placed a high value on theology, but it also included natural science, medicine, and mathematics. Deeper concepts of Christianity encouraged science, including the view that nature is good and that humankind is made in the image and likeness of God. With this Christian emphasis on science, up until the nineteenth century discussions and controversies were conducted and resolved largely within a Christian worldview. For example, from the fourth to the seventh centuries a controversy arose among Christian writers whether the Bible interprets the universe as rectangular or round. This controversy led to a Christianization of the Greek cosmos that combined the spherical and geocentric universe of **Aristotle** with the Christian and biblical concepts of a created world, which located hell, heaven, and God within the cosmos. Later controversies between science and religion included the thirteenth-century challenge to the Aristotelian theory that the world is eternal and the trial, in the early seventeenth century, of **Galileo Galilei** (1564–1642), who challenged the Catholic Church's commitment to a geocentric universe. Each of these controversies was slowly resolved through careful biblical interpretation, or through science seeking a more appropriate understanding of faith.

This situation changed radically in the nineteenth century largely because of the rise of secular biblical criticism and the theory of evolution of **Charles Darwin**, which offered a naturalistic explanation of life, including humankind. In the second half of the nineteenth century a body of professional scientists arose, many of whose leaders (e.g., Thomas Huxley in England and Ernst Haeckel in Germany) set themselves against the central beliefs of Christianity. They espoused a form of materialistic **naturalism** that claimed that the scientific method is the only means to acquire true knowledge. In the West the late nineteenth century saw the high point of militant hostility within the sciences toward religion. Andrew White, the president of Cornell University, published in 1896 the *History of the Warfare between Science and Religion*. In Continental Europe, this period was associated with larger movements in which church properties and education were secularized, and political movements hostile to Christianity arose, such as Marxism.

During the twentieth century professional science became more differentiated, with individual attitudes toward religion varying from hostility to indifference, interest, and religious commitment. The life sciences were generally hostile to religion, but physics and mathematics tended to be more sympathetic. However, the ethos of much of science remained resolutely secular. In the twentieth century, heated controversies arose, particularly in America, between evolution and Christian **fundamentalism**. Creationism (see **creation/creationism**) and **intelligent design** emerged from this controversy. The mainline churches in the West, however, have found various ways to reconcile Christian belief with the theory of evolution, and also modern psychology and neuroscience.

From the late twentieth century to the present, many scientists have become increasingly aware of the significance of religion within their disciplines. Many medical faculties saw the importance of spirituality in the healing process. Psychologists began to recognize that religion was an authentic part of the life of the mind. Sociologists recognized the importance of faith communities in resolving social problems. Philosophers of science recognized that religion deeply influences the worldview of scientists. Postmodernism recognized that a narrow scientific empiricism could no longer be sustained. The influence of religion in the fields of ethics, genetics, the environment, and weaponry is considerable.

Also in the late twentieth century, science and religion began to emerge as a scholarly discipline, with academic appointments, undergraduate and graduate courses, an enormous literature both scholarly and popular, along with journals, conferences, scholarly centers, and national and international academies. But this seems to have had little impact on the popular view that science and religion are incompatible.

Further Reading

Brooke, John H. 1991. *Science and Religion: Some Historical Perspectives*. Cambridge: Cambridge University Press.

> The most scholarly and authoritative history of science and religion, especially for the nineteenth century and for Darwin.

Dembski, William A. 2004. *The Design Revolution*. Downers Grove, IL: InterVarsity.

> An original and intelligent thinker's powerful new terminology and analysis of the circumstance in which design occurs in systems. He applies this to the emergence of life. Unfortunately, the controversy over his theory almost overwhelms rational critique. This is an accessible book, but in a slightly polemical style.

Johnson, Eric L., and Stanton L. Jones, eds. 2000. *Psychology and Christianity: Four Views*. Downers Grove, IL: InterVarsity.

> Represents a wide range of perspectives on how Christianity interacts with psychology.

Koenig, Harold G. 2002. *Spirituality in Patient Care: Why, How, When, and What.* Philadelphia: Templeton Foundation Press.

> A very authoritative figure in spirituality and medical care.

Lindberg, David C., and Ronald L. Numbers, eds. 1986. *God and Nature: Historical Essays on the Encounters between Christianity and Science.* Berkeley: University of California Press.

> Ushered in a new historical approach to the relationships between science and religion. This text helped make historians of science more aware of the importance of religion in the evolution of science. It also challenged the warfare metaphor.

Numbers, Ronald L. 1992. *The Creationists: The Evolution of Scientific Creationism.* New York: Knopf.

> The classic history of American creationism. It involves a sympathetic analysis of a very controversial period in American culture.

Peters, Ted. 1997. *Playing God? Genetic Determinism and Human Freedom.* New York: Routledge.

> Discussion of how scientific facts may be open to multiple theological interpretations.

John Roche, Linacre College, University of Oxford

☐ Science (Scientist, Scientism)

Science is the means of knowing that involves collecting data from observation or experiment, and deriving rules that aim to explain observed phenomena. From these facts and rules scientists can then make predictions about other situations and move on to test these new predictions. Scientific knowledge can be seen as an ever-growing giant. Many scientists, from the seventeenth century onward, have claimed that their ability to understand more than previous generations, to see farther than the giant, is because they are like dwarfs standing on the giant's shoulders. This acknowledges their creativity but shows their dependence on previous work.

As a pursuit, science tends to be divided into categories of study, such as physics, chemistry, or biology, and their various subdisciplines. While historically scientists were natural philosophers (see **natural philosophy**) who combined these activities, today scientists tend to be divided into those who specialize in observation or experimentation and those who develop theories. The healthy development of science requires an effective interaction between these two groups.

The process by which science takes place is seldom uniform, but includes the acquiring and development of hypotheses to interpret the data, and the testing of these hypotheses with other data (see **scientific method**).

Scientism refers to the belief that the only reality that exists is the material universe, which is at least potentially analyzable by science. Followers of this perspective therefore deny the existence of a spiritual universe (see **materialism** and **naturalism**). Scientism does not necessarily follow from science and is a philosophical interpretation over and above it; however, there is often confusion between scientism and science in the eyes of many who are of a religious persuasion and among scientific atheists.

Key Points/Challenges

- The claim of the vast majority of the scientific community is that science is in some sense the study of an objective reality, for which the identity, life history, and spiritual condition of the individual scientist are irrelevant. This point of view is disputed by various postmodern interpretations, which cite historical examples where the personal influence of an eminent scientist may have stifled the development of a field. The standard response to this would be to acknowledge that scientists are influenced by their personal social, political, and religious convictions, but that this does not affect the underlying objective reality of the material universe.

- Religious followers may dispute the effectiveness of science since it is concerned solely with the material universe. If the universe has been made by a spiritual being, then an interpretation of it that focuses purely on the material and ignores the spiritual cannot be complete.

- Scientists, who may be unconcerned with the philosophical basis or implications of the scientific approach, will generally point to science's successes. **Quantum physics**, for example, has a remarkable record in the interpretation and prediction of phenomena in the atomic and subatomic realms, leading to many technological advances, manifested most obviously in the computer revolution. There is a tendency to regard science as needing no other justification than that obtained from its success.

- Scientists may also emphasize that science itself, while leading to an expanding body of knowledge, is always open to correction and modification. This "falsifiability" of science thereby acknowledges that mistakes can be made and that personal bias of eminent leaders in the field may distort perceptions of reality, but that science itself therefore remains the only method for studying the objective phenomena of the material universe.

- Some commentators say that falsifiability distinguishes science from religion, in that while science can be tested and corrected, religions are based on revelation that, once given, may not be corrected. Others, however, say that religious revelation is itself an ongoing process, where former understandings are tested and new ideas developed. As such, the distinction between science and religion becomes blurred.

Further Reading

Barton, Andrew. 1999. *Questions of Science: Exploring the Interaction between Science and Faith.* Eastbourne, UK: Kingsway.

> Fifty questions describing the underlying principles of science and showing why the author, a scientist and Christian, sees them as complementary pursuits. The format is simple, but the ideas are fairly rich.

Okasha, Samir. 2002. *Philosophy of Science: A Very Short Introduction.* Oxford: Oxford Paperbacks.

> A quick but clear introduction to the history and philosophy of science, explaining the nature of scientific reasoning, scientific explanation, revolutions in science, and theories such as realism and antirealism. The book reviews some of the issues that relate to particular sciences, such as biology's problem of classification, and the nature of space and time in physics. The book takes a brief look at the conflicts between science and religion, and questions whether science is always beneficial.

Stenmark, Mikael. 2001. *Scientism: Science, Ethics and Religion.* London: Ashgate.

> Looks at scientism in detail, showing its variety of forms. Overall, it argues against a strong scientism position.

Pete Moore, Trinity College, Bristol

☐ Scientific Method

The core of scientific methodology across fields might be described as an insistence on experimental or observational testing of scientific hypotheses in order to confirm or reject a theory about how the world works. Only theories that produce testable predictions are regarded as scientific. However, professional scientists creatively invent specific methods that are relevant to each field. While this certainly fosters innovation, it also means that beyond this core, there is no general scientific method.

To understand how science actually operates requires a historical and autobiographical perspective. Most scientific discoveries rely on a vast background of cultural creations such as civic culture, number writing, and the creation of logical argument. Greek science in antiquity created large elements of scientific method as we understand it today, including the concept of "natural explanation," which involved systematic observation, systematic theory, and logic. Greek science tried to remove the magical and mythical from natural explanations and to explain the unknown in terms of the better known in nature. For example, Anaximander (610–ca. 546 BC) describes the sun as a fiery wheel. Greek science also introduced minimalism in the explanatory entities of nature, including the four elements (earth, water, air, and fire) and the ether.

While the Greeks used souls and a prime mover in heaven as part of their model for explaining nature, there were some materialistic currents, usually associated with atomism. Mathematics, medicine, and astronomy were the main areas of discovery in

Greek science. The Greek-inspired scientific method developed further in Islam and the medieval West. William of Occam (ca. 1285–1349) introduced the principle of parsimony (the explanation involving the fewest elements is preferred), which he used to eliminate unobservable entities. This remains a highly important methodological principle in working science.

With the seventeenth-century scientific revolution came new and powerful scientific methods. **Francis Bacon** (1561 1626) pioneered "experimental philosophy" and "scientific induction." This involved gathering evidence and analysis. Improving the induction needs a controlled experimental inquiry, which leads to further testing and eventually to a mature theory. Bacon insisted that scientific research should be useful to humankind. **Galileo** (1564–1642) developed a modified physics, which synthesized mathematics, experimentation, and idealized physical concepts. **René Descartes** (1596–1650) introduced *systematic doubt* to clear away old theories. He introduced a new model of scientific naturalism, using the machine as a model for exploring and explaining nature. Refined, this remains the model of much scientific naturalism today. Also, **Robert Boyle** (1627–91) effectively introduced the concept of a scientific hypothesis as we understand it today, as a candidate for a true statement about nature.

In the nineteenth century some scientists began to articulate philosophical theories of scientific method, and by the early twentieth century the "philosophy of science" became a distinct profession. August Comte (1798–1857) introduced **positivism**, which emphasized that only verifiable natural phenomena can be known, and rejected metaphysical and theological concepts.

From the late nineteenth century to the late twentieth century, positivism and philosophical skepticism merged. The philosophy of science then generated a remarkable variety of forms of skeptical positivism, most linked to a rejection of "objective knowledge" or a "real world." For example, Ernst Mach (1838–1916) argued that scientific laws are summaries of facts. He refused to posit a realm of "reality" behind the phenomena, and was hostile to hypotheses. Pierre Duhem (1861–1916, see **Quine-Duhem thesis**), a physicist, historian of science, and committed Catholic, argued that there are no irreducible facts devoid of all theory. By weakening the claims of objective science, Duhem argued that there can be no conflict between objective religious propositions and physical theories. Carl Hempel (1905–97) went farther and argued that scientific method is based on hypotheses rather than on observations. For Karl Popper (1902–1994), the source of hypotheses is irrelevant; testing is all that matters. Hypotheses cannot be confirmed, and scientists should seek only to falsify hypotheses. A theory that survives rigorous falsification has been "corroborated." Paul Feyerabend (1924–94) denied that there is such a thing as scientific method. He declared that "anything goes." Feyerabend effectively brought the twentieth-century positivist tradition to a close. Thomas Kuhn (1922–96) emphasized the historical and social setting of scientific theories. He argued that scientific revolutions involve "paradigm shifts," a disciplinary shift in the whole culture of a scientific field. The new theory may well be incommensurable with the old. Gradually method becomes more routine and moves into a "problem-solving mode." Kuhn's theory of science admits a strong element of **antirealism** and social constructivism.

To summarize, professional scientific research combines creativity and methodology. Scientists tend to absorb their working methodology from their laboratory culture and from research teams, rather than from the literature of the philosophy of science. Nevertheless, many philosophers of science, from Bacon to Comte and Popper, have deeply influenced the foundations of scientific method.

Key Points/Challenges

- In a unique approach, **Michael Polanyi** (1891–1976) stressed the personal and tacit knowledge of the scientific thinker. Scientists follow rules of which they may be hardly aware.
- Recent decades have seen a turn toward **critical realism** in the philosophy of science and a shift away from a physically based philosophy of science to one more biologically based. Some of the leaders in the field of science and religion, including Ian Barbour (1923–), Arthur Peacocke (1924–2006), and John Polkinghorne (1930–), are professional scientists who have also been partly influenced by various movements in the philosophy of science.

Further Reading

Crombie, Alistair C. 1994. *Styles of Scientific Thinking in the European Tradition: The History of Argument and Explanation, Especially in the Mathematical and Biomedical Sciences and Arts.* London: Duckworth.

> Stresses the objectivity of much of science, and reacts against the philosophical skepticism of much of twentieth-century philosophy of science.

Losee, John. 1993. *A Historical Introduction to the Philosophy of Science.* Oxford: Oxford University Press.

> A history of scientific method, understood as a theory of scientific method as developed by professional philosophers.

Pannenberg, Wolfhart. 1976. *Theology and the Philosophy of Science.* Translated by Francis McDonagh. Philadelphia: Westminster.

> Argues that theology is the science of God, and that it is not possible to understand the processes of nature appropriately without any reference to God.

John Roche, Linacre College, University of Oxford

□ Scientific Revolution

The scientific revolution is dated roughly to the sixteenth and seventeenth centuries, but some people see elements as early as the fourteenth century and the last stages as late as the eighteenth and nineteenth centuries. This time period saw a fundamental transformation in scientific ideas in astronomy, physics, and biology, in the institutions supporting scientific investigation, and in a worldview of the universe. The standard view is that this was a singular event that overturned the authority in science of previously respected writers of the Middle Ages and also of the ancient world, involving a fundamental change in worldview. It is claimed that the way scientists worked radically changed, from highly Aristotelian to mechanical and empirical approaches. **Aristotle** had recognized the teleological concept of "final cause" (see **causation** and **teleology**). **Descartes** rejected all goals, emotion, and intelligence in nature. He held that the universe is a mechanical system that can be described in mechanical terms. Whereas before the scientific revolution nature had been imagined to be analogous to a living identity, thereafter nature was generally viewed as akin to a machine following physical laws. God became more remote and nature less sacrosanct (beyond criticism or analysis). The standard view, however, fails to recognize that many of the key figures shaping this revolution saw themselves as working within a worldview that contained a God. For example, **Newton** argued that the solar system and the fixed stars were designed and maintained by an all-pervading Intelligence.

Key Points/Challenges

- Many writers contemporary to the event (e.g., John Donne), together with modern historians (e.g., Herbert Butterfield), have claimed that this period saw a revolutionary change in worldview, examples being the replacement of the Earth by the sun as the center of the universe, and the challenge to the Aristotelian theory that matter is continuous.

- Key new developments that emerged during the scientific revolution include **Nicholas Copernicus's** (1473–1543) argument for a heliocentric theory, and **Galileo Galilei's** (1564–1642) and **Johannes Kepler's** (1571–1630) revolutionary theories of planetary motion. Andreas Vesalius (1514–64) and William Harvey (1578–1657) discredited Galen's views on human physiology, while the microscope of Antony van Leeuwenhoek (1632–1723) opened up the microworld of biology. **René Descartes** (1596–1650) emphasized the use of deductive reasoning to test hypotheses. **Isaac Newton** (1642–1727) developed calculus and advanced the theory of universal gravitation.

- **Francis Bacon's** inductive approach to nature replaced Aristotelian deduction as the common procedure for scientific investigation. Although the Aristotelian sciences were based on observation, under Bacon's influence a more systematic empirical and experimental tradition was developed during the seventeenth century. In practice, however, many scientists believed that a mixture of induction and deduction was needed. Nevertheless, by the end of the scientific revolution the organic world of philosophers had been largely replaced by a mechanical, mathematical world to be known through experiments.

- An important factor in the scientific revolution was the rise of learned societies and academies in various countries. These provided opportunities for the publication and discussion of scientific results. Science was socialized and given a more stable international voice.

- Thomas Kuhn's *The Structure of Scientific Revolutions* colored the way modern historians view the scientific revolution. However, it is not at all clear that there was a single or unitary revolution in Kuhn's sense.

- There is a danger of a Whiggish reading of history—reading back what has become important later—so that the scientific revolution is seen as a uniformly good thing, moving us from a state of scientific ignorance dominated by philosophical and religious ideas to something based on hard facts. Indeed, the very notion of a scientific revolution is somewhat Whiggish. The standard view has exaggerated the importance of purely intellectual factors, seen to be independent of cultural and economic changes.

Further Reading

Butterfield, Herbert. 1949. *The Origins of Modern Science, 1300–1800*. London: Bell.
  A classic account.
Hall, A. Rupert. 1983. *The Revolution in Science, 1500–1750*. London: Longman.
  The standard view, largely developed from Butterfield's work.
Lindberg, David C., and Robert S. Westman, eds. 1990. *Reappraisals of the Scientific Revolution*. Cambridge: Cambridge University Press.
  Multiauthored work offering broad reflections on a range of aspects, reappraising the prevailing metaphor of a singular revolution.
Shapin, Stephen. 1996. *The Scientific Revolution*. Chicago: University of Chicago Press.
  Concise critical account, with an extensive bibliographic essay.

Donald A. Nield, University of Auckland

☐ Secularization

Secularization in its traditional form is a sociological theory. It states that a scientific worldview has brought about social changes leading to the decline of religion and will result in the disappearance of religion as a powerful voice in society. The word *secularization* comes from the Latin *saeculum* meaning "the world" and so distinguishes affairs in the world from the sacred.

Early sociologists such as Max Weber (1864–1920) argued that religion in Europe once strongly influenced many aspects of society (such as politics, law, economic affairs, education, health services, and family life). Although Protestant religion, together with modern science and technology, led to capitalism, according to Weber, there was a decline in religion as the government and other social institutions took over most of the roles once held by religion. Because of the increase of power of nonreligious (secular) institutions, the authority of religion in society has declined and people are becoming less religious. The decline in personal religion could occur in two ways. First, as religious organizations lose authority they have less control over the behavior and beliefs of adherents (Chaves 1994). Second, scientific worldviews seem to have greater plausibility than religious worldviews in modern society, and people will absorb and choose from a greater array of possible meaning-systems, leading to many forms of nontraditional personal meaning-systems (Luckmann 1967). Both pathways suggest people will espouse beliefs and behaviors that conform less and less to the doctrines and prescriptions of established religion.

Key Points/Challenges

- Some social scientists (e.g., Mary Douglas, Rodney Stark) argue there was no "golden age" when religion had great power over social structures and people's beliefs, and so it is misguided to speak about secularization as a radical decline in religious authority.

- Whereas church attendance and personal belief in God may be declining in Europe, there is no such pattern in the United States, and an increase in personal spirituality and new religious movements can be seen in different developed countries (Peter Berger, Daniele Hervieu-Leger). In addition, religion is re-emerging as a strong voice in local and global politics (William Swatos and Kevin Christiano). Hence the causal chain from modernity to inevitable religious decline is not supported.

- Secularization is not a theory but a description of society at a very broad (macro-theoretical) level. It can explain challenges to contemporary religion but cannot predict specific outcomes of religion (Peter Beyer).

- Many contemporary sociologists and historians of religion advocate a more complex view of religion in society, with periods of religious influence, loss of influence, religious adaptations, and revivals (Yves Lambert, David Martin, Alister McGrath).

- Secularization theory provides an important social context for contemporary science/religion dialogue. Traditional secularization theory treats religion as a declining social power. In addition, it depicts theology as losing ground to a scientific worldview. However, the more complex, recent analyses of religion in society suggest that religion is not defeated by science, but rather is changed and can be renewed by its engagement with a science-based society.

Further Reading

Berger, Peter. 2001. "Reflections on the Sociology of Religion Today: The 2000 Paul Hanly Furfey Lecture." *Sociology of Religion* 62:443–55.

> Excellent review by a sociologist who initially proposed a version of secularization theory but has since denied the "inevitable demise of religion" view.

Chaves, Mark. 1994. "Secularization as Declining Religious Authority." *Social Forces* 72:749–74.

> Good example of a neosecularization theory that suggests levels of secularization and hence does not assert that the decline of religion as a social institution necessarily results in less individual religiosity.

Hervieu-Leger, Daniele. 2000. "The Sociology of Religions in France: From the Sociology of Secularization to the Sociology of Religious Modernity." In *La Sociologie Francaise Contemporaine*, 241–50. Paris: Presses Universitaires France.

> A compelling account of the religious restructuring, with emphasis on community-based religion that focuses on personal experience.

Lambert, Yves. 1999. "Religion in Modernity as a New Axial Age: Secularization or New Religious Forms?" *Sociology of Religion* 60:303–33.

> This paper carefully distinguishes between institutional and personal effects of modernity and supports religious reshaping rather than religious decline.

Luckmann, Thomas. 1967. *The Invisible Religion*. New York: Macmillan.

> Classic account of how religion moves from a public to private system of meaning.

Martin, David. 2005. *On Secularization: Towards a Revised General Theory*. Aldershot, UK: Ashgate.

> Comprehensive theoretical and historical theory of secularization, but not easy to read. For an accessible summary of Martin's views, see the foreword by Charles Taylor (ix–x) and the introduction (1–13).

McGrath, Alister. 2004. *The Twilight of Atheism: The Rise and Fall of Disbelief in the Modern World*. New York: Doubleday.

> A readable account of atheism, defined narrowly as disbelief, from the perspective of a Christian historical theologian.

Sommerville, John. 2002. "Stark's Age of Faith Argument and the Secularization of Things: A Commentary." *Sociology of Religion* 63:361–73.

> A critique of Stark, but also an excellent discussion of the complexity of religion. Sommerville proposes a modified, multilevel account of secularization.

Stark, Rodney. 1999. "Secularization, R.I.P." *Sociology of Religion* 60:249–73.

> Very readable argument denying a "golden age" for religion.

Swatos, William H., Jr., and Kevin J. Christiano. 1999. "Secularization Theory: The Course of a Concept." *Sociology of Religion* 60:209–28.

> This is a very clear discussion of the term "secularization" and what would constitute evidence for and against secularization as a theory.

Weber, Max. 1976. *The Protestant Ethic and the Spirit of Capitalism*. Translated by Talcott Parsons. 2nd ed. London: Allen & Unwin.

A classic text for those interested in primary sources.

Maureen Miner, University of Western Sydney

□ Social Sciences

The social sciences are a cohort of disciplines given to the study of human behavior and social phenomena. Anthropology, economics, education, geography, linguistics, political science, psychology, and sociology are commonly identified as social sciences. Social sciences are distinguished from the humanities through application of scientific methods to social problems. In contrast to the "hard" scientific methods of physics and biology, social sciences use "soft" approaches that consider subjective human experience. This may be accomplished with *quantitative* statistical methods applied through laboratory experiments, survey questionnaires, and demographic analyses. Alternatively, social scientists in several disciplines employ *qualitative* methods to analyze the stories, experiences, and practices of others. These methods differ considerably, reflecting ongoing tensions within the social sciences regarding the extent to which objectivity is possible when studying human complexity.

Although the seeds of social science are centuries old, it was not until Auguste Comte (1797–1857) that attempts were made to systematize the field. The work of **Charles Darwin** was widely influential, raising the possibility that human behavior is genetically derived. Biological aspects of individual and group behavior became an emphasis for social science of the late nineteenth and early twentieth centuries. Keeping in step with Darwin, thinkers such as John Dewey, Sigmund Freud, William James, and B. F. Skinner advocated a social scientific rigor that would parallel the harder sciences. In the latter half of the twentieth century these ideas were subjected to increasing criticism. Early critics of Darwinian social science argued that culture rather than genes provided a principal basis for understanding human adaptation and behavior. More recently critics argued that humans are inherently unpredictable and cannot be effectively studied using hypothesis testing. For quantitative social scientists, this criticism encouraged researchers to back away from causal interpretations in favor of "correlation" between social variables. Qualitative social scientists used the criticism as justification for doing away with hypothesis testing altogether.

Key Points/Challenges

- Social scientists are currently underrepresented in the contemporary science/religion dialogue. Religion was a key focus for early social scientists, particularly sociologists such as Durkheim, Marx, and Weber. However, arguments for "harder" methodologies drove religion to the margins of social scientific practice for much of the twentieth century. This skew is only recently changing, focused primarily on experiences of spirituality.

- A critical issue for the field relates to rapidly changing methodologies and perspectives. New developments in the brain sciences make interdisciplinary thinking mandatory for social scientists. Cutting-edge examples include social cognitive neuroscience (the study of brains in social context), social network analysis (using power-scale mathematics to quantify behavior in social systems), and computational linguistics (using computers to mimic human knowledge).

- Because of their ability to consider human experience at individual and group levels, social scientists routinely access data of interest to the science/religion dialogue. Human studies in spirituality, altruism, gratitude, and virtue bring together social scientific and religious concerns. Some social scientists are looking for novel explanations of human behavior that reconcile scientific and religious interests. Nonreductive physicalism is one example, an idea that humans do not have a disembodied soul but instead generate "emergent" soulish properties out of lower-level processes in the brain (see **mind/body problem**).

Further Reading

Balswick, Jack O., Pamela E. King, and Kevin S. Reimer. 2005. *The Reciprocating Self: Human Development in Theological Perspective*. Downers Grove, IL: InterVarsity.

> A social scientific survey of lifespan human development from an explicitly religious perspective, claiming that the person or self is understood principally on the basis of relationship with others.

Brown, Warren S., Nancey Murphy, and H. Newton Malony, eds. 1998. *Whatever Happened to the Soul? Scientific and Theological Portraits of Human Nature*. Minneapolis: Fortress.

> A landmark publication in its consideration of nonreductive physicalism across social scientific knowledge bases.

Emmons, Robert A. 1999. *The Psychology of Ultimate Concerns*. New York: Guilford.

> A leading social and personality psychologist applying best quantitative practices of social science to the study of spiritual goals in human experience.

McAdams, Daniel P. 1997. *The Stories We Live By: Personal Myths and the Making of the Self*. New York: Guilford.

> Considers the significance of narrative and meaning-making through qualitative social scientific methods.

Post, Stephen G., Lynn G. Underwood, Jeffrey Schloss, and William B. Hurlbut, eds. 2002. *Altruism and Altruistic Love: Science, Philosophy, and Religion in Dialogue*. New York: Oxford University Press.

An excellent social scientific overview of human compassion to extend classic philosophical and theological scholarship on the topic.

Sheldon, Kennon M. 2004. *Optimal Human Being: An Integrated Multi-Level Perspective*. Mahwah, NJ: Erlbaum.

This book is an ambitious attempt to use social science for a comprehensive explanation of human behavior.

Kevin Reimer, Azusa Pacific University

☐ Soteriology

Soteriology is the study of salvation in Christian theology and includes also a theory of what ails humanity. The traditional, Genesis-inspired Christian narrative teaches that in the beginning God created a perfect world. Humans, in turning away from God, brought themselves and the rest of creation into brokenness, often referred to as *the fall*. The fall, including death, brought an inevitability to further sin in all the descendants of the first pair of humans. Christian salvation tells the story of God's coming in Jesus to save humans from death and to restore the perfection of Eden. In Christian history this story has been understood in a variety of ways—symbolically, allegorically, and literally—but has always included a historic and eschatological dimension (see **eschatology**), especially as it relates to the coming of Christ.

The manner in which salvation is accomplished is known as atonement. Sacrificial motifs of Jesus's salvation, borrowed from Old Testament law, hold that Jesus was the divine sacrifice of God as expiation for human sin, by which, in being wholly perfect and good, Jesus satisfied the need for an infinite compensation for human wrongdoing. Early church *Christus Victor* theories of atonement see God as having achieved victory over the devil, into whose hands all of humankind had fallen. Christ is a payment or ransom made to the devil by God on humanity's behalf.

Penal theories of atonement were developed in eleventh-century Britain by Anselm of Canterbury and draw on feudal understandings of honor. God's honor has been undermined by human sin and needs satisfaction. This satisfaction is made by Jesus, who is able to do so as God and who is required to do so as human. In contrast, Abelard, Anselm's contemporary, argued that Jesus's death was a divine act of love, and this love is sufficient to change and hence save humankind. Developments of this idea are called the moral influence theory.

Key Points/Challenges

- Science has thrown light on the long prehistory of humanity and on the brokenness of the natural world before humans emerged. Science has revealed a natural world "red in tooth and claw," full of death and apparent deliberate violence among some of the higher primates. The concept of a fall as a historic event has thus been compromised, as has the link between death and sin. At one extreme the fall is now considered existentially as symbolic of the individual in every age coming to full moral consciousness. Others reinterpret all tendencies to sin as resulting from an accumulation of the consequences of human action over time. **Fundamentalists**, however, have resisted these interpretations and insist that the science of prehistory is wrong and the fall is a historic event. Thus salvation, the solution to the fall, is now also diversely understood.

- Soteriology has historically concentrated only on the salvation of humans. In the present context of relatively detailed knowledge of our long evolutionary development, a new reading of soteriology attempts to glimpse the biblical vision of salvation for the whole cosmos. The book of Romans speaks of the whole creation groaning as it awaits its redemption (Rom. 8:22). Isaiah tells of the peaceable kingdom in which lamb and wolf will feed together (Isa. 11:6; 65:25). The book of Revelation describes a new heaven and a new earth, but in continuity with this earth and located here rather than in some other realm (Rev. 21). However, some Christians reject the antiquity of the earth and still proclaim the older, narrower version of salvation presented above.

- Salvation as traditionally understood was salvation from death, with an emphasis on the afterlife. The tension between salvation and justice in this life, rather than in another realm, was enormously heightened in the late twentieth century. Marx was critical of the Christian need for an afterlife as an "opiate" for suffering in this life. Christianity has tended to polarize between a liberalism that deemphasized eternal life and a world-denying fundamentalism that rejects science and believes that Christians will be raptured out of the world in the end, when the earth will be burned, and a new heaven and a new earth brought into being.

Further Reading

Brueggemann, Walter. 2002. *Reverberations of Faith: A Theological Handbook of Old Testament Themes.* Louisville: Westminster John Knox.

A discussion of Old Testament themes with scientific theories in mind.

Korsmeyer, Jerry D. 1998. *Evolution and Eden: Balancing Original Sin and Contemporary Science.* Mahwah, NJ: Paulist Press.

A look at original sin from a scientific perspective.

Peters, Ted, and Martinez Hewlett. 2006. *Can You Believe in God and Evolution? A Guide for the Perplexed.* Nashville: Abingdon.

An introduction to some of the theological consequences of evolutionary theory.

Stackhouse, John G., Jr., ed. 2002. *What Does It Mean to Be Saved: Broadening Evangelical Horizons of Salvation*. Grand Rapids: Baker Academic.

Open evangelical theologians expounding broader understandings of salvation.

Nicola Hoggard Creegan, Laidlaw College

☐ Spinoza, Baruch/Benedict (1632–77)

Spinoza was a Jewish philosopher, trained as a rabbi but excommunicated by his religious community for his teachings. He was of Portuguese-Moorish descent but lived in Holland for most of his life. He was initially influenced by Cartesian philosophy (see **Descartes**), although the Cartesians in Holland later denounced him for his views. He made his living as a lens grinder. His most famous work, *Ethics Geometrically Demonstrated*, was published posthumously due to the controversies related to his thinking. Although he was persecuted a great deal, friends praised his integrity and high moral character. He influenced modern philosophy profoundly (despite often being repudiated by the very thinkers who were most shaped by his thought). He is often considered a pantheist (see **pantheism**), equating God with the world and defending a deterministic worldview. Spinoza was condemned as an "arch-atheist" during his lifetime, yet was later called the "God-intoxicated man" due to the important role God played in his system (interpreting all matter and spirit as an extension of the divine).

Key Points/Challenges

- Spinoza argued against the then-common separation of the natural and the supernatural. He denied that miracles constitute a proof for God's existence. He rejected any "supernatural" miracles and instead interpreted "nature" as an expression of God's will and laws. Even Christ's resurrection is to be understood in a "spiritual," not a literal, sense.

- Spinoza is regarded as one of the founders of the science of biblical criticism. He viewed the Scriptures as a literary text that must be interpreted as would any other text.

- For Spinoza (modifying Descartes), there is only one supreme substance (the divine) of which we know two expressions: matter (extension) and spirit (mind). There might, however, be countless other dimensions of which we are presently unaware.

- Spinoza rejected the Cartesian need for founding knowledge either in God's existence/the divine will or in the human cogito. The world is rational and can be known by humans (primarily through mathematics). Even ethics can be demonstrated geometrically.

- Spinoza is particularly famous for applying the idea of the *conatus essendi*—the principle that what is in existence will always desire to continue—to humans. Suicide thus becomes a logical contradiction.

- Spinoza's God, which is more or less identical with nature, is a kind of free-flowing energy propelling the universe. It is both *natura naturans* (active force) and *natura naturata* (divine product). God fully actualizes all possibilities of existence and views all things *sub specie aeternitatis* (under the view of eternity).

- Spinoza did much work on identifying and categorizing human emotion. The highest kind of knowledge is one that combines theoretical science and intuitive knowing of sense perception coupled with empathy.

- His systematic and elegant system of knowledge in many ways defined the spirit of the new science of his day (especially as expressed in **Galileo**, **Kepler**, and **Newton**).

Further Reading

Garret, Don, ed. 1996. *The Cambridge Companion to Spinoza*. New York: Cambridge University Press.

> A collection of essays aimed at both specialists and novices. See especially Alan Gabbey, "Spinoza's Natural Science and Methodology"; Alan Donagan, "Spinoza's Theology"; and Richard H. Popkin, "Spinoza and Bible Scholarship."

Grene, Marjorie, and Debra Nails, eds. 1986. *Spinoza and the Sciences*. Dordrecht: Kluwer.

> An anthology exploring the influence of Spinoza on seventeenth-century science. Essays cover the natural and human sciences and generally suggest that Spinoza's influence on science was quite limited.

Mason, Richard. 1997. *The God of Spinoza*. New York: Cambridge University Press.

> One of the best and clearest studies of Spinoza's views of God and religion.

Christina M. Gschwandtner, University of Scranton

□ Supervenience (Top-down Causation)

In 1952 R. M. Hare introduced *supervenience* as a technical term in philosophy and **ethics** to relate evaluative/ethical judgments to descriptive judgments:

> First, let us take that characteristic of "good" which has been called its supervenience. Suppose that we say, "St. Francis was a good man." It is logically impossible to say this

and to maintain at the same time that there might have been another man *placed exactly in the same circumstances* as St. Francis, and who behaved in exactly the same way, but who differed from St. Francis in this respect only, that he was not a good man. (cited by Horgan 1995, 778)

Since 1970 the term has been widely used in philosophy of mind, but there is no agreement on its definition. Terrence Horgan writes:

The concept of supervenience, as a relation between properties, is essentially this: Properties of type A are supervenient on properties of type B if and only if two objects cannot differ with respect to their A-properties without also differing with respect to their B-properties. Properties that allegedly are supervenient on others are often called consequential properties, especially in ethics; the idea is that if something instantiates a moral property, then it does so *in virtue of,* i.e., as a (noncausal) *consequence of,* instantiating some lower-level property on which the moral property supervenes. (1995, 778)

There are two distinguishable notions of supervenience here. In the first sentence—substituting "S" for "A" for clarity, so that S-properties are *supervenient* and B-properties are subvenient or *base* properties—one can summarize:

1. Properties of type S are supervenient on properties of type B if, and only if, two objects cannot differ with respect to their S-properties without also differing with respect to their B-properties.

But from the last sentence we can construct the following definition:

2. Properties of type S are supervenient on properties of type B if, and only if, something instantiates S-properties in virtue of (as a noncausal consequence of) its instantiating some B-properties.

These definitions are not equivalent; the reason can be seen in Hare's use of the term. Francis's actions (B-properties) constitute him (or someone like him) a good person (an S-property) only *under certain circumstances.* It is conceivable that identical behavior in different circumstances would *not* constitute goodness. Thus I offer the following:

3. Property S is supervenient on property B if, and only if, something's being B constitutes its being S under circumstance C.

Recognition of the role of the broader circumstances in which the supervenient property is involved relates the discussion of supervenience to that of downward causation—which is the effect of a more complex (or "higher level") system on its constituents—so it might better be called whole-part constraint, as when an organism, embedded in a higher-level system that includes its environment, is affected by the environment. If a property is supervenient in the third sense, this means that it is what it is in part due to its embeddedness in a higher-order system. Its relation to the higher-order system involves it in causal relations that it would not otherwise obtain. For example, current flowing in a wire (a base-level event) may also be the transmission of (supervenient) information if it is a part of an appropriate system. As information it has causal effects that the current flow would not otherwise have.

Key Points/Challenges

- The definition of supervenience is important to religion/science discussions because it bears on issues of reduction (see **reductionism**) and **emergence**. If defined in the first way this ensures the reducibility of the higher level to the lower; if in the third sense, reduction is not a necessary consequence, and this supports the idea of S-emergence.
- The reality of downward causation is accepted in some scientific disciplines such as psychology but is hotly debated in philosophy. Again the issue of reductionism is at stake, with implications for human freedom and divine action (see **determinism and free will**).

Further Reading

Horgan, Terrence E. 1995. "Supervenience." In *The Cambridge Dictionary of Philosophy*, edited by R. Audi, 778–79. Cambridge: Cambridge University Press.

    A brief but excellent survey of the issues; see also related entries in the same volume.

Kim, Jaegwon. 2005. *Physicalism, or Something Near Enough*. Princeton, NJ: Princeton University Press.

    A defense of the first sort of definition from the most prolific writer on supervenience.

Murphy, Nancey, and Warren S. Brown. 2007. *Did My Neurons Make Me Do It? Philosophical and Neurobiological Perspectives on Moral Responsibility and Free Will*. Oxford: Oxford University Press.

    A somewhat technical defense of downward causation with explanation of the relevance of supervenience.

Van Gulick, Robert. 1995. "Who's in Charge Here? And Who's Doing All the Work?" In *Mental Causation*, edited by J. Heil and A. Mele, 233–56. Oxford: Clarendon.

    A brief and clear argument for downward causation; see also other essays in the volume.

Nancey Murphy, Fuller Theological Seminary

☐ Technology

Technology may refer to an artifact (object), a skill (knowledge), an activity (making), or a volition (power). Etymologically, the word comes from the Greek root *technē*, which refers to the practical or industrial arts and is distinguished from categories such as nature, knowledge, poetry, and the fine arts. If the natural sciences entail the acquisition of knowledge, then technology is the application of knowledge for practical purposes. The human knower, *Homo sapiens*, is by nature a maker or crafter, *Homo faber*. The use of tools to hunt, fish, plant, harvest, breed, invent, transport, communicate, or manufacture is technology. John Kenneth Galbraith defined technology as "the application of organized knowledge" (1967, 12).

Most contemporary philosophers of technology understand that technology may refer either to "a specific form of human cultural activity; to the content of technology, consisting of the ensemble of technologies used to make the various kinds of material products and procedural schemes in use in a society at a particular time; or to the sum total of the technics in use in a given society at a particular time" (Hannay and McGinn 1980, 28). In the past, for instance, the sociocultural understanding of technology would have conjured up images of farmers applying a scythe to shocks of wheat; later of grease-covered laborers in a factory; and today of biotechnologists in protective white coats and masks standing at the bench in a lab or of information technologists sitting in front of a computer screen.

Key Points/Challenges

- For Heidegger (1977), technology was a way to inhabit the world with the goal of mastery and efficiency.
- Some scholars, such as Stephen V. Monsma and colleagues, argue from a theistic perspective that "we can define technology as a distinct human cultural activity in which humans exercise freedom and responsibility in response to God by forming and transforming the natural creation, with the aid of tools and procedures, for practical ends and purposes" (1986, 19).
- Some individuals view technologies as value-free, understanding the rightness or wrongness of a given technology to reside in its application. At least since Jacques Ellul's (1964) critique of the technological society, however, most agree with historian of technology David E. Nye that "technologies are social constructions. Machines are not like meteors that come unbidden from outside and have an 'impact.' Rather, human beings make choices when inventing, marketing, and using a new device" (quoted in Mack 2001, 122), and those choices are inherently value-laden. Values inform which technologies to develop over others, whether to use certain materials over others, and whether to use certain forms of energy and not others.

- The pervasiveness and influence of technology in contemporary society has made it an important topic within current theology. Concerns are often voiced about the seductiveness of new technologies, dehumanization occurring through the use of mediated techniques or tools, and the problematic values of efficiency and mastery promoted by technology.

- Theologians such as Ron Cole-Turner and Brent Waters as well as philosophers such as Carl Mitchum and Albert Borgmann note these problematic aspects of technology, especially in relation to the Christian tradition, and seek to link the discussion to technology's relationship to our humanness and theological concepts such as grace, the created order, and the sacred.

Further Reading

Ellul, Jacques. 1964. *The Technological Society.* New York: Knopf.

> One of the most influential analyses of technology in the twentieth century. As a sociologist, Ellul examines the way "technique" becomes an all-consuming end in itself.

Galbraith, John Kenneth. 1967. *The New Industrial State.* Boston: Houghton Mifflin.

> Classic analysis of corporate "technostructure" by one of North America's best-known economists.

Grant, George Parkin. 1984. *Technology and Justice.* Notre Dame, IN: University of Notre Dame Press.

> An insightful study of the trajectory of technological infatuation, written by a Canadian philosopher.

Hannay, N. Bruce, and G. Robert McGinn. 1980. "The Anatomy of Modern Technology: Prolegomenon to an Improved Public Policy for the Social Management of Technology." *Daedalus: Journal of the American Academy of Arts and Sciences* 109 (1):25–53.

> A benchmark essay on channeling technology for the common good.

Heidegger, Martin. 1977. *The Question Concerning Technology and Other Essays.* Translated by William Lovitt. New York: Harper & Row.

> Neither a Luddite nor a romantic, Heidegger makes it possible to question technology.

Mack, Arien, ed. 2001. *Technology and the Rest of Culture.* Columbus: Ohio State University Press.

> A series of diverse essays on the social and ethical implications of burgeoning technology.

Monsma, Stephen V., ed. 1986. *Responsible Technology: A Christian Perspective.* Grand Rapids: Eerdmans.

> The product of a symposium held by the Calvin Center for Christian Scholarship at Calvin College; argues for technological stewardship.

Nye, David E. 2004. *America as Second Creation: Technology and Narratives of New Beginnings.* Cambridge, MA: MIT Press.

> An examination of technological stories that inform the way individuals and cultures inhabit the world, with particular emphasis on the American ethos.

C. Ben Mitchell, Trinity International University

☐ Teleology

Teleology is the notion that the universe has a plan, purpose, or predetermined goal. The term derives from the Greek word *telos*, which carries a variety of nuances, including end, achievement, and final destiny. Teleology is intimately related to the concept of **intelligent design** in nature, the view that the structures and processes of the physical world reflect rationality, and ultimately a creative mind.

Historically, teleology is often associated with **Aristotle** and his four kinds of causes in nature: material, formal, efficient, and final (see **causation**). Aristotle thought that an Unmoved Mover was the final cause behind the world, while the atomists rejected the concept of final cause and restricted the operation of nature to irrational necessity. During the Middle Ages Aristotelian categories were integrated within Jewish, Christian, and Muslim scholarship, and final cause was explicitly identified as being rooted in the Creator. Notably **Thomas Aquinas** offered proofs for the existence of God and appealed to an ultimate First Cause for the cosmos.

In the late eighteenth century, teleological arguments were challenged by philosophers, including David Hume. However, a purposeful view of nature remained the standard approach at the turn of the century as illustrated by the work of **William Paley** (see **natural theology**). A perceived blow against teleology occurred with **Charles Darwin**'s theory of **evolution**. Darwin noted in his *Autobiography*, "The old argument of design in Nature, as given by Paley, which formerly seemed to me so conclusive, fails, now that the law of natural selection has been discovered" ([1876], 1958, 87). As a result, biological evolution was rendered susceptible to a dysteleological interpretation of nature, a worldview in which there was no ultimate plan, purpose, or final goal.

With the rise of **secularism** and **scientism** during the first part of the twentieth century, teleology came under direct attack. To acknowledge the seemingly purposeful characteristics in nature, yet at the same time dissociate these from final causes and a Creator, new categories emerged. The term *teleonomic* refers to a goal-directed biological process that depends on a genetic program. For example, embryological development follows a plan directed by genes being expressed in an orderly fashion. However, the origin of these programs is said to be rooted ultimately in the blind process of natural selection. *Teleomatic* is a category that qualifies the processes of inanimate objects that arrive at an end. That is, as a rock falls to the ground it eventually reaches an endpoint. This process is neither intentional nor goal-seeking but is simply the operation of natural laws. The *telos* reflected in these terms is intrinsic to the living organism or inanimate object, while the traditional conception of teleology argues that its ultimate origin is extrinsic to nature.

The emergence of a science/religion dialogue in the late twentieth century has initiated a reassessment of the reality of teleology in nature. Modern physics reveals that the fundamental laws and constants in the evolution of the cosmos appear to be finely tuned. Some contend that this points to a teleological universe, one which was designed ultimately for humans to evolve (see **anthropic principle**). Natural selection is acknowledged as an important evolutionary mechanism, but not the ultimate causal factor.

Key Points/Challenges

- Teleology is a metaphysical notion and thus not detectable by the methods of science. However, the use of scientific evidence to argue the case for a teleological world is epistemologically appropriate. Undoubtedly a personal precommitment for or against a Creator is a powerful factor in this discussion.

- Natural selection is often believed to be the panacea for teleology. However, it is only a selective mechanism. The ultimate origin of biological variability opens the possibility of a teleological reality ordaining the laws of nature.

- Popular opinion assumes that teleology in nature is necessarily associated with divine interventions, as seen, for example, in **intelligent design** theory. However, natural processes may account for teleology-reflecting features in the world, dismissing the need for a God-of-the-gaps (see **ideas of God**).

Further Reading

Darwin, Charles. 1958. *The Autobiography of Charles Darwin, 1809–1882*. Edited by Nora Barlow. London: Collins.

    A section titled "Religious Beliefs" reveals that Darwin did not embrace a dysteleological view of evolution.

Davies, Paul W. C. 1983. *God and the New Physics*. London: Penguin.

    A popular introduction to the anthropic principle and a teleological view of nature.

Dawkins, Richard. 1986. *The Blind Watchmaker*. London: Penguin.

    A well-known book on dysteleological evolution.

Denton, Michael J. 1998. *Nature's Destiny: How the Laws of Biology Reveal Purpose in the Universe*. New York: Free Press.

    An introduction to a teleological approach to evolution.

Mayr, Ernst. 1982. *The Growth of Biological Thought: Diversity, Evolution and Inheritance*. Cambridge, MA: Belknap Press.

> A classic work on the history and philosophy of biology written from the perspective of scientism. Introduces the notions of teleonomic and teleomatic processes.

Denis O. Lamoureux, St. Joseph's College, University of Alberta

□ Theodicy (Evil)

The word *theodicy* derives from the Greek *theos* (god) and *díkē* (justice), referring to "the justice of God." More simply, a theodicy analyzes the problem of evil. It is an exercise in which theologians and philosophers attempt to reconcile a belief in a benevolent, omnipotent being with the existence of evil in the world.

Almost every culture has a tradition to explain the existence of evil. Within the Western tradition, the best-known theodicy is in the Hebrew Bible (Old Testament). The book of Job presents the story of a perfectly righteous and faithful man who suffers a series of personal and physical disasters. The book questions whether the universe operates on a principle of reward and punishment. It also outlines discussions for appropriate responses to innocent suffering. In the end, the book does not advocate an answer to the problem of evil; instead, the author admits that there are times when suffering remains a mystery.

In early Christianity, **Augustine** addressed the question of evil with his "free will defense," whereby he argued that creation initially reflected God's goodness and that humanity was created without sin but with free will. As such, Adam and Eve's choice to eat the forbidden fruit (Gen. 3:6) brought about evil and, as the common origin of humanity, their fall has affected subsequent generations of humanity. In the thirteenth century **Thomas Aquinas** built upon Augustine's concept that evil is a deviation from the good. Aquinas denied the ontological existence of evil, contending instead that evil is an absence of goodness in some thing. Thus, as in Augustine's thought, God has no role in the creation of evil because evil is not a thing in itself, but merely a privation (lack) of goodness in a thing.

Gottfried Wilhelm von Leibniz is a key figure in the later European theodicy debates. Leibniz outlined an "optimist" position in which he admitted that while evil exists in the world, this world is still the best of all possible worlds because a perfect God created it. Philosophers such as John Mackie countered Leibniz, arguing that God could have created a world in which people would make better choices. Alvin Plantinga responds to Mackie's challenge with his contention that there are limits to divine omnipotence (for example, God cannot make $1 + 1 = 4$), and because of human free will God could not have created Mackie's "better choices world."

Key Points/Challenges

- Almost every Christian theodicy begins with an argument for God's existence, followed by a discussion about the nature of God.

- Questions of human free will (see **determinism**) and divine freedom often play an important role in discussions about theodicy. Proponents of free will argue that God does not interfere with human actions.

- The Holocaust, Euro-American colonialism, the history of slavery, and ethnic cleansing campaigns have all posed difficult questions for twentieth-century theologians seeking a coherent theodicy.

- Some philosophers contend that, if any theodicy were valid, there would be no system of morality because any evil event would be rationalized as permitted or affected by God. Others contend that the problem of evil is incompatible with discussions about divine nature.

- Recently, process and evolutionary theodicies reframe the question in terms of God's participation in creation, asserting that the means by which creation occurs allows for the existence of evil at least temporarily (see **process philosophy/ theology**).

Further Reading

Cohn-Sherbok, Dan. 2002. *Holocaust Theology: A Reader*. Exeter, UK: University of Exeter Press.

> Contains several points of view by significant Jewish and Christian theologians and philosophers responding to the Holocaust.

Farley, Wendy. 1990. *Tragic Vision and Divine Compassion: A Contemporary Theodicy*. Louisville: Westminster John Knox.

> Representative of recent theodicies rejecting the question of why there is suffering and evil in a world created by an omnipotent and loving God, instead seeking out God's response to suffering and evil.

Habel, N. C. 1985. *The Book of Job: A Commentary*. Old Testament Library. Louisville: Westminster John Knox.

> Introductory commentary on a biblical text wrestling with the problem of God, injustice, and suffering in the world.

Kant, Immanuel. 1999. *Critique of Pure Reason*. Translated by P. Guyer and A. Wood. Cambridge: Cambridge University Press.

> German philosopher's seminal text containing his approach to God and position on moral order.

Leibniz, G. W. von. 2001. *Theodicy: Essays on the Goodness of God, the Freedom of Man, and the Origin of Evil*. Edited by Austin Farrer. Eugene, OR: Wipf and Stock.

> Contains Leibniz's key writings on theodicy.

Mackie, J. L. 1955. "Evil and Omnipotence." *Mind* 64 (254):200–212.

> Now classic essay that prompted the development of several logical proofs concerning the problem of theism and the existence of evil.

Plantinga, Alvin. 1974. *God, Freedom and Evil.* New York: Harper & Row.

> Analytical approaches to theodicy from an American Protestant philosopher and major figure in the field.

C. Shaun Longstreet, University of Texas at Dallas

□ Trinity (Perichoresis)

The belief that God is Trinity—Father, Son, and Spirit—presents an inescapable tension within Christian monotheism, which can seem an outright contradiction but possesses great creative potential. Pondering trinitarian unity and diversity, an infinite commonality of nature marked by distinctiveness of **person**s, has not only spawned the historical development of the concept of human personhood, it has also highlighted the beauty of interrelatedness.

While the term *trinity* does not occur in Scripture, it is implied by the high Christology of John, "In the beginning was the Word, and the Word was with God, and the Word was God" (John 1:1 NRSV) and by the call to baptize people from every nation "in the name of the Father and of the Son and of the Holy Spirit" (Matt. 28:19 NRSV). Belief in the Trinity arose from the belief that the Son and the Spirit are fully equal to God the Father but in some manner distinct from the Father and from one another.

The full development of trinitarian doctrine was not completed until some 350 years after the crucifixion. Eventually the church settled on the formula of one substance (*ousia*) and three persons (*hypostasis*, plural, *hypostaseis*). The Cappadocians, Basil, Gregory of Nazianzus, and Gregory of Nyssa (all ca. 330–95), were the first to work out an explicit understanding of the fully equal divinity and status of Father, Son, and Spirit. Gregory of Nazianzus was also the first to use the term *perichoresis* to explain the interrelated unity of the three persons.

The great "payoff" to trinitarian doctrine is the relational identity of God. Because the unity of divine nature is perfectly and infinitely shared by Father, Son, and Spirit, each person is fully understood, fully expressed, fully loved. Only God can understand the infinite fullness of divine perfection; thus, only the persons of the Trinity can fully understand one another. We can imagine a human person capable of great thought or portraying great beauty, but what if there were no one who could fully understand the thought or beauty that was expressed? Such a situation could lead only to frustration and deep loneliness. The greatness of trinitarian doctrine is that it incorporates the inherently relational being of God, so that God is understood as three distinct persons who share one divine nature.

Among the Greek fathers *perichoresis* (Latin, *circumincessio*) has been used to explain trinitarian relations, the relations of the two natures of Christ, and the relationship of God to sanctified humans. The most widely accepted translation, *interpenetration* or *coinherence*, allows for keeping both unity and diversity in our understanding of the Trinity. If the three persons are understood to interpenetrate or coinhere in one another, any tendency toward tritheism (three gods) is minimized.

Key Points/Challenges

- While we may discover a certain consonance between aspects of the material world and our understanding of God as Trinity, no one should expect to find a direct line of solid proof that links the two. The Trinity is first and foremost a question of revelation rather than reason. Nevertheless, we might hope to find some vestiges of trinitarian interrelatedness in the creation.
- For example, a quantum phenomenon known as the EPR effect (named after its discoverers, Einstein, Podolski, and Rosen) demonstrates the pervasiveness and profundity of interactive relationality. When an excited atom emits two previously interrelated photons, the photons remain related even when separated by tremendous distance, so that a measurement made on one of the separated photons instantaneously affects the other—a strange and counterintuitive phenomenon. In the EPR effect and the Heisenberg Uncertainty Principle, there is a surprising and/or elusive aspect to much of contemporary science. If aspects of the material world resist being understood by linear, algorithmic thinking, then perhaps it is not so strange that the trinitarian God who makes science possible is likewise not subject to full human comprehension.

Further Reading

Harrison, Verna. 2006. "Perichoresis in the Greek Fathers." *St. Vladimir's Theological Quarterly* 35:53–65.

   A lucid account of the history and meaning of perichoresis.

Olson, Roger E., and Christopher A. Hall. 2002. *The Trinity*. Grand Rapids: Eerdmans.

   An excellent source for beginners and a useful reference and summary for more advanced students. It includes a very helpful annotated bibliography.

Philip A. Rolnick, University of St. Thomas

☐ Verification Principle

The verification principle grew out of the meetings of a group of philosophers and scientists, known as the Vienna Circle, who gathered regularly in Vienna during the 1920s. With Moritz Schlick generally leading, they focused on the work of Wittgenstein, who wrote in his *Tractatus Logico-Philosophicus*, "The world is the totality of facts and not of things." Several notable figures attended, some more regularly than others, including Carnap, Feigl, Frank, Gödel, and Quine, although not all attendees were "official" members. A central activity was to propagate their thinking, which they attributed to the contents of the *Tractatus*. Ironically, Wittgenstein did not agree with this use of his *Tractatus*. In any case, the movement growing out of the efforts of the Vienna Circle is called logical **positivism**, and its fundamental tenet is known as the verification principle.

In a nutshell, the verification principle states that, in order to have meaning, a statement must either be a tautology (i.e., something that is true by definition) or be capable of empirical verification. Such a notion poses a threat to numerous religious statements and to metaphysical speculations more generally, as many claims in those domains seem to lie beyond the demands of the verificationist criterion. For example, if one allowed eyewitness testimony and historical records to count as empirical evidence, in principle it might be possible to verify the claim, "Jesus Christ rose from the dead." By contrast, the statement, "God raised Jesus Christ from the dead" poses challenges, unless one were to appeal to some type of eschatological verification where presumably direct testimony could be established in the afterlife.

The main criticism of the verification principle is that it falls under its own weight: the verification principle itself cannot be empirically verified. Ironically, although Gödel attended many meetings of the Vienna Circle, he did not agree with the verification principle, and it has been argued that his famous "incompleteness theorem" of 1931 undercut its claims. The theorem states, briefly, that (assuming a basic theory of arithmetic is consistent) there are true (and meaningful) arithmetical statements that cannot be proved to be true (i.e., cannot be verified in that system).

Key Points/Challenges

- While most contemporary philosophers consider logical positivism to be a dead issue, many practicing scientists, consciously or unconsciously, still adhere to its dogma. Thus when engaging in theological discussions with practicing scientists, it should not be assumed that verificationism is inoperative as a paradigm for knowledge.
- The current antirealist (see **realism, antirealism**) movement is in some ways a derivative of logical positivism.
- The verification principle is relevant to the notion of meaning in language, as it attempted to promote a strict empirical criterion for meaning itself.

- The principle is also relevant to the analytic versus synthetic distinction, terms made popular by the philosopher Immanuel Kant. For Kant, an analytic truth is represented by the statement "all bachelors are unmarried." The meaning of the subject term (in this case *bachelors*) is contained in the predicate term (*unmarried*). The truth of such a statement is known independently of experience, as it can be gleaned simply by an analysis of the meanings of terms. A synthetic statement is one like "Sacramento is the capital of California." The meaning of the subject term (*Sacramento*) is not contained in the predicate (*capital of California*). Certainly it is true that Sacramento is the capital of California, but the concept "being the capital of California" is not implied by the meaning of *Sacramento*. Kant thought that most synthetic statements are known a posteriori, that is, on the basis of experience. But he also thought that mathematical truths could be both synthetic and a priori, meaning that they are known prior to experience. Proponents of the verification principle would likely object to this last distinction. Many philosophers subsequently developed these ideas in a movement now known as analytic philosophy. One of the main tasks of this effort was to engage in a logical or linguistic analysis of concepts by breaking them down into more basic terms. For example, Gottlob Frege and Bertrand Russell collectively helped develop modern logic, and A. J. Ayer (in his *Language, Truth and Logic* [1936]) mapped out a refined version of logical positivism, which he called "logical empiricism."

Further Reading

Alston, William P. 2005. "Religious Language." In *The Oxford Handbook of Philosophy of Religion*. Edited by William J. Wainwright, 222. Oxford: Oxford University Press.

> Discusses the verification principle in the context of religious language on page 222. See also the chapter by William Hasker, "Analytic Philosophy of Religion," 425.

Feferman, S., et al., eds. 1986. *Kurt Gödel: Collected Works*. Vol. 1, *Publications, 1929–1936*. Oxford: Oxford University Press.

> Contains Gödel's famous 1931 paper, "Über Formal Unentscheidbare Stäze der Principia Mathematica und Verwandter Systeme," (i.e., "On Formally Undecidable Propositions of Principia Mathematica and Related Systems"), and other works.

Hume, D. 2004. *An Enquiry Concerning Human Understanding*. Whitefish, MT: Kessinger.

> Many people consider Hume to be a forerunner of Wittgenstein. Hume believed that meaningful concepts came either from sense experience or basic "relations among ideas."

Isaacson, D. 2004. "Quine and Logical Positivism." In *The Cambridge Companion to Quine*. Edited by R. Gibson, 214–69. Cambridge: Cambridge University Press.

> An analysis of Quine's thinking, with historical comments relating to the Vienna Circle.

Wittgenstein, L. [1961] 1974. *Tractatus Logico-Philosophicus*. London: Routledge & Kegan Paul.

> The basis for the discussions of the Vienna Circle. This book unpacks Wittgenstein's belief that the problems of philosophy are linguistic. He believed that "what can be said at all can be said clearly, and what we cannot talk about we must pass over in silence" (7).

Russell W. Howell, Westmont College

Contributors

Wolfgang Achtner, PhD, professor of systematic theology, Justus Liebig University, Giessen, Germany

Peter Barker, PhD, professor of the history of science, University of Oklahoma

Ruth Barton, PhD, associate professor of history, University of Auckland

Robert C. Bishop, PhD, associate professor of physics and philosophy and John and Madeleine McIntyre Professor of History and Philosophy of Science, Wheaton College

Hessel Bouma III, PhD, professor of biology, Calvin College

Craig A. Boyd, PhD, professor of philosophy, Azusa Pacific University

Costica Bradatan, PhD, assistant professor of philosophy, Texas Tech University

Daniel K. Brannan, PhD, professor of biology, Abilene Christian University

Paul D. Brown, PhD, associate professor of chemistry and environmental studies, Trinity Western University

Heidi A. Campbell, PhD, assistant professor of communication, Texas A&M University

Steve Clarke, PhD, senior research fellow, Centre for Applied Philosophy and Public Ethics, Charles Sturt University, and James Martin Research Fellow, Program on the Ethics of the Biosciences, James Martin 21st Century School, University of Oxford

Nicola Hoggard Creegan, PhD, lecturer in systematic theology, Laidlaw College

Edward B. Davis, PhD, professor of the history of science, Messiah College

Celia Deane-Drummond, PhD, chair in theology and the biological sciences, University of Chester, UK

Steve Delamarter, PhD, professor of Old Testament, George Fox Evangelical Seminary

Jeffrey Dudiak, PhD, associate professor of philosophy, The King's University College

Denis Edwards, STD, senior lecturer in theology, Flinders University

Stephen Garner, PhD, lecturer in practical theology, School of Theology, University of Auckland

Carl Gillett, PhD, associate professor of philosophy, Northern Illinois University

Christina M. Gschwandtner, PhD, assistant professor of philosophy, University of Scranton

Peter Harrison, PhD, Andreas Idreos Professor of Science and Religion, Harris Manchester College, University of Oxford

John Henry, PhD, director of science studies, University of Edinburgh

Russell W. Howell, PhD, professor of mathematics, Westmont College

Larissa Johnson-Aldridge, lecturer in history and philosophy of science, University of New South Wales

Neal Judisch, PhD, assistant professor of philosophy, University of Oklahoma

David M. Knight, PhD, professor of the history of science, Durham University

Denis O. Lamoureux, PhD, assistant professor of science and religion, St. Joseph's College, University of Alberta

C. Shaun Longstreet, PhD, coordinator of educational enhancement, University of Texas at Dallas

Heather Looy, PhD, associate professor of psychology, The King's University College

Brian Martin, PhD, professor of physics and astronomy, The King's University College

Patrick McDonald, PhD, assistant professor of philosophy, Seattle Pacific University

Alister McGrath, DPhil, DD, professor of historical theology, University of Oxford

Ernan McMullin, PhD, professor emeritus, University of Notre Dame

Hubert Meisinger, PhD, associate lecturer in systematic theology, Center for Social Responsibility, Mainz, and Protestant Academy, Arnoldshain

Maureen Miner, PhD, lecturer in psychology, University of Western Sydney

C. Ben Mitchell, PhD, associate professor of bioethics and contemporary culture, Trinity International University

Pete Moore, PhD, visiting lecturer in ethics, Trinity College, Bristol

Phil Mullins, PhD, professor of religious studies and humanities, Missouri Western State University

Nancey Murphy, PhD, ThD, professor of Christian philosophy, Fuller Theological Seminary

Donald A. Nield, PhD, associate professor of engineering, University of Auckland

Graham J. O'Brien, PhD, Anglican Diocese of Nelson, Adelaide, Australia: ATF

Dennis Okholm, PhD, professor of theology and philosophy, Azusa Pacific University

Thomas Jay Oord, PhD, professor of philosophy and theology, Northwest Nazarene University

Kuruvilla Pandikattu, PhD, professor of philosophy, Jnana-Deepa Vidyapeeth (Papal Seminary)

Gregory R. Peterson, PhD, associate professor of philosophy and theology, South Dakota State University

Michael L. Peterson, PhD, professor of philosophy, Asbury College

Samuel M. Powell, PhD, professor of philosophy and religion, Point Loma Nazarene University

C. P. Ragland, PhD, assistant professor of philosophy, Saint Louis University

Del Ratzsch, PhD, professor of philosophy, Calvin College

Kevin Reimer, PhD, professor of graduate psychology, Azusa Pacific University

John Roche, PhD, professor of physics and history of science, Linacre College, University of Oxford

Philip A. Rolnick, PhD, professor of theology, University of St. Thomas

Holmes Rolston III, PhD, University Distinguished Professor of Philosophy, Colorado State University

Duncan L. Roper, PhD, adjunct fellow, University of Western Sydney

Robert J. Russell, PhD, founder and director, Center for Theology and the Natural Sciences, and professor of theology and science in residence, the Graduate Theological Union, Berkeley

Kevin Seybold, PhD, professor of psychology, Grove City College

F. LeRon Shults, PhD, professor of theology, University of Agder, Kristiansand

Arnold E. Sikkema, PhD, associate professor of physics, Trinity Western University

James K. Simmons, PhD, assistant professor of physics, Shawnee State University

Stephen D. Snobelen, PhD, associate professor of humanities and social sciences, University of King's College, Halifax

Rodney L. Stiling, PhD, associate professor of history, Seattle Pacific University

James B. Stump, PhD, professor of philosophy, Bethel College, Indiana

Henry S. Tillinghast, PhD, chair of the Division of Natural Sciences and Mathematics, Ottawa University

Nivaldo J. Tro, PhD, professor of chemistry, Westmont College

Willem P. Van De Merwe, PhD, professor of physics, Indiana Wesleyan University

Brent Waters, DPhil, associate professor of Christian social ethics, Garrett-Evangelical Theological Seminary

Philip K. Wilson, PhD, associate professor of humanities and science, technology, and society, Penn State University College of Medicine

John R. Wood, PhD, professor of biology and environmental studies, The King's University College, The Au Sable Institute of Environmental Studies

Thomas W. Woolley, PhD, professor of statistics, Samford University

Index

Note: Boldface entries and page numbers indicate complete primer articles devoted to the topic.